324

15p

7/6

THE HAPPY HIGHWAYS

By the Same Author

In this Series

Earlier
    The Gardens of Camelot
    The Altar in the Loft
    The Drums of Morning
    The Glittering Pastures
    The Numbers Came
    The Last of Spring
    The Purple Streak
    The Wild Hills

Later
    The Moon in My Pocket
    The Life for Me
    The Blood-Red Island
    The Verdict of You All
    The Tangerine House
    The Quest for Quixote
    The Wintry Sea
    The Gorgeous East

THE HAPPY HIGHWAYS

by

Rupert Croft-Cooke

W. H. ALLEN

LONDON
1967

To
The Memory of Vincy Schwarz

That is the land of lost content,
I see it shining plain,
The happy highways where I went
And cannot come again.
A Shropshire Lad

Contents

I	Smarden Grange	9
II	Attitudes, 1937	20
III	A Collection of Letters	30
IV	Friends	48
V	Parnassus N.W.8	62
VI	Work and Freedom	77
VII	Ernst Thoma	91
VIII	The Circus Has No Home	104
IX	Tenting	118
X	The Man in Europe Street	131
XI	Belgium and Holland	141
XII	Germany	152
XIII	Czechoslovakia	173
XIV	Austria	184
XV	Hungary	191
XVI	Yugoslavia	211
XVII	Italy	220
XVIII	France and Home	234
	L'Envoi	246

CONTENTS

CHAPTER ONE

Smarden Grange

[1]

THE YEAR 1937 was one of the most extravagantly eventful of my life. I saw the new year in on a ship coming home from South America, and regretfully watched it go out while I was travelling in a living-waggon through the third of nine European countries I was visiting, accompanied by two circus performers, in an attempt to interview the European man-in-the-street. Between these two exotic midnights I leased and moved into a Kentish manor-house which was far too large for me, published a novel, a travel book and a collection of short stories, was viciously attacked in the Anglo-Argentine press, opened a third antiquarian bookshop this time in Gravesend, wrote a weekly feature in a Sunday paper, met an unusual variety of people, stayed a month in Germany at the very time of Mussolini's visit to Hitler, fell in with and followed a circus in England and prepared the expedition on which at the end of the year I was engaged. Also I had my thirty-fourth birthday and supposed that with it I achieved the status of a mature and responsible man, a successful writer and solid householder, whereas in truth I remained little more than an energetic adolescent.

The house was called Smarden Grange and it stood on a cross-roads a mile away from an attractive Wealden village. There are those who consider the levels of the Weald of Kent, the land of the 'dens'—Marden, Biddenden, Tenterden, Benenden and the rest—too flat and tranquil, or who find in this last agricultural stronghold, untouched by industrial enterprise, a countryside too grimly rural for sophisticated habitation. But I had loved it since boyhood when I had discovered it by cycling from Tonbridge.

9

It is flat, but not without undulations and sudden rises, and its land is almost entirely given to fruit and hops and vegetables. But it has leafy roads, a few winding streams and some of the most unspectacularly beautiful villages in England. Its people are dedicated to the land, except for a few retired folk from the cities who have chosen its restful solitudes as their home and the doctors, schoolmasters, clergymen, publicans and shop-keepers who minister to them. It merits all the kindest clichés—it is out of date, off the map, behind the times, even perhaps beyond the pale. It is fertile; vivid with mile upon mile of fruit blossom in spring and scented with hops and heavy with apples and plums in autumn, the true garden of England. Its tempo is plodding, its atmosphere benign, its landscapes unpretentious.

In the very heart of the Weald was Smarden to which my father had come a year before his death to make the last of his many homes in a house on its outskirts. He died in this house, as I have related in *The Wild Hills*, and it had remained empty since. The Weald had lost its prosperity along with English agriculture and nobody wanted to rent, still less to buy, a house out of reach of London, three miles from a railway station itself on a slow line, a mile from the village and entirely sur-rounded by orchards. But I did not even re-examine the house before signing the lease and moving in.

It was built in early Victorian times on a square eighteenth-century model, with a pillar'd portico to redeem its flat surface, red and blue brick walls and a slate roof. I always intended to buy it, plaster its surface and put in eight-paned windows when it would have become, to all appearances, a Georgian house. It was much too large for me, with three sitting-rooms, one of which had been added as a billiard-room and was enormous, a vast kitchen, four bedrooms and a bathroom over the older rooms, and a big separate bedroom and bathroom over the one-time billiard-room. It had a garden of flowering shrubs and an orchard of Conference pears. There was a green-house built against the south wall, too extensive and utilitarian to be called a conservatory and a pair of cottages, their upper floors constructed of hideous corrugated iron, behind it in the garden. There was also a swimming-pool made with no means of changing the water and inhabited by a few lazy carp.

The house was dry and in splendid repair but the whole place needed, indeed cried out for money to be spent on it if it was to become a 'gentleman's residence'. The staircase was mean and narrow and started to ascend two paces from the front door. The portico should have been shifted to make one of the small rooms downstairs an entrance hall. The upper floors of the cottages should have been removed and the pool made usable. None of this would have cost much money at that time and I had an option to purchase the house for £1200. If . . . but there is no more fatuous kind of hypothesis for people of my age than that which supposes the clever investment of money before the Second World War. Moreover if I had possessed the place it would have robbed my six years in the army of their delightful rootlessness and irresponsibility.

Not that my living in that house seemed impermanent or makeshift to me. I took it, as my father had taken all his houses, with the intention of remaining there for the rest of my life, and throughout my occupancy I was forever planning improvements to be made when I had achieved the literary fortune which (inevitably, I still believed) would one day be mine. I did not see myself as squatting with insufficient furniture in a home which was beyond my means and too large for quiet possessive comfort. It was miraculous to me that I had achieved this tenancy, however precariously, by what I liked doing best, writing books.

[2]

I even received afternoon calls and it was as well that I had brought from Gloucestershire the manservant-cook whom I had employed there for the last three years, because he was ready to enter into the spirit of the thing, even to wear a white coat and open the front door. Eric Harwood, as I have recalled in *The Wild Hills*, was a born cook and by now a highly practised and skilled one. He was a Cotswold village baker's son and though too humorous and independent, too much of a rustic Sam Weller to make the kind of dim ceremonious servant still then in vogue, his imaginative cooking made daily meals a series of delightful minor events, as meals should be. Eric was no longer the gauche boy who had come and asked for a job but an accomplished young man who as a servant was, like the house, beyond my means.

The callers were few but punctilious, only the male of each household arriving and leaving a card on departure. The Rector, who had buried my father some twenty months earlier, was as my father had found, 'a splendid old fellow'. He gazed at my books already ranged round the walls of the largest room and said they reminded him of a problem, a puzzle that he knew. I secretly yawned for I detest mathematical problems, but the Rector refused to be put off and proceeded to communicate one of the best teasers or brains tests, as they were later called, that I have ever heard.

"On the shelf", said the Rector, "you have the volumes of a set ranged in correct order, volumes one, say, to five. For the sake of argument let us suppose that the covers are a quarter of an inch thick and the accumulated pages of each volume make an inch of thickness, so that each volume, standing upright, occupies one inch and a half of shelf.

"Now there is a little bookworm who always eats his way in a dead straight line. He starts at the first page of volume one and eats his way to the last page of volume two. How far has he travelled?"

I, like everyone else who has not heard the answer, made my faulty guess. Two and a half inches I think I said. The Rector shook his head, for what I failed to remember even as I stared at two such volumes was that the first page is to the right of a volume as it stands, the last page to the left, so as the Rector triumphantly demonstrated, the bookworm had travelled half an inch.

Another caller was a retired army officer from a villa along the road who was reputed to practise nudism in his own home. This amused Eric who imagined himself taking the day's orders from the Major in the kitchen and warning him in good Rabelaisian terms against going too near the hot stove. There were other formal callers from among the families who had chosen the large local houses as retreats, but I had not time to do more than make the ritual counter-call, wondering that such conventions survived. The only friends I had in the region before arriving there were Maurice and Greta Clifford who were farming over at Headcorn. Maurice had been at the King's School Rochester when I had my bookshop there. At seventeen he was already secretly engaged to Greta, 'the prettiest school-girl in the Medway towns', so that they had used my shop as a meeting-place. I now went often to their fine Tudor farmhouse.

For a month I was wholly absorbed in household affairs and the animals I had brought from Gloucestershire. Chief among these was Dingo my yellow Alsatian, now three years old, a most beautiful and lovable creature who seldom left my heels. I had also brought Guy and Pauline, the peacock and his mate who made the early mornings shrill. Guy at once chose the garage roof as his perching place and hung his long brilliant feathers down its slope to be seen from the road, a position recommended by his vanity. When Eric discovered that beyond the kitchen there was a brick oven so that he could bake in the only way that produces really fine bread, and when I had accustomed myself to writing at a window which overlooked my own pear trees, and when an unrealized wistaria suddenly covered two walls of the house with blue luxuriance, my new home gave me all I could ask of felicity and interest.

[3]

Two hundred yards down the road, on the edge of an almost uninhabited area stretching five miles or more, was a pub called the Bell. It seemed to me then, and seems now in recollection, to have all that I most value in the tradition of the English inn. It was an old timbered building but its antiquity was not speciously preserved or stressed, its public rooms were not cluttered with antiques, it was not quaint or old-world but a sensibly furnished, cheerful, well-kept tavern in which for three centuries liquor had been sold without fuss or folksiness to the local farmers, their men and a few passing travellers.

There was, I believe, some kind of private or saloon bar, or some room removed from the ordinary business of the place, but I never saw it and I never heard of it being used. There was one bar-room used by us all whatever our station; it had a bare board floor, a bright fire in winter, hard wooden-seated chairs, a dart-board and faded chintz curtains.

Since the Bell Inn was a mile or more from Smarden, it was free from intrigue and envious rivalry that are found when there are several pubs or taverns in a single village. It had its regular customers and I knew them all, was indeed one of them, but there was no chit-chat brought to it from other licensed premises in the vicinity.

The landlord was a youngish man as landlords go, tall, vigorous, combative. His father, a neighbouring farmer, 'Old Mr Hughes', used to visit the Bell, driving over in a pony and trap, wearing gaiters and looking every inch a character in a Hardy novel, perhaps the Mayor of Casterbridge himself. I can remember him hoisting himself up to the driving seat of his trap long after nightfall when his carriage-lamps were lit, and with a click of the teeth to his pony and a wave of his whip to his son disappear into the dusk for a nine-mile drive home. Gordon Hughes the landlord, who was married and had a son and daughter, was of a go-ahead and enterprising turn and because the Bell Inn, for all its comfort and homeliness and devoted patrons, could give no more than a living, he had made kennels for racing greyhounds in his yard and himself bred dogs and entered them in races. But this made him no less a landlord, welcoming to his customers, quick to serve an honest measure, expert in the care and treatment of beer, opinionated and impatient with the self-important, but humorous and noisy with his friends. He was a skilled dart-player, a ready gambler and a good loser.

There gathered in his bar at night a number of men so well worth knowing, so sharply contrasted within the small compass of the time and the place, so typed and yet so individual, that each remains in my mind like a lifelong friend, each is here in this room with me two thousand miles and thirty years away.

There was first a piece of physical wreckage and indomitable cheerfulness named Syd. In the army at sixteen during the First World War, he endured three years almost continuously in the trenches and on demobilization found himself totally unskilled in anything but the use of a rifle and a gasmask. He spent the wretched few pounds he was awarded for his services in as many days and without family or chance of employment he drifted penuriously till a chance to join the Royal Irish Constabulary, the Black and Tans, to get into uniform again, seemed to him a godsend. He had little knowledge of Ireland or the issues concerned, he felt no malice or shame in joining that abominable gang, knowing nothing of the indignation it had roused in England as well as Ireland. He was shot to pieces in an ambush, left for dead, nursed by nuns back to a half-life of crutches and lacerated lungs and now hobbled round, emaciated and deformed, existing on a tiny pension. He had somehow found his way to the Bell Inn and Gordon Hughes and his wife had adopted him as a boarder.

With a fine, sensitive face, a faint but pleasant voice, deepset thoughtful eyes, he had an almost uncanny talent for modelling and carving, shaping any available material to his whims. From the children's plasticine he produced, his narrow fingers working with confidence, whole families of exquisitely shaped grotesques. He would sit shaping a piece of wood with a knife or chisel or moulding clay to fanciful figures from his own imagination. He spoke little but his whole gentle nature was in his smile when he looked up from his work. This was the last year of his wrecked life for he died without self-pity in the following winter.

Bob Parker was a cripple too, but a lustier figure altogether. He had sailed before the mast and lost the use of a leg in an accident at sea, but could lever himself on to a bicycle and at closing-time ride swearing away to the shack he occupied on a piece of wasteland. Swearing, but without foul or blasphemous language for he had great ingenuity in abuse and malediction, using old-fashioned fulminations without any of the uglier four-lettered words. He was a tall man with a tight-lipped mouth and somewhat harsh expression that broke often into a grim smile and he wore steel-rimmed glasses. Something of a raconteur, he made the best of his past to give us, on occasion, accounts of sailing-ships or tell us far-fetched stories of incidents in foreign ports.

Just after the First World War he had fallen a victim to one of those plot-of-land swindles which took the gratuities from officers and other ranks alike. A so-called property company had bought for almost nothing a few acres of poor ground near Smarden and spent some money on drawing up an elaborate prospectus which promised plot-purchasers a new city of shops and industries. A large-scale map was published showing where 'market', 'church' and 'hotel' would stand, and a public auction disposed of some hundred 'plots' of bare meadowland a few miles from a railway or any house or place of business.

Every other purchaser soon realized he had been duped and abandoned his hopes, but Bob Parker was an obstinate man and undeterred by finding that his plot was in the middle of a wilderness, he built himself a wooden shack there and started a smallholding. As the years passed and the surrounding sites remained barren he took over more ground and invested in a few sheep. Occasionally, as he used to tell us, one of the original mugs would arrive to see the state of his investment but he was usually glad to sell Bob his elaborately drawn up deed for a pound or two and Bob remained in possesion. His 'estate' was a couple of miles from the Bell and he would come in almost nightly, looking shabby and sullen till with the first pint or two he became garrulous. At weekends his wife, who was a shorthand typist with a good post in London, came down, plump, pretty and urban, to stay a night or two in Bob's primitive bungalow.

Less attractive were the owners of the greyhounds which Gordon Hughes boarded, dull and prosperous shopkeepers from Maidstone or Chatham with dressy wives. But their invasions, the women wearing that unhappy combination, fur coats from department store windows and artificial pearls, and the men seeking to buy pints for the yokels, did not much change the atmosphere of the Bell. They came and left in their smart little saloon cars without disrupting our games of darts or my conversation with Edgar or Harry Homewood.

These were two of the three bachelor brothers who shared a little house nearby, the last Englishmen I have known in my life who could fairly be said, without condescension or sentimentality, to belong to that ancient and now vanished class, the yeomanry. Born in the house they still inhabited, with a holding not large enough to support them, they had worked from childhood on the land of others, but with a certain independence of outlook. Harry, the oldest, was a merry little gnome of a man, less than five foot tall, rubicund, white-haired, watery-eyed, who rarely shaved and stumped into the bar to spend a few pence nightly on cider. His passions were shooting and fishing of the most elementary kind—he would sit day-long by the stream nearby waiting for a bite from the few coarse fish that it held, or one would see him with his gun tramping on his short legs to some distant spinney. In his thick Kentish speech he would tell stories of long-ago shoots or triumphs of his own with an ancestor of the ferrets he kept at home. He was never without a sack which sometimes contained ground game. I suspect that he could not read or write but as he did not need to do either, but sat perky and innocent staring at his pint, I do not know for certain. When I saw Walt Disney's *Snow White* I recognized Harry in all seven of the dwarfs, but they had not his earthiness, his beautiful, blank, childish ignorance of the world, or his knowledge of wild creatures.

Lebby, the second brother, had lost a leg in the First World War and walked on a wooden stump, having refused to accommodate himself to an artificial limb. He cooked and cleaned the cottage for the other two and in spite of his pension and the proximity of his home he never came to the Bell. ("Too mean", it was said.) Lebby was well-read and loved to lean over the five-barred gate of his holding, talking with any passer-by who had time to spare.

The youngest brother, Edgar, was in his fifties then, I suppose. Unlike Harry, he had once left the district—that was as an infantryman in the First World War, when he had been taken prisoner in 1916 and, as he told me, had his 'guts ruined for life' by the starvation diet of turnips he remembered. Edgar with his dyspeptic lined face and sullen dark eyes, his moustache and the defiant set of his old cap, was the least sociable of the three, drinking his pint in silence or grumbling to the rest of us about his brother Lebby. He seemed a grim misanthropic man and surprised the customers of the Bell three years later by escaping his brother's housekeeping for good and marrying a local widow some years younger than himself. She adored him and used to call at the Bell for a bottle to take home for 'my Edgar'.

Grand fellows the Homewood brothers seemed to me, calling me 'Mus'r Cooke' and talking to me, Edgar of his troubles and Harry of the day's bag, as we sat by the Bell fire at night throughout that chilly March. Less admirable, perhaps, but no less amiable, was Big Jim. It would not be fair to call him the village wastrel for he had no vices, harmed nobody and was not incapable of work, but left an orphan and brought up by an indulgent aunt ("The sunshine comes out the back of his arse for *her*", it was picturesquely said), he had never been dependent for his very living on the work he did and had therefore idled, and lost jobs, tried this or that occupation and now in his forties 'did a few days work here or there' to the secret envy of his more industrious fellows. He was called Big Jim because he was tall, but he was not proportionately powerful, thinnish rather, with a long anserine face that had a perpetual smile of good-nature on it. He still lived with his aunt who was reputed to 'have a few pennies', and he was rarely short of beer money.

There were others who came less regularly, among them a working blacksmith, for there was a smithy in full blast a few yards away, a butcher named Ledger who rented a part of the Bell yard for his shop and made the best pork sausages I have eaten, a farmer named Millin with his two sturdy sons and some youngsters from the village who came out on cycles. Few of these had been farther from home than Ashford market and few might afterwards have done so if the war had not come to break the continuity of their placid lives.

[4]

The Bell was along the road from my house but there was a shorter way to reach it across the orchards and before the spring was over I had worn a wavering footpath to it through the grass. Lost to the more exigent society of my respectable neighbours I once again settled to a life which suited me well, working through the morning, eating Eric's too-luxurious food, resting or gardening till it was time to drink several cups of China tea, writing again and before seven o'clock crossing the orchard to spend three hours in dart-playing or conversation.

This was enough for a month or two until impulses of energy, trivial ambition or sheer restlessness sent me farther afield.

CHAPTER TWO

Attitudes, 1937

[1]

IN FEBRUARY was published *Kingdom Come,* a novel I had written in the previous year in rather curious circumstances. I had met and become friendly with a young film star named Douglass Montgomery whose work, particularly in the film *Little Man, What Now?* I had long admired. I have already related how he wanted me to write a play for him, how we discussed an idea for it and worked it out in some detail, but how afterwards, when Douglass had returned to America, I decided to write it as a novel. Now it came out and met a kind of criticism which surprised me.

Hitherto I had been treated with the indulgence usually shown to young writers who seem to be trying. There had been predictions of future success rather than (from significant critics) any very weighty approval of what had appeared. But this was my tenth novel and reviewers now began to accept me as established somewhere in the hierarchy, and to refer to earlier books in considering this one. I had, in fact, secured a place among regularly publishing novelists. In spite of the fact that my books came from one of Walter Hutchinson's group of companies, they were seriously judged as more than the *jeux d'esprit* with which I had started.

Kingdom Come received this treatment from a number of critics whose names meant a good deal then and from one or two whose names are still effulgent. Leo Walmsley, C. B. Rees, Wilson Pope, Richard Church, James Agate, Roger Pippett, D. S. Meldrum, Howard Spring, Francis Burdett and Wilfred Gibson were all gentle with its faults and in general commendatory, while it was noticed by anonymous reviewers in *The Times*, *Times Literary Supplement*, *Punch* and a good many more. It was also, for what that was worth, a Book Society Recommendation.

Easily beguiled by printed approbation in those days, I took all this quite seriously, but soon found that there was a fly in the ointment and one with a particularly virulent sting in its tail. Cecil Day-Lewis had picked out two of the embarrassingly purple passages which appeared too often in my prose and quoted them mercilessly in the *Daily Telegraph*. "I can stand a good deal," he wrote, "but my nerve gives way when faced with phrases like . . ." No, I will not repeat them here. It is sufficient to say that Day-Lewis's choice of my words was deadly, and that I can sympathize with his irritation. An enthusiastic story-teller who had no editorial guidance, I was apt to write at the top of my voice in a style which I find exacerbating to my nervous system today when I come on it in the works of Lesley Branch and Iris Murdoch. But it was the form of the reproof which was most wounding, for no one likes being made to look foolish out of his own mouth and I could not but admit that I had supplied the material.

I was accustomed to blasts. Two good critics, Frank Swinnerton and Winifred Holtby, had virtually told me to go to hell from the first, and two others, John Brophy and Dudley Carew, had pursued my books with what I was pleased to call catcalls through the columns of various unimportant periodicals. But what Day-Lewis wrote was far more effective and painful because I could recognize it as justified.

The little gibe, which I ought to have considered all in the day's work of any novelist, took on an absurd significance in my mind. I did not know Day-Lewis personally—I did not in fact meet him till twelve years later when I found him an affable and intelligent person who would have been disturbed to know that he had caused such a fluttering of dovecotes—but I was aware that he belonged to a group of poets and political writers just then beginning to make themselves known, gathered as they were round the editorial figure of John Lehmann whose quarterly *New Writing* was rousing considerable interest. These poets and polemicists were of my own age and had mostly known one another since school or university days; they had Left Wing sympathies though they did not call themselves Communists and if any one of them was aware of my existence as a writer he probably considered me a fuddy-duddy novelist who was published with far too much ill-earned profit.

Now I had begun my career by contributing poetry to the reviews which a few years before were considered *avant garde* but which had now been largely superseded by *New Writing*. These were the *London Mercury*, the *New Coterie*, *Poetry* (Chicago), the *Adelphi*, the *Chapbook* and the *English Review*. The poetry which Lehmann was publishing, in a new poetic idiom, made those early verses of mine look like the work of a very minor Georgian, born too late. Moreover the writers of an older generation I had known, Kipling, Galsworthy, Chesterton, were no more and the editors who had encouraged me, Squire, Orage, Chesterton, Middleton Murray, Monro were dead or out of business. I began to feel already excluded from the Forward movements at the age of thirty-three and to build up a youthful and petulant resentment towards that powerful body of the time, the Left Wing Intelligentsia.

It was not until after the war that I contributed to *New Writing* and came to know, appreciate and like John Lehmann himself. In 1937 there were many factors which isolated me from writers belonging to all the more interesting coteries of that epoch. What reputation I had was forbidding—that of a popular novelist. (I was even being mistaken for a best-selling one.) It was a damning thing to be published by one of the Hutchinson group at that time and even fifteen years later when Macmillans were publishing my books a director of the firm warned me that in the opinion of their travellers this early affiliation had categorized me for life. Then, I had lived in the deepest country districts for the last five years and knew almost no one in the mysterious and busy state called 'in the swim'.

Although in that year I spent some time in London and met a few people in the world of books it was usually under the aegis of Louis Golding who certainly did write best-sellers and was very much out of intellectual fashion. More than this, I was not actively associated with any political movement and this to the idealistic young men of the years just before the war was un-forgivable, or perhaps incomprehensible. Secretly I considered my particular kind of sympathy with the needy proletarian world of the time, my facility for being accepted among the least literate or articulate of people, my proudly achieved class-lessness after a severely bourgeois upbringing, the novel I had written about the unemployed, my sincere liking for the vulgar and common-place in things, people, places, all these to be worth more than a display of solidarity with 'the workers' voiced by literary supporters of Left Wing policies. I was consoled by this but it did nothing to recommend me to the ardent crusaders who looked to Russia for their inspiration.

A more potent factor was my belief in professionalism as an end and triumph in itself. I had to wait nearly twenty years before I met, in John Lodwick, anybody who shared this. To him, as to me, the profession of letters was a proud one and he felt a strong personal loyalty to its members. 'But he's a *writer*', he used to say of someone criticized in other capacities. I have always detested amateurism and believed that a man should have the self-sacrifice and courage to make himself dependent on his work. I believed that a fine book was more likely to come from a writer who had worked his way up from mediocrity and pot-boiling than from one who spent his leisure in the scrupulous polishing of some precious *oeuvre*. I was prepared to forgive a writer anything but the fear of committing himself wholly to his profession and I respected those of the past and the few contemporaries to whom writing was all that mattered, who could match painters and composers in their wholeheartedness. This belief in professionalism as a creed and an essential is totally unfashionable today when no more than a score or two of men and women in England are determined to earn a chancy living solely by the writing of books rather than hire themselves out as the improvisers of television and radio scripts or advertising copy and film dialogue, as participants in radio guessing games, as dons, public lecturers, television artists or politicians. Even at the time I am recalling when it was possible for young people to live wholly by writing, my respect for professionalism was not understood and I felt lonely in it.

But there was something more critical than any of these which cut me off from all who felt political or sentimental obligations, even from many of my fellow Catholics. That was my attitude to the Spanish Civil War which was then in its second tragic year.

I had loved Spain since boyhood. I had lived there five years earlier and had stoutly believed in the Republic and its power to overcome its enormous difficulties. I had proclaimed this belief in a naïvely fervent article in the *Review of Reviews* in 1933. When the Republic failed to govern, that is to give the most elementary protection to the rights of the individual, I felt it as a tragedy but I did not deceive myself about that failure and I wonder now (admittedly with hindsight), how anyone can have done so who watched events during the year before Franco's uprising. When, during the war itself, the Government ceased to be legal and was taken over by mortally competing groups of doctrinaires I lost all sentiment of loyalty to it.

My position would have been simple if I had been able to accept Franco as a potential saviour of Spain, but this I could not do. Had his rebellion been what he proclaimed it to be, a truly popular rising, the mass movement of a whole great people exasperated by chaos, incendiarism, murder and deadly quarrels between political parties, had it in other words succeeded immediately and without great bloodshed, it might have been another matter, but this was not so. So, though most of my Spanish friends actively supported Franco and though there was much in his cause with which I sympathized, I could not join it.

What then remained? For me only one ideal, a passionate

belief in non-intervention, not as a political measure or a subject for international conferences, but as a personal credo and obligation which became more insistent as the war went on. It was perhaps natural for me who had long since purged myself of trust in political parties. The only Communism that my generation had then seen in action was that of Stalin, a murderous stultification of all men's higher aspirations, a denial —not merely in emergency but for all time—of the essential rights of humankind to live, think, pray, create and aspire. The only Fascism we knew was the macaronic and makeshift gangsterism of Mussolini while the horrors of Nazism could only be guessed from the spoken or written ravings of Hitler. How could men believe in any of these, I asked myself, so ardently that they would go and kill Spaniards for the sake of them? The Spaniards themselves had no remedy. It was largely a question of geography and they were roped into whichever forces held the district in which they found themselves. But that foreigners should volunteer, for the sake of a philosophical or political preference, to join in a civil war seemed to me immoral, however much heroism they might show in doing so. I determined—and it was not an easy resolution to make—that I would take no part even by word in that conflict. That I became tiresome and self-righteous in this is shown by some high falutin nonsense I wrote in my Introduction to the war memoirs[a] of Colonel Casado, the last head of the Government who surrendered Madrid to Franco.

'In this country, throughout the war, the intelligentsia were "taking sides" like preparatory schoolboys on Boat Race Day, while a nation was committing suicide. To those of us who love Spain and her people the idiot oratory of "Save Spain" meetings was as painful as the "Christian Gentleman" talk of the Franquistas. We did nothing, either as a nation or as human beings, to serve the only cause in Spain, or anywhere else, which was worth serving—the cause of peace. While

[a] *The Last Days of Madrid* by Colonel S. Casado. Translated with an Introduction by Rupert Croft-Cooke (Peter Davies 1939).

young Spaniards shot one another, we bandied words like
quarrelling neighbours, and the literature in this country in
defence of one side or the other was a disgrace.'

This was over-written and pawky, but the basic sentiment
expressed remained throughout the Spanish Civil War—somewhat vociferously I fear—my own.

This made me unpopular with people I knew on all sides.
The young writers of the Left, just in their epoch of greatest
influence in London intellectual life, would have found it easier
to forgive downright support for Franco than this belief that
embroilment was a crime. I was a Catholic and in England
people seem to look for something mysterious, something quite
unaccountable by accepted standards, from their Catholic
minority.

Nobody who knew me would have blamed me for being a
Franquista, but almost everyone I knew blamed me for refusing
to take sides even in my own mind. Since no conflict in which
the country was not directly involved has ever stirred the
British as this one did, so that one could never escape discussion
of it for long, I felt when I was in London almost a pariah.

But I was not often in London, remaining among people to
whom John Lehmann and his *New Writing* were as remote as
Jesús Hernandez and his *Mundo Obrero*.

[2]

So, cut off from the causes and activities of my contemporaries
by inclination, by temperament, by conviction, by economic
considerations and by sheer distance, I created in obscurity a
stance of my own which in the following years was in danger
of becoming a pose. I was a country-dweller not in the capacity
of a naturalist or authority on agriculture, which I was far from
being, but as one who preferred what was left of rural England
to the metropolitan life which his fellows found fertile and

inspiring. I was a public-bar man who had written the only book on darts. I was a novelist whose stories were about un-eccentric and undistinguished people in several countries, void of intellectualism or philosophy, and who began rather mon-strously to maintain that fiction should be like this, quoting Hardy, Conrad, Kipling and others as models. I was a traveller who sought to know people of the streets abroad, and I kept in touch with the friends I had made in France, Germany, Spain, Switzerland, Argentina, and others from still more countries whom I had met at the Institut Montana, none of them intellectuals or artists. As a writer of non-fiction I worked first for the Freedom Association for whom I turned out article after article upholding small personal liberties, and in those years I also began to write on food and wine. Shortly I would become a wordy partisan of the circus and spend months tenting with a family concern. Later I was to travel with gypsies and write several books about them. All this was my private and unvoiced answer to the illuminati and it gave a certain shape and meaning to my life in the years before the war. I liked to think that they—by whom I meant pretty well all young men whose names were booming just then, Auden, Spencer, Day-Lewis, Isherwood, MacNeice and the rest—were making a cult of poetry and a certain kind of literature while I would make a cult of experience which would find its own expression in time. It was a false and foolish presumption made in solitude by one who unconsciously longed for and needed literary fellowship, but its after-effects have never quite left me. I was far too little known to create this as an image in the public eye but by the time I joined the army, and ceased to write or think much about letters for six years, I had gone some way towards doing so.

I would not have it thought that these were deliberate or even fully conscious resolutions, the result of fierce introspection and self-criticism. On the contrary I was far too zestfully con-cerned with everyday life, with many projects and new interests, to brood morbidly over my own or anyone else's work, or to question myself about the future. I wrote, without too many heavy considerations of purpose, things that I wanted to write. I enjoyed writing as I enjoyed almost everything else and sat down at my desk with light-hearted gusto rather than the agony and despair which so many writers claim to feel when they are faced with pen and paper. Whatever my subconscious may have been up to, I was aware only of a cheerful disrespect for the earnest pronouncements of the politically obsessed and a lack of sympathy for their aims in poetry as in life. But this awareness was not a dark or invidious thing—it gave me an extrovert's good-natured and exaggerated hilarity. At this time I bought and carefully studied Michael Roberts's *Faber Book of Modern Verse* and took honest pleasure in much of it, was impressed by its sincerity of purpose and irritated by the affectations and sillier obscurities in its manner. Much of it seemed self-conscious, much hysterical, but I had to admit that there was unexpected beauty, if of a sporadic, unsatisfying kind. That anthology, in the years of which I am writing, was considered a fair symposium of one group's achievements and it did not justify, I felt, the solemnity and awe with which its poets were treated, and with which too often they seemed to treat themselves. They could still be considered comic as well as pathetic figures in their desperate concern with intellectual causes and their attempts to satisfy poetic aspirations with a dreary system of economics. I found no reason in their writings, or in any of the foreboding and portentous writings of the time, to check the vaultings of my optimism.

[3]

It was perhaps not surprising that the only novel I wrote that year was a light-hearted satire of English contemporary life. The framework of it was derived from the circumstances in which my French friend Robert Cahiza had come to England a year or two earlier—the exchange system under which French and English students spent alternate months in one another's home. I used my French visitor as a Gulliver, and by the simple device of making the two brothers who entertained him one philistine and the other intellectual I could ridicule both. When it was published nearly a year later it displeased critics in the press of both Right and Left and Humbert Wolfe announced with Victorian hauteur that he was not entertained. But it tickled the uncommitted like Sean O'Faolian who after saying that I was sometimes a sentimentalist ("So is every writer who happens to believe in something and gets driven off his balance now and again by the guffaws of the hard-boiled") pointed out that I got my own back, with interest, on the anti-sentimentalists, while Desmond Shawe-Taylor in the *New Statesman* called it horribly veracious. It was, at any rate, an easy and enjoyable book to write and expressed my own far too frivolous state of mind.

For dates are deceptive. Looking now at the ciphers '1937' one could suppose that we were already, and consciously, on the very eve of war, or at least that we knew war to be inevitable. This would be a false impression. In spite of claims of foresight made in after years, few people during that spring and summer were resigned to the prospect and most who realized some of the megalomania of Hitler believed it would be satisfied by the adulation of his own people. His occupation of the Rhineland had seemed understandable if not justifiable to the majority of the English and he had as yet made no territorial claims, while by his pact with Schuschnigg in the previous year he appeared to respect Austrian sovereignty. The Spanish war looked like being confined to Spain and a world war, so far from seeming inevitable, could still be thought a contingency too outrageous to be adopted even by Hitler, though there were percipient people whom we called pessimists who never doubted its imminence. If Spain as a country had been unknown to me and unloved there would have been nothing in the international situation to distract me from work and the diversions of a life without imposed discipline.

B

CHAPTER THREE

A Collection of Letters

[1]

AS IF I WAS NOT already fully occupied, with a large house on my hands and the necessity to write enough to bring me a living, I decided to start another bookshop. There was in those years a strong vein of the dealer in me; I loved a bargain and the adventure of looking for it. My younger brother Laurie and I had built up quite a considerable business in old and rare books in Rochester and sold it well in 1931, to return to book-dealing spasmodically at various times since then. It was a pleasant and interesting trade and, with our hardly acquired knowledge of values and a certain flair for finding unusual books, a profitable one. I do not think we were greedy or mean-spirited in this though I suppose all forms of direct buying and selling involve some hard-headedness. I like to think it was the sheer fun of it that appealed to us, the pursuit, the discovery, the acquisition and the disposal of treasure, and the pitting of our wits and energies against those of men in a shrewd, competitive and distortedly knowledgeable profession.

When we had a shop in Rochester in 1928–30 one of our most fruitful hunting grounds was the town of Gravesend. It had an air of vanished grandeur for it had flourished as a river port in Victorian times and piers were erected, a promenade laid out and many solid grey houses built with verandahs overlooking the river and the flats of the Essex coast. Prosperity had not yet returned with the great paper mills and Gravesend's pretentious houses concealed a good deal of poverty. The atmosphere of the place was somewhat grim, but it had character. There was a maze of narrow streets near the river which had once held ships' chandlers' and fishing tackle shops, even, when I first knew it, some salty old inhabitants who might have come from the writings of W. W. Jacobs. Most in keeping with the general decay was the empty shell of a theatre, in disuse in 1937, but in 1925 when I lived a few miles away, visited by the last of the old touring companies staging forgotten melodramas and pre-Wilde 'society plays' acted by penurious unfortunates in soiled costumes.

Such a town promised well for us, since the business of the provincial antiquarian bookseller was then paradoxically to *buy*. His 'shop trade' he regarded as a means of getting rid of some of the books he had been forced to acquire in auction in order to obtain that one, or those few books in an auctioneers' lot which he could sell by catalogue. In the mouldering drawing-rooms of Gravesend, we argued, must be plenty of good stuff and we were right in this. Our mistake was to open a shop at all for we had to keep an assistant and the few books we sold to passers-by did not pay his wages or the shop rent. We should have been satisfied to comb the town and others as we had done before and to catalogue the stuff from my home at Smarden, throwing out or re-auctioning everything that was not worth cataloguing.

But we found premises and in doing so came on one of those anomalies which affect shop-keepers everywhere. Why, it is asked, are certain streets of a town or even certain *sides* of streets useless for the retailer while others, in appearance no more promising, are properous? One can produce a hundred arguments to prove that a street *should* be the most thriving in the whole area, it is on the way from *this* to *that*, its shop-fronts are well-constructed, it is not a wind-trap or a place of gloom, it is used by moneyed people, but somehow it is just not a good street for a shop and nothing, it seems, can make it one. In such a street our shop was opened and failed within the year.

But in that time it entailed a large expense of energy and petrol, for Gravesend was more than thirty miles from my home. My brother and I, or more often my brother alone, attended auctions, followed clues, gained access to houses in which were collections of books that might be bought, but somehow it failed to interest us as it had once done, perhaps because we were seven years older, perhaps because I at least could not give my whole time to it.

[2]

To counteract this onset of partial failure I used what connections I had as a writer to increase our trade in a way which would have brought us success twenty-five years later. I realized that there were collectors for authors' manuscripts and I put in one of our catalogues the complete holograph manuscript of Louis Golding's *Magnolia Street* for £75, of which (if we sold if) Louis was to pay us £25. I intended to follow this with other authors' manuscripts, a scheme ahead of its time for in recent years American libraries have taken to buying these on a vast and generous scale. *Magnolia Street* in fact did not pass through our hands for Sir Louis Sterling, an eccentric industrialist of the time, hearing of it in our catalogue bought it direct from Louis Golding (who honoured his agreement with us). But this incident led to a remarkable purchase which I have never regretted.

In the early years of this century an American literary agent named Curtis Brown had come to London, gathered a number of distinguished authors to the agency he founded and become friends with many of them. After his death his younger son Spencer Curtis Brown had continued the business and now agreed to sell us a large number of letters of bibliographical interest which had been written to his father, chiefly between the years 1910 and 1923. My brother spent a couple of weeks in the basement or cellar of the firm's premises in Covent Garden, going through dusty files and picking what was of interest to collectors, and purchasing them in bundles. When he arrived at Smarden at night, dusty and tired but triumphant, we would go through the day's bag before walking through the orchard to the Bell.

There was fascination but also something distressing about these records of long-ago disputes with publishers, anxieties over money due, arguments about royalties, despair about the difficulties of gaining a livelihood felt by the poorer authors and dictatorial demands by the more successful ones. How painfully alike were all authors' letters to their agent, how like my own I thought uneasily, how much concerned with the same old questions of percentages or outright sales, of translations, film rights or cheap editions. Reading these should have been enough to discourage any young writer from the profession of letters, in spite of the lordly addresses of the few best-selling authors of the day. Even now as I look at them I feel, as then, deeply interested and somewhat dispirited. They reveal so much of 'old unhappy far-off things and battles long ago'.

Taking them in alphabetical order, I find William Archer in 1918 using the immemorial terms of reproach about a publisher which surely every author once at least in his career has used. He has a very strong impression that Hutchinson have *grossly* neglected *India and the Future*. If it has not sold well he is convinced it is their fault. "Since it was published I have not seen a *single* advt. of it." In the next year he wants to write a book called *The Coming Cosmos* which he believes will attract some attention as its ideas go far beyond those which are likely to be realized in the 'League of Nations actually set on foot by the Peace Congress'. A month later he feels that world affairs are moving so quickly 'that it is almost impossible to say anything on the new world-order at present' and decides to drop the idea.

Michael Arlen's letters included thanks from him and 'the girl who is reckless enough to marry me' for a wedding present in 1928, and an angry letter from Paris when he has seen in the papers that the play of *The Green Hat* is on somewhere in London twice nightly though he has been told *absolutely nothing* about this. "I consider it perfectly amazing that I should hear of this first in the newspapers."

Daisy Ashford also expects she will be married before next autumn (of 1920) and thinks perhaps 'the excitement about the book' (presumably *The Young Visiters*), may have died down by then. Lady Oxford and Asquith in 1917 wonders if the representative of some periodical would give her any money if she gave him a long interview on every sort of thing. "The fact is that I am very hard up." It was difficult enough in Downing Street but more difficult now, as till she dies she will bring her husband's adorers to the house and in times like these who can say that a brain like his will not be needed again? Two years later she is planning the publication of her Diaries which she considers of great value not because she thinks them clever or herself remarkable but because they deal accurately 'over many years of tremendous times in the history of this country'. She did not however write her autobiography until three years later when Thornton Butterworth, according to a footnote on this letter, paid her £11,000 for it. But when the question arises of Asquith himself writing an autobiography she thinks £15,000 too little. No Prime Minister in England's history has held the office for so long at one time or led such a difficult and clever party through such momentous times. It will be the calmest men and not 'the town-criers' who will ultimately stop 'this horrible war'.

Lady Astor, on the other hand, writing in 1935, does not 'believe more in Memoirs to order' and cannot even entertain such a suggestion.

Of greater interest to me were a number of letters from that lively writer Stacey Aumonier. I had long had first editions of his collections of short stories and took delight—as I can today—in such little masterpieces as *Which was Wych Street?*, *Miss Bracegirdle Remembers* and *The Great Unimpressionable*. He sent the typescript of the last to Curtis Brown with a covering letter of two words—"Another dud?"

Sir J. M. Barrie writing from Adelphi Terrace House in 1935

is upset because 'a son of a nephew' of his with the same name as himself is signing business letters from Curtis Brown's address with his own name. What the author of *Peter Pan* wants to know is whether this is to stop. "He can of course use his name if he makes it clear that I am not the writer."

Max Beerbohm will 'appear in your presence' as soon as he is quit of the preparations for his show at the Leicester Galleries in November 1928. Stella Benson in California in 1919 cannot imagine London under peace conditions and wonders about the chances of her new book *Living Alone*. Marjorie Bowen in long, involved letters from Pound Farm, Wittersham, Kent, quotes solicitors, rival publishers and editors. She finds that she can place all the work she writes as quickly as she writes it, on terms that are quite agreeable to her, so that, she says, the most sensible thing for her is to work without bothering an agent at all.

Francis Yeats Brown in 1919 writes from the Bath Club in a businesslike way about a number of articles he has written on his imprisonment in Turkey and wants to know whether the *Daily Mail* will publish an article illustrated by a photo of himself dressed as a girl. Oscar Browning, writing from the Palazzo Simonetti, Via Pietro Cavallini, Rome, in 1920, bemoans changes at Cassells which now buy the copyright of 'flashy books like Wells' *World History* of no solid value whatever'. He is working hard on the Mediaeval Section of his own *History of the Modern World*.

Sir Hall Caine in 1925 has been offered 'huge fees, more than once a hundred pounds' to say what the drift of his new book is to be but he has refused. He is handicapped by the 'appalling ignorance' of members of his own craft about religion and looks forward with pride to sweeping 99 per cent of theologians off the earth. In Masefield's *Trial of Jesus* he finds an historical error on every second page and asked: "If the public accept Masefield, what have I spent so many years of my life for?"

Edward Carpenter sends a cheque for 13s. 3d. Noel Coward is 'working like a dog' at 111 Ebury Street in 1937. Desmond Coke notes that the sales of his two skits produce 3d. for Curtis

Brown less 1½d. postage and 2s. 6d. for himself and considers it a farce.

There were five letters from Lord Alfred Douglas. It is extraordinary that when I was tapping all possible sources for material for my *Life* of Douglas I should have forgotten these. They would have meant only one correction—Bosie received only £300 (not £500 as I stated) for his beastly book *Oscar Wilde and Myself* and of this Crosland, who did most of the writing, had half.

In characteristic phraseology Sir Arthur Conan Doyle considered in 1909 that the crime of the (then) King Leopold of the Belgians in the Congolands was 'the greatest which has ever been known to human annals'. In a homelier note Theodore Dreiser regrets that another meeting is 'out' as tomorrow he is lunching with George Moore and Friday he has promised to Michael Sadleir while on Saturday he sails for New York. This was in June 1928. John Drinkwater is pleased in 1919 that German and Scandinavian rights in *Abraham Lincoln* have been sold, but goes into endless correspondence lasting through the spring of 1927 about half the royalties for a performance of his adaptation of Hardy's *Mayor of Casterbridge* which was put on for a special matinée at Weymouth, 'an infernal nuisance over a matter of a few pence' which 'in principle' cannot be allowed to stand.

Ashley Dukes in 1922 was concerned about the publication rights of a play by Georg Kaiser he had translated, presumably *From Dawn To Midnight*. Lion Feuchtwanger, writing from Hohenzollerndamm 34, Berlin, in 1928 (that is five years before he was fortunate enough to be expelled from Germany by Hitler), is in difficulties over the ownership of the dramatic rights of *Jew Süss* which Matheson Lang wants to produce as a play in London. He writes in German.

John Galsworthy had his problems, too. A Spanish translation of *Strife*, a production of one of his plays in America in which 'the mistake was made of substituting certain American for certain English expressions' and changing the milieu to Pittsburgh 'which is absurd', and a 5 per cent charge made by an English management for collection of American royalties. Moreover the arrival of talking films apparently played hell with American contracts as is shown in letters in 1929. Somebody wants an agreement which would leave Basil Dean 'only control of the talking part of the film' of Galsworthy's *Escape*. Ada Galsworthy, writing after her husband's death, agrees that *Indian Summer* is the loveliest short story that ever was.

William Gerhardi in 1922 is 'awfully interested' in the new novel he is writing and has 'come across that celebrated person, Beverley Nichols'. Sir Philip Gibbs lost an article he had written 'on the top of an omnibus' and recovered it from Scotland Yard. He does not want to undertake a school-book on the heroic deeds of the Scots in the Great War as the only thing he wants to write about the war is 'the plain unvarnished truth of its misery and abomination'. Ian Hay, he thinks, might be glad to do it. Sir W. S. Gilbert in July 1910 asks Curtis Brown down to Grim's Dyke, Harrow Weald, to discuss 'the proposed revivals'.

Kenneth Grahame's letters, mostly from Boham's, Blewbury, between 1911 and 1920, were of particular interest to me, for I had long collected his work and had heard much of him from his friend and biographer Patrick Chalmers. Also, although the addressee remained 'Mr Curtis Brown' I knew that the two men had been friends. Grahame writes first from the Old Government House Hotel Guernsey where he has arrived after a holiday in Brittany which was 'very interesting—so much as the stormy weather allowed us to see', the food always good— 'we revelled in oysters, mussels, langoustes and other sea truck', but the people were 'rough and mannerless'. Just after the outbreak of war (in October 1914) Grahame went for a day to Oxford hoping it would cheer him up. It was 'beautiful beyond words' but it did him no good. 'I was bleeding at the heart for these poor Belgians.' Not till 1918 is much business discussed, then it is of Nelson's 2s. edition of *Dream Days* and *The Golden Age* which causes some debate but 'you will not find me obstructive so long as I can do the right thing by all parties concerned'. In May 20 is a letter of thanks for Brown's

B*

condolences on Grahame's loss of his only son who died while an undergraduate at Oxford.

In September 1925, writing from The Laundry, Easton Park, Dunmow, Philip Geudalla wants to sue the Hearst organization over some articles. The proceedings would be in London 'where the wealth or importance of Mr. Hearst would not make the slightest difference'. Guedalla doesn't care whether Hearst prints or resells the articles but requires that he should pay for the goods he has bought. On another occasion he 'assembled the publishers and talked to them like a father'. But there's a wordy dispute about a copyright fee of £2 8s. od.

Of greatest interest to literature were some surprisingly businesslike letters of Thomas Hardy. He accepts an offer of £2 for the German rights of each story in *A Group of Noble Dames* in 1904 and in 1918 gives permission to an anthologist, Brand Whitlock, to quote from his poem *The Darkling Thrush*. In June 1928 Hardy's widow writes to Brown saying that she has in her possession the manuscript of an unpublished story by T. H. It was intended to be included in *Life's Little Ironies* but 'for certain reasons' was withheld. It is not even typed. Four days later it is sent in duplicate, and after another four days we learn that it is called *Old Mrs Chundle* and that Mrs Hardy wants to sell the manuscript. Yet another four days, and Counsel's opinion has been taken on Hardy's will, for there is a dispute with Sydney Cockerell, Florence Hardy's joint executor and *Old Mrs Chundle* cannot be sold. Cockerill thinks the story is a poor one but says that if a competent judge, 'E. M. Forster for example', approves he will agree to publication. Florence Hardy is thinking of resigning her executorship as she finds it impossible to work with Mr Cockerell.

Joseph Hergersheimer writes from the Dower House, West Chester, Pennsylvania in 1922 to say that J. C. Squire is to have *A Sprig of Lemon Verbena* for the *London Mercury* for whatever he is able to pay. "It is the handsomest appearing magazine I know and I am extremely interested to see myself in such digni-fied type." He is that day (June 5th, 1922) beginning a study of

Western America to make a book of 80,000 words called *The Magnetic West*. This will appear first in *The Saturday Evening Post*. The creator of Raffles, E. W. Hornung 'c/o Y.M.C.A. Army of the Rhine' in 1919, is indignant because a publisher has tried to change 'Notes' to 'Notebook' in a title of his. "This is an infernal liberty which of course I won't stand for a moment: if persisted in I shall seek legal redress without hesitation." Back at Midway Cottage, Partridge Green, Sussex, later in the year, Hornung does not like allowing an edition of 20,000 to be printed of *Fathers of Men* to be sold at 2s. with 2d. a copy to him. "Try if you cannot get it down to 5000 or 10,000 with an enhanced royalty beyond that." W. D. Howells in May 1918 received a 'joyful surprise' of 118 dollars from the French edition of *The Leatherwood Gods*. He begins to hope the war may end suddenly though in America 'we are preparing to fight it for a thousand years on unbridled billions of Liberty Bonds'.

Ford Madox Ford, still Ford Madox Hueffer in 1919, accepts £8 for *Pink Flannel* from *Land and Water*, 'all right as it's old stuff', while Richard Hughes in 1924 is not surprised that a story called *Martha* has not sold—it was the first short story he ever wrote at 18 or so.

E. M. Hull who created *The Sheik*, wants Brown's support in an interview with Thornton Butterworth. "I was so scared at having to see you yesterday that I must have appeared about as intelligent as an oyster." Another once popular writer, Fergus Hume, 'to get cash' has sold many books outright at prices ranging from £50 to £100 but now (1919) wishes to make a new start and pull up his prices to something reasonable, but two chapters of his new novel are lost in transit or at his publisher's office and he has to re-write them. "It is the deuce to re-write detective stories, which have so many links to be carried forward. People undervalue these tales, but they are the most difficult to write of any composition." Yet another best-seller of half a century ago, C. J. Cutcliffe Hyne, whose Captain Kettle thrilled so many of us as boys, writes from

Heaton Lodge, Bradford, in 1918, to say that he does not think his Kettle stories have been offered to the proper markets in America as they are 'going like hot cakes,' here. An 'irresponsible humourist' in America 'calling himself Chief Postal Censor' has returned one of his stories since he has not complied with certain regulations. And £5 has been offered for Swedish rights in 'some Kettle books'. In this company, too, is Jerome K. Jerome who has much to say about the plays he has to offer in 1919, *Nicholas Snyders, Tommy and Co, The Russian Vagabond* and others. Is Cyril Maude interested?

Margaret Kennedy missed rehearsals for Basil Dean's revival of *The Constant Nymph* in 1928 as Basil Dean did not let her know when or where they were taking place and Edward Knoblock did not want any of his plays 'novelized'. D. H. Lawrence, writing from Del Monte Ranch, Questa, New Mexico, shows that he can be as closely concerned with the business side of authorship as any lesser writer. American rights, an offer accepted from a publisher giving the whole royalty scale but thirteen copies *not* to count as twelve, for (underlined) "I won't sign any further contract with this thirteen-count-as-twelve-clause". He considers *The Plumed Serpent* his most important novel so far. Three years later he writes from Villa Bernarda, Spotorno, Prov. di Genoa to say that he may take a walking tour with Brewster in Capri, and three months later from Florence he hopes Secker will let Cape reprint *Sea and Sardinia*. He is reading up the old Etruscans and may write a book about them, half travel, half description of Etruscan things. In November of 1926 he writes to an American publisher asking why he looked for a best-seller from him. He is the wrong bird. "Blame me if you like, for leaving you. But blame yourself, now as ever, for not knowing how to be simple and open with me."

T. E. Lawrence writes from Cloud's Hill, Moreton, on December 4th, 1924, in answer to a request from Brown to be allowed to purchase a copy of the original edition of *Seven Pillars of Wisdom* which was to have been limited to a hundred copies and sold at 30 guineas. He warns that it may be late in 1925 before it's ready, that it may be necessary to print as many as 120 copies to cover the printing expenses, that he is giving plain texts to the people mentioned in the text who shared the campaign with him. If Brown still wants a copy he must send £15 15s. od. to 'Seven Pillars Account' at Bank of Liverpool and Martins, 63 Lombard Street. The other 15 guineas will be due on publication. Lawrence puts no restriction on writing about the book, or lending it, or selling it. He signs himself T. E. Shaw.

I suppose few of the younger generation will know the name W. J. Locke but before, during and immediately after the First World War he was an enormously successful romantic novelist whose books, *The Beloved Vagabond*, *The Wonderful Year* and the rest ran through countless editions. He writes that it is 'dam silly' to think that every publisher and agent must be considered a rogue. "There are a few wrong-uns in every profession; there are again those who without running crooked are hard bargainers and merciless exactors of the uttermost farthing, but the bulk of every profession is honest and reasonable." In another letter from Corner Hall, Hemel Hempstead in 1918 he regrets that he can add nothing to the *Who's Who* account of his 'eventless' life.

Rose Macaulay was disappointed in 1921 that her publishers had refused to pay a higher advance. "It was worth trying but I suppose no use." She is doing some articles for *Nash's*; the terms are good but the articles a bore. A cheque for royalties on *Dangerous Ages* in 1922 came as a 'pleasant shock'. Sir Edward Marsh forwards an offer made by Viola Tree for the rights of *Lithuania*, a one-act play by Rupert Brooke whose literary executor he was. Another letter from Marsh elucidates this. He is not sure that in a contract he ought to be described as executor to the estate. (In fact he was nothing of the sort.) Rupert Brooke died intestate, he goes on, having expressed in an informal letter (to his mother) the wish that Marsh should be his *literary* executor. Other letters of Marsh's are written from the War Office when he was Churchill's secretary in 1920 and 1921 and from the Colonial Office in 1921. They refer to Churchill's contract with *The Times* and a cheque for Churchill from Scribner's. Finally Marsh writes that he has been spending Sunday with the Poet Laureate Dr Robert Bridges and has discovered that he has never had a literary agent. He wants to write some articles on poetry for America and has recently (1922 at the age of 78) written some short lyrics which are 'quite startlingly beautiful'. Dr Bridges is genuinely indifferent to popularity and he has a 'strong rather old-fashioned sense of personal dignity' but he would like to make some money.

John Masefield writes from 13 Well Walk, Hampstead in 1915 to refuse an unidentified Vice-Presidency Brown had offered him, and W. Somerset Maugham in a letter from 27 Carlisle Mansions, Westminster, in which he does not give the year of writing, declines Brown's offer to act for him in America as his affairs there are in the hands of Mr Morris Colles of the Authors' Syndicate.

There were then several letters from W. B. Maxwell, an author who has—undeservedly perhaps—gone quite out of fashion. I remember Michael Sadlier once telling me that he collected his first editions. He has written a play called *Winged Birds* (in 1921) of which Cyril Maude thinks highly. Later Miss Gladys Cooper considers it and Maxwell thinks the appeal of the play would be irresistible if made through her.

A. A. Milne also writes about a play in the first of his many letters between 1917 and 1919. *Belinda* must be delayed till Irene Vanbrugh can play in it. Boucicault thinks Milne is too 'refined' and 'delicate' but may change his opinion if *Wurzel-Flummery* goes well at the Coliseum. Milne encloses the first act and scenario of a play called *The Great Broxopp* in 1918 (it was not produced till 1923); also *The Lucky One* which should go to America first. He finishes *The Great Broxopp* (August 7th, 1918) and 'dotes on' the first act. He can see three men doing it in order of merit: Bouchier, Ainley, Eadie. Next day he writes again to say Owen Nares wants *The Boy Comes Home* but Brown must stick out for a weekly fee. 'I want a lot. I want £15 if you can get it.' And in a post-script 'On second thoughts £20'. In September Nares dines with the Milnes at 15 Embankment Gardens and is described as 'a nice person'. Milne wants to see Brown about amateur rights—he (Milne) ought to have no trouble with them 'beyond paying in the cheques'. Endless complications with managers and stars continue, Butt, Bouchier, Aubrey Smith, du Maurier, Daniel Mayer, Beerbohm, Hawtry, Tearle, Miss McCarthy drop in and out of the correspondence which concerns *Mr Pim Passes By*, *The Great Broxopp* and *The Boy Comes Home*, giving a curious vista of London theatre affairs immediately after the 1914–18 war.

George Moore writing a long letter from 121 Ebury Street in 1917 states that no publisher ever published a book by him if he read the manuscript. Scribner, Harper and Appleton all three refused *Esther Waters* and when the book was published in England and it became apparent that the public liked it, Scribner, Harper and Appleton sent their agents to Moore to ask if they might publish. He gives several other examples of the folly of letting publishers see manuscripts before they have agreed to publish. The original writer (as opposed to one who writes like other authors) must insist that the publisher shall not see the book till the contract is signed.

Beverley Nichols sends his second novel *Patchwork* from Cleave Court, Torquay, in 1921; Baroness Orczy, signing herself 'Emmuska Orczy' and writing from Villa Bijou, Monte Carlo in 1921 wants to know why the American sales of *By the Gods Beloved* have suddenly gone up and Sean O'Casey (letter undated) says 'Steady up! Steady up!' A novelized version of *Juno and the Paycock* is a big question and he intends to keep at a fairly safe distance from it. God forbid, God forbid that *Juno* has a long run in the States. 'The production is apparently such that one must pray for the mercy of Almighty God' to give the play a sudden and unprovided death.

Eden Philpotts is delighted with a commission to do some short stories in 1917 and writes several times about his stories

The Witch, Peter Paul, A Near Shave for Mary Jane, and about magazines of the time in England and America, the *Graphic, Harpers, Cornhill, Windsor,* the *Century.* Sir Arthur Pinero does not want his play *The Freak* 'hawked round' in America.

There were a number of letters from that great old literary trooper of forty years ago, William le Queux, who wrote about European royal courts and spies, travelling in places difficult of access, Algeria, the Balkans, the Arctic and the Sudan. Brown acted for him in America and receives the proofs of *Love Intrigues of the Kaiser's Sons* in 1917 and *Behind the German Lines* in the following year. Le Queux was then (1917–19) living at The Hermitage, Guildown, Guilford. *The Secret Life of the Ex-Tsaritsa* leads to offers from Italy and Holland and Le Queux follows it with *The Minister of Evil,* a second book about Rasputin, his first *Rasputin the Monk* having sold (he says) 200,000. His letters are all curt and businesslike unlike those of Sir Arthur Quiller-Couch who gets involved with that hoary figure in author publisher relations—the man who cannot obtain some books of the author's at the bookstalls and has written to tell the author so. Quiller-Couch is immersed in all the rest of the traditional fussings of authorship—trivial corrections to be made should there be a second edition, hopes that the trade will 'handle' a book well, expenses of press corrections, one publisher who is 'playing tricks with the sale of a book', names of characters to be changed in the typescript, questions of the publisher raising or lowering the price of a book, publishers' cheques a month overdue, lawyers involved, the *lot,* and when Q's wife joins in there are more complications.

Then came a fascinating set of letters from that obscure but significant stream-of-consciousness novelist Dorothy M. Richardson. It has been said of her that first editions of her novels fetch more than she received for them from her publishers. She appears to have received £15 each as advance on her novels *Honeycomb* and *Backwater* and proposes to ask £15 for *The Tunnel.* Little wonder that in October 1917 she is appalled at the state of her finances, and cannot imagine how she is going to pay her way next year. "Oh, for a few months complete security and tranquillity!"

But her publishers rescued her with 'a regular living on possible future royalties'—a most generous contract she thinks. She is glad to hear on May 1st, 1919 of Knopf's plans for *The Tunnel* and trusts his courage will meet with its reward. Later (July 28th, 1919) she hears from a 'small bird recently returned from New York' that Mr Knopf is going ahead in the publishing world. The fact that he is issuing all her books together disarms her, nevertheless she feels she must make an effort to get him to treat her as generously as possible. "I must find £10 before September".

Her last letter came on January 1st, 1920 from Rose Cottage, Trevone, Padstow, North Cornwall, where I was to meet her ten years later, as I have described in my book *The Last of Spring*.

Followed some optimistic letters from Cecil Roberts in America in 1920—he looks like being the 'pet fashion' the way things are going. Rafael Sabatini sends a cutting about his play *The Rattlesnake*. Bernard Shaw (in 1927) says that Brown knew he was a man 'fossilized in the conviction that no agent ever does anything properly' and in 1929 warns Brown that the book (unspecified) will be a tissue of seditious and blasphemous libels from beginning to end.

I found then a long and to me fascinating series of letters from May Sinclair, a novelist I have always thought excellent and of late neglected. Between August 1917 and April 1923 she wrote no less than 42 letters about her work in progress, her discovery of and delight in Stow-on-the-Wold which became the Wyck of her fine novel *Mr. Waddington of Wyck*, about serial rights of her novels which seem always to have been sold, translations into French, a row in the Society of Authors of which she appears to have been a committee-woman and other professional and personal matters. She thinks scenarios and serials are 'the very devil himself', using the word 'scenario', before it was adopted by the film industry, to mean a synopsis. The correspondence ends with a letter (from 1 Blenheim Road, N.W.8, her address during the later correspondence) with a

synopsis of her novel *The Cure of Souls* which closes on a characteristically pithy note. "Chapter XXI. The unveiling of the
War Memorial—and of the Rector."

Upton Sinclair in 1917 suggests that the sequel to *King Coal*
which he has almost completed should be combined with it
making a volume of 270,000 words, but is later deterred by his
publishers. He would like a play made of *Sylvia's Marriage*.
John Galsworthy will not write a preface to *King Coal*; may the
typescript be sent to Bernard Shaw?

J. C. Squire, editing *The New Statesman* in 1918 writes huffily
about a typescript by (Clifford?) Bax. Brown had sent it without return postage. It is, Squire thinks, an imposition to ask the
paper to pay return postage on unsolicited manuscripts. Herbert
Strang is interested in translations of his books—he has already
sold *Kobo* in Sweden, Denmark, Norway, and Germany. Booth
Tarkington writing from Kennebunkport in 1917 gave (to me,
at least) a touch of nostalgia because he is concerned with the
French rights of his novel *Seventeen* and one of my earliest film-
going memories was of Jack Pickford (Mary Pickford's younger
brother who died shortly afterwards) in the film of this.
Russell Thorndyke has received a cheque with great joy and
surprise. It would have done Brown good to see his sister, his
wife and himself dancing round the studio. I must say I found
this suggestion of Brown as a postal Santa Claus a little hard
to take. Herbert French wants the correct version of *The Battle
of the Marne* used for magazine offer as it has some extra lines.
G. N. Trevelyan seemed to be anticipating in September 6th,
1918 that the war may end at any moment and cannot say what
he will undertake when it is over.

Horace Annesley Vachell, whose letters all start 'My dear
old man', regrets that his last letter was dashed off in a moment
of heat. 'Let heat destroy it' he asks, and Brown apparently did
so for there is no angry letter here. On the contrary he is pleased
with suggestions for a play and will 'probably let Farleigh come
on and egged on by Agatha have a fight with Lady Susan'. He
cannot be the only writer who has been 'very uneasy about

Cochran', or wondered if he had 'cold feet'. What can be got for the Polish rights of *The Other Side*?

Alec Waugh would be glad of a German translation of *The Prisoners of Mainz*. He has not got a school story actually by himself (in 1919) but will soon write one about one of the characters in *The Loom of Youth*. Mary Webb, an unsuccessful novelist who was later brought into sudden prominence by a reference to her work in a public speech of Stanley Baldwin's during his Premiership, wants Brown to phone her bank so that she can get an overdraft, and is another author to grumble about her non-appearance in publishers' advertisements. May her poems be returned *at once*, by return of post, registered? Hers are the most near-hysterical letters in the collection and Ella Wheeler Wilcox, writing from 349 West 58th Street in 1909 to Mr. Merrill, is calm and humorous in comparison. She wants back the picture which was entrusted to his 'handsome and gentlemanly young reporter', as it is the only evidence she has that she was ever a child.

Leonard Woolf in 1920 sends the English translation of Gorki's *Reminiscences* of Tolstoi which, he says, is the first Russian literary work to reach the outside world from Soviet Russia. Israel Zangwill will not send scripts abroad, since foreign managers could easily find reliable agents in England.

So writers argued, threatened, haggled forty and fifty years ago and so, I have no doubt, we are arguing, threatening and haggling still. An agent's files reveal the meanest side of the writing profession—more even than the files of most publishers, I imagine—but even so it was not pleasant to find so many men and women who occupied dignified places in literature behaving no better, though certainly no worse than their publishers. Nor was it pleasant to know that in similar files were countless letters of my own, as anxious and as argumentative as these though perhaps less articulate than most of them, and that some bookseller of the future might come on them and think them worth chucking in with the rest of a mixed bag. But this did not cure me of writing either books or letters to agents.

CHAPTER FOUR

Friends

[1]

I PLAYED ON MY PROFICIENCY at the game of darts for all it was worth, not as a detail in some subtle plan, for I was innocent of any such scheming, but as part of the attitude to life and literature which I had assumed—that of a public bar man, a lover of the commonplace for its own sake, a writer about 'ordinary people'. Darts had an almost mystic importance in my life. Besides, I was good at the game. I was once awarded the silver darts offered by the *News of the World* each week for the most unusual feat reported to them by a publican. (Mine was to get three darts into one treble three times in one week.)

This brought me a freakish reputation that year and I was in danger of becoming a 'darts writer' as better writers than I had found their scope narrowed by editorial demands to cricket or golf or bridge. I had written a book *Darts* which had been published with clever illustrations in the previous year and when the *Sunday Chronicle* finished its serialization, the editor asked me to continue the series with weekly articles. I found myself judging darts anecdotes sent in by readers, discussing the disadvantages of boards made without a space for trebles, and towards autumn of that year predicting that this would be 'the biggest darts season we have ever had'.

Then a periodical started called *Darts Weekly News* and I became its chief contributor with a much-featured series of articles called *An Evening at . . .* in which I could write up my favourite pubs up and down the country. I look a little sardonic-ally at these articles now, each illustrated with a picture of the pub, the Smarden Bell, the Pound and One in Bruton Mews, the Puesdown Inn in Gloucestershire, the Royal Oak Beckley, Sussex, and many others. They are not bad, as articles go, and a good deal less embarrassing to reconsider than some of the more luridly purple patches in my novels, but where, I wonder thirty years later, did I find the enthusiasm to write so light-heartedly, so flamboyantly on a subject so basically homespun? I enjoyed it all immensely—no doubt of that. With no more alcohol in me than a pint or two of beer, with no more reward than the few guineas paid me (till it failed, owing me for several articles) by *Darts Weekly News*, I ran about the countryside in my old Lee-Francis open car, talking to publicans and their customers, writing their stories, competing with them at darts, garrulous and callow.

[2]

Some twelve miles away, on the Kent and Sussex border, was a small area with which I had strong ties, both immediate and of the past, that of the villages of Northiam and Beckley. At Northiam my sister was teaching at a then famous girls' school called Brickwall and my mother, now a widow, had taken a bungalow in the village to be near her. At Beckley was the Royal Oak, that idealized hostelry of my boyhood, which I had reached on an abortive walking-tour in my eighteenth year, to remain there, sleeping in a four-poster, instead of tramping on as I had planned.[b]

The landlord was an unusual man named Charles Goddard who took over the licence in 1900 and so when he died at the end of the last war had held it for nearly half a century, which was by way of being a record, particularly for a bachelor publican. An unusual man? To me as a boy he seemed so, so unfailingly genial and hospitable, so paternal with the young men of the village, so humorous and kindly in all he said and

[b] See *The Glittering Pastures* (Putnam 1962).

did. He lived for his pub, proud of its wholly rural tradition and the fact that the Romney Marsh Hunt met there twice a season. It had an ugly modern front but behind this were ancient rooms which had been those of the village poor-house and there was a fireplace four foot deep with a twelve foot beam across it. The bedrooms had uneven oak floors and the furniture of the place, a jumble of ancient and Victorian pieces, had been accumulating haphazardly since the inn was first licensed in the eighteenth century. When I had found it as a boy it seemed to me the most romantic of inns and even in 1937 its true purpose, the providence of liquor to the local farm-workers, had never been lost. It was an inn such as one read about in old novels, and Charlie Goddard, with no self-consciousness, was one of the few landlords who might have served as a model to Cobbett or Borrow, if not to Fielding. With the years I had learned his failings, the miserliness that lay behind his genial manner and what led him to choose young boys from orphanages as his resident barmen, but he was still to me a 'character' and to return to the Royal Oak was to recapture some of the bookish plagiarized emotion which had led me once to walk through Sussex looking for wayside adventures, and afterwards to return many times with friends of my own age to drink and stay in a 'real old Sussex inn', as I must have thought it—and not so stupidly thought it, after all.

To the Royal Oak at Beckley, then, I used to go and to the Six Bells at Northiam which was kept by an ex-quartermaster of the First World War named Parker, who had flourished so bravely in the R.A.S.C. that he had bought this as a village pub and turned it into a prosperous hotel. My mother, though a little lost after forty years of my father's insistence on 'arranging' things, was beginning to enjoy her long widowhood, playing the piano when she felt like it, buying her own clothes, mistress of her own small affairs. My sister was content to teach games and riding at Brickwall for she had plenty of good horses and could ride to hounds in the holidays. The headmistress was a remarkable woman named Heath who would have made it one of the first three girls' school in England if an unfortunate experiment in nudism in the rose-garden by an enthusiastic young couple, conducted without the parents' permission, had not almost emptied the school a few terms later.

For Whitsun I decided to stay at the Royal Oak for a few days, stipulating with Charlie Goddard that I should have the room with the four-poster which I had occupied sixteen years earlier, a sentimental preference for which no excuse is needed. From this bed I again heard that rumble of conversation outside the pub after closing time which went on sometimes till 1 o'clock in the morning between men unwilling to go home, and I again smelt mushrooms being fried for breakfast in the kitchen below.

To bathe I would not go down to Camber, for the ruined tower of Camber Castle which had stood in an uninhabited and almost unvisited wasteland when I was a boy was now the centre of a bungaloid bedlam, but I found a place farther along the coast which was less crowded and such was the heat of that early summer that I was laid low for a day or two with sunstroke.

But on Sunday I went to hear Mass in the little chapel which Sheila Kaye-Smith had built near her home, and so added yet another tie with the district, for 'the Sussex novelist', as she was almost universally called, gave me her gentle, reserved but enduring friendship which lasted till her death a quarter of a century later, though there were many years of that time in which we did not meet.

How good are her novels? I wonder now, not in disloyalty but with curiosity, for I have not seen one of the earlier books since I read them spellbound in my early twenties. *Sussex Gorse, Green Apple Harvest, The End of the House of Alard, Joanna Godden*, I remember them all, and 'almost as good as Hardy' they seemed to me as an adolescent, for the comparison was inevitable. Later I found them being used as the merchandise of booksellers who specialized in modern first editions and that made them somewhat suspect in my eyes, so wide of the mark was the judgement of these mercenary arbiters.

Perhaps I am a little afraid to read them again because I loved and revered Sheila and she gave me a good reason to do so when I faced a crisis sixteen years after meeting her that warm Sunday morning of early summer in the year I am recalling.

I loved her home, too, and it seemed to me a proper reward for her success as a novelist. Constructed from a group of ancient oast-houses in a fold of the hills a few miles from Northiam, it was not a grand or a period house but it had the charm of a home lovingly constructed with care, ingenuity and great feeling for the countryside in which it was set. It was a novelists' house and it was comforting to me that novelists should have beautiful houses and be able, as the fruits of labour, to furnish and run them as hospitably and as generously as Sheila and her husband ran Little Doucegrove.

The daughter of a Hastings doctor, she had begun to write early and her young face, the forehead covered by a fringe, was familiar in pictures in illustrated and literary papers before the First World War. She had been an ardent Anglican as her early books reveal, and had married a High Church curate who was considered to have a brilliant ecclesiastical career before him. Their London home was for a long time a rather famous meeting-place for distinguished members of their two professions where go-ahead bishops met rising writers and there was much good talk and perhaps—my conjecture—a little hilarity at the expense of the Bloomsbury drawing-rooms of the time. Then Sheila and her husband caused something of a sensation by becoming Catholics and moving down to the Sussex in which all Sheila's novels were set. For many years Sheila reviewed books for the *Sunday Express* and had been kind to my early novels, though she called the first 'corseted'.

She had grown a little matronly by the time I met her and it may be that the best of her work was done. It has been said that the *genre* of her early novels could not survive Stella Gibbons's naughty parody of it, *Cold Comfort Farm*, but Sheila was still publishing a novel every year or two with success and remained an important contemporary figure. She became for me what Kipling and Galsworthy had been in their lifetimes, one of the people I knew and respected at the top of my profession.

It was never an intimate friendship, though, and I do not think anyone except her husband could claim to have that with Sheila. Even other women writers who had been acquainted with her for many years never seemed to me to know much of her mind.

It may seem that I am guilty of whimsy in recalling the other-worldliness one felt in Sheila's presence but it was too real and cogent for that. There was a remoteness about her which persisted behind all the polite part she took in the conversation, an introvert's look which suggested something fay or occult. Her expression was not far-away so much as hooded. She was not absent-minded—on the contrary she was very much with us in the room. She talked quite readily and often very well—about books, people, the external and practical aspects of religion, of local myths and affairs and of Sussex itself. Her comments were shrewd, sometimes devastating and she had a quick though kindly sense of humour. Yet it always seemed that she had just come from somewhere else and was waiting to return there, some place to which no one could follow her, in which her real life was lived. Perhaps it was the world of her books.

[3]

Bosie Douglas, with whom I spent a long day that summer, lived in no other world—not even the world of the past. He was sixty-seven years old now and one of the most endearing things about him was his sense of actuality, his acute interest in the present, in his own circumstances and his own ambitions. These last he kept to the end of his life. He was delighted a few years later when his poems were broadcast, with others by A. E. Houseman and Hilaire Belloc, as those of poets who had kept the tradition, and delighted when he was invited to address the Royal Society of Literature. But he had the smaller ambitions of the inveterate gambler and punted on every day's racing, never losing his hope of riches.

His mother had died two years earlier and his nephew, Francis Queensberry, who had recovered some of the family's fortune squandered by the Scarlet Marquis and Bosie's amiable brother Percy, had taken a flat for him in a modern block in Hove. It was on the ground floor of a rather pleasant red brick building in Nizell's Avenue and Bosie had furnished it with some pieces from his mother's home.

I found him cheerful and vivacious, pleased with his new home and a little proud of it. It was the first time he had been a householder since 1913 when his wife had left him and he gave up their home in Church Row and went to live with his mother. He never lost an amused and amusing vanity about his good looks in youth and showed me a pastel portrait of himself as a most beautiful little boy. He was being cultivated at this time by all sorts of people, from curiosity or sympathy or admiration. James Agate had sought him out and been down to see him that spring; Evan Tredegar had made his acquaintance, Richard Rumbold was cagily devoted to him and he was on excellent terms with his family. He seemed to me to have changed little in appearance during the fifteen years I had known him and kept the same clear skin which was quick to flush, the same restless, jerky manner, the sudden, high-pitched laugh.

Our friendship was an easy one. Based on my early hero-worship and devotion at a time when he was generally despised and outlawed, it had grown through the years to be a many-sided relationship. There were people met, and places visited, and experiences shared to discuss for I was one of the very few of his later friends who had known such oddities as Herbert Moore Pim and Alfred Rose and other people of the past, who had liked Bosie's son Raymond before his mental breakdown, who had read Bosie's last desperate weekly papers *Plain English* and *Plain Speech*, who had known Bosie himself and his mother before his imprisonment.

With another devoted friend of his, Sorley Brown, he had quarrelled that spring over a correspondence in Sorley's paper *The Border Standard*. Sorley, who had stood by Bosie in all his troubles had now 'let him down', Bosie told me, by allowing an anonymous correspondent to 'insult' him in the columns of his paper. These were serious matters for the ageing duellist who had suffered so much in the past by his own and others' eristics. There was a reconciliation later with Sorley Brown but as we walked down to meet Bosie's wife Olive that day he was voluble about poor Sorley's misdeeds.

Olive Douglas was plump and talkative, rather witty and fond of laughing. Her literary passion was Byron and her own poems, first published by Lane in the Nineties, are still collected among the more precious and *fin-de-siècle* work of the time. But there was nothing intense or soulful about her or about her good practical warm friendship with Bosie. They lived in separate flats at different ends of the town and met almost daily on mutual ground for lunch. Olive, the only daughter of a rich man now deceased, made Bosie an allowance.

Bosie insisted on a walk along the promenade that afternoon, after Olive had returned to her pretty flat full of Byroniana. He wore heavy boots, as was his habit, a battered felt hat and a raincoat. He walked with quick shortish steps and I had to make some effort to keep up with him.

He kept a schoolboy greediness for cakes in the afternoon and there was always a variety of those small rather sickly sweetmeats which confectioners call 'pastries' on the dining-room table at tea-time. He pressed me to stay on—for dinner or for the night—but I had to return, for some forgotten reason, and left him alone there at the door, smiling as he gave me his small hand. "Good-bye, old chap." He always said 'old chap', not as hearty men in pubs did but almost caressingly. "Come again soon." Then, just as I reached the public footpath three yards from him—"Have you published anything lately?"

This was so typical of Bosie that I drove away smiling. He had talked of his book on Shakespeare's Sonnets, he had explained how he would be vindicated in the Life of Wilde which A. J. A. Symons was working on as he had already been vindicated in a book by Sherard called *Bernard Shaw, Frank Harris and Oscar Wilde* which had just been, or was about to be published. He had explained that he was working on a book to be called *Without Apology*, and had told me in which countries rights of his books had been sold and what their royalties amounted to, but he had not once asked (even out of politeness) about anything I might be writing. I quite understood this. It would not have occurred to Bosie to think that I might have an interest in my own work comparable with my passionate curiosity about the smallest detail of his. I understood and accepted this. Then, just as I was leaving him, was about to get into my car, his natural courtesy prompted him and he asked that smiling, incurious question. I gave him an evasive answer which quite satisfied him and left him waving a quick and jerky, but affectionate good-bye. There was an inarticulate, quite undemonstrative but deep-based love between us, especially since he had—in all essential senses—lost his son. The nearest it ever came to being expressed was when, during the war, I was on a troopship bound for the landings in Madagascar and I wrote saying I felt 'sentimental' about our (then) quarter century of friendship. "Don't apologize for being sentimental", he wrote back. "I have always been inclined that way myself."

[4]

Two other old friends I saw that year, both for the last time as it turned out. They were both men of personality who will be familiar to readers of earlier books in this sequence, both had influenced my life, both were now in their sixties, but in character, appearance, background they had nothing in common.

Of Derwent Miall I have written that he was one of the young men of the Nineties who had called themselves Decadents and wrote poetry which owed its feeling to the French Decadents and maintained a sort of *rive gauche* existence on the borders of Soho. Miall had indeed taken me to the café (long since demolished) in what had become Cranleigh Street where he had sat with Dowson and Arthur Symons while the mother of Cynara dried her washing in front of the fire. But Dowson had died in 1900 and eight years later Symons was certified insane, and in the meantime Derwent Miall had married and settled to a life of literary drudgery, writing short stories at a few guineas a thousand for the rest of his life, while his brother Bernard Miall who had been better known in the Nineties than Derwent, and had published a book of his poems, took to the no less onerous and unrewarding work of translation.

When I knew Derwent Miall he had no aura of Decadence and it would have been a clever man who could guess that the tall, gentle, unassuming man with sharp, rather noble features and piercing blue eyes had once been a comrade of the poetic hell-rakers of the Nineties. If he suggested any associations with that time it was with a gaslit London of music-halls and a Strand and Fleet Street like those illustrated on the cover of the *Strand Magazine*. With his narrow sensitive face he might have been Sherlock Holmes and his London was that of Conan Doyle and Jerome K. Jerome rather than of Dorian Gray. He was a man of robust tastes and brilliant conventional humour.

As I write this in my Tangier home with the first sunlight of 1966 pouring in at my windows, I have before me the two books of his which he gave me and I examine them a little ruefully. Here, in an ugly yellow cover and issued by the long-vanished publisher Everett and Co., is *The Strange Case of Vincent Hume* by Derwent Miall, 'author of *The Powers of Darkness*' (whatever that may have been). It is a story of an ordinary young man with a gift of prophecy, written half facetiously, half melodramatically and it would be unreadable but for those touches of period, those glimpses of Victorian London which

make Sherlock Holmes stories endurable to me. I read of a man
in the audience of a music-hall—"He had a bald head and
side-whiskers, and a Gladstonian collar . . . His wife who sat
beside him, had her veil pushed up and her bonnet strings
untied, and a glass of stout stood in the rack in front of her."
On the next page is a flash-back—literally—to the first motion
pictures. "The band crashed into a cheerful march, the house
was darkened, and a white sheet on the stage was forthwith
covered with very animated figures. Shivering horses, be-
stridden by shivering jockeys, leapt into limbo over shivering
hedges; a shivering regiment marched by, to a lively quick step
to be followed by a royal procession; and the woman in front
of Vincent said again and again, 'Ain't it life-like?' and 'I can't
think how they do it!' " I read on, of a 'swell mobsman', of a
young man who says, 'you must dine with me. But, of course
you're engaged three-deep. No? That's ripping. Shall we say
Perugi's at eight, and we'll see if they've any of the '95 wine
left, my dear old boy'. 'The string band in the gallery of the
restaurant was playing a cake-walk when Vincent and Aston-
Blake sat down.' 'With his face towards Vincent was a young
man, pale, heavy-eyed, dissolute. Vincent's eyes rested on the
lad's handsome face, marred by indulgence.' Later in a tram,
'his straying glance rested at last upon a comfortable matron
in black and bugles, who sat in the corner near the door. In
her hand she held a reticule, which, so Vincent felt assured,
contained her best lace cap; she was on her way to a visit of
ceremony to one of the little bay windowed houses.' ' "Drive
straight on—drive like blazes," cried Vincent as the cabman
opened the trap.' 'Vincent had been East of Temple Bar, and
was regaling himself with tea and muffins in a tea-shop, and
wondering why a place devoted to the consumption of such
homely provender should be got up to resemble a palace, with
ceiling gilded—especially as the customers seemed to be prin-
cipally ink-splashed office boys, who hailed from Brixton.'
'Vincent ushered his guest into his small sitting-room, and they
sat down on opposite sides of the hearth, with cigars and

capacious tumblers.' 'I think' says a financier to Vincent, 'you have other interests in life than emptying bottles and filling the pockets of the bookmakers. Is that aquarelle yours?' 'Yes, I have a studio down Chelsea way.' 'Big Ben's harsh voice sounded twice. Two o'clock, and fresh, country smell stealing into the street from the park: lights still showing in club windows, a few rubber-tyred carriages driven home, and men with a hose, sluicing the pavement in Cockspur Street.' 'Outside the street was bathed in moonlight, a breath of summer wind drifted into the room, and the sound of a footman's voice, calling carriages, rose above the trample of horses' feet. A long queue of carriages stretched down the street, a long array of orange eyes of flame. Warm, crowded, moonlit Vanity Fair was pulsating with life, though the season was waning; and its gauds might well glitter attractively in the eyes of a man who had the wherewithal to buy of them without stint.'

The other book is later and consists of a number of short stories linked by a single main character, a device popular at the time—1912. The stories are all reprinted from *London Opinion* and I remember poor Miall telling me that he had received nothing for the book rights, the editor having paid him well, three guineas each, as the stories appeared. The central character is a press agent, the first to appear in fiction. His name is Mr Pusher Long and what he gets up to for publicity's sake is nobody's business. An artist's one-man show is made to boom by the slashing of one of the pictures representing a women with evil eyes, an unknown actress is made a star by the delivery at her suburban door of an elephant, the 'gift of a Maharajah', a hunger-duel in a boarding house to advertise what would now be called vitamin tablets, twelve stories in all, in a little 12mo book on paper that dries and turns to powder.

I suppose these two volumes, if one can call them so, represent the literary lifework of a man who began as a poet of the Nineties. There must be hundreds, perhaps thousands of his short stories scattered among the bookstall magazines of the first three decades of this century, those magazines which fell out of the running one after another till today there is none left.

When I first knew him Miall lived with his family at Worthing but he moved to a house near the Alexandra Palace, then an empty shell surrounded by gloomy grounds and asphalt paths. I went with him to some bar in the place and we carried our beer-mugs into the open air to drink. Then we walked to his semi-detached home and I met his wife and tall son and daughter. But what I remember about that house was a deep cupboard as tall as the room, stuffed with magazines and weeklies containing Miall's stories. I was impressed and envious for I was twenty-one at the time and rejection slips were still tragedies while to appear in print anywhere, in any publication, was a triumph. But by 1937 I could see the pathos of that stuffed cupboard.

Miall was now living at Sutton and I asked him if he could come down to Smarden for a few days. He replied that he would cycle down, taking his time. (He was now sixty-three years old.) Such cycling, I felt, would belong to his period, that of Mr Polly's cycling adventures. I welcomed this but he arrived eventually in the motor-car of a Sutton resident who was coming to visit me.

I can see him now as he sat over tea in my home, his hawklike face breaking often into restrained smiles and in his cultured voice, which sometimes ran up to a treble squeak, he brought out some chuckling witticism such as might have roused laughter in a Fleet Street bar in 1910. He was never shabby but he dressed in a neat old-fashioned way for he was one of those men who make their clothes last for years, and are proud of it. In London he wore for many years a bowler hat of the old pattern, shallow in the crown, wide in the brim fore and aft. He was, more than anyone I have known, a man of his time, of his background and of his calling.

[5]

But Bede Jack Bentley, who also came down to Smarden
that year, was not stamped by period and dropped into no
category that I could name. He was a younger, somewhat
ne'er-do-well son of John Francis Bentley the architect of
Westminster Cathedral and he knew a great deal about old
furniture, metalwork and pottery. He was intolerant in this
as in many other matters, loving things for their intrinsic
beauty and to hell with décor. He was also a liar, not of the
mean pretentious kind but on a grand romantic Münchhausen
scale. It was difficult to mention a place, a person or an incident
to Jack Bentley without hearing him identify himself with all
three by some ingenious anecdote.

But he was, I found that spring, a better host than guest. He
had quarrelled with my father some years earlier—a piece of
skulduggery by Jack Bentley who had tried to entice my
father's garden boy to work for him—and now took pleasure
in criticizing whatever my father had done to the house.
Squatting in a low armchair of his own decaying Tudor farmhouse, with his dogs at his feet and his big pipe well lit, telling
some fabulous story of how he had snubbed Bernard Shaw or
eaten crocodile flesh, Jack was a ripe and entertaining man,
sincere in his love of beautiful things and devoted to his eccentric wife. But here, crabbing my father's decorations and telling
me the house was Victorian and that some cherished piece of
furniture of mine was brand-new, I did not find him so amiable.

CHAPTER FIVE

Parnassus N.W.8

MY LONG FRIENDSHIP with Louis Golding, if a relationship
which volleyed so often between sympathy and antipathy may
be called a friendship, was at its most positive in 1937. There
were few if any of those wordily polite recriminations which
Louis so enjoyed—'You see, old chap, I don't think you quite
appreciate . . .' 'Surely it must have occurred to you that I am
not the sort of person . . .' 'I'm sure you had no intention of
causing me pain, but . . .' and so on with immense ingenuity
and persistence. Louis was at the top of his form as a man, as a
talker, and as a best-selling writer. The books he was turning
out were competent and profitable and he enormously enjoyed
his success. His best work as a novelist had been done before
Magnolia Street when his cosmopolitanism was a faith and an
inspiration rather than a useful adjunct to story-telling as it
became in his later books, and his peculiar breathless and
magniloquent style was something essential and intrinsic and
not an affectation. *The Miracle Boy*, now ten years behind him,
has always seemed to me his best book. But 'the author of
Magnolia Street', as Louis had become, was in many ways a more
amiable person than the early novelist.

I saw a great deal of him that year for he liked coming down
to Smarden for week-ends, bringing one or two friends, and in
return would put me up in London whenever I wanted to stay
there.

Louis throve on the companionship of the young uneducated
cockney and the first of these whom he had idolized was a boxer,
so now, with an urge to reproduce the hallowed past which any

Freudian could recognize, he sought cockney boxers as his companions and tried to find in each relationship the felicity that had once been his when as a penurious and little-known writer he had explored middle European countries and the Mediterranean seaboard with that good-natured friend. He was fortunate for the most part and the young men I used to meet at his house or see diving in the stagnant water of the pool in my garden, were good-hearted easy-going fellows who treated Louis with a slightly cynical tolerance and that mixture of pity and awe with which the immature, ignorant and healthy view the intellectual, unbeautiful and ageing. He idealized each of them, not only in his own mind but in conversation with his friends, many of whom were unsympathetic to such confidences. Each was an Appollo, a sparkling source of natural humour with a character full of beautiful generosity and gentleness revealed only to his intimates, and each—this the important thing—was a very Achates in his devotion to Louis.

There was no harm in all this for Louis gave those common-place young men a great deal in sheer education, in experience and in furtherance of their modest ambitions and though in a sense they gave him more it was with open eyes and as part of a perfectly understood bargain. He encouraged them to get married because, as he once confided to me, this made them far more dependent on his benevolence. In those pre-war years he was content with a small circle of these friends and did not look beyond it or seek restlessly to increase it. No, there was no harm in it, and it only became a bore when one was alone with Louis and he wanted to gush with confidences about his friends' perfections. When they themselves were present they were fastidious and humorous enough to imply apologies for the infatuation of Louis and shrug it away as an embarrassment.

They treated Louis's literary friends, particularly those who did not share his yearnings towards themselves, with the natural good manners which are part of the cockney's character. The household in Hamilton Terrace, though it must have seemed an odd one to the conventionally-minded, was at this time happy and welcoming, and I think of it nostalgically.

It was the year when the *Lambeth Walk* had a universal folk-song kind of popularity and one of Louis's circle, a tough crop-headed lightweight from Lambeth, used to chant it as he did his stint of housework.

> *Any time you're Lamberf way*
> *Any evening, any day*
> *You'll find them all*
> *Doing the Lamberf walk . . .*

his voice would rise raucously.

"I shall hear that to the end of my life", said Louis, with a smiling touch of whimsy.

[2]

But other, very different people came to Louis's home, old friends of his from Manchester or Oxford days or fellow writers newly met. He gave small dinner parties at which his guests were waited on by one of the boxers, and Louis's charm and wit made up for any deficiency in hospitality. He rarely drank spirits himself and shrank from the prodigality of offering them to his guests, but without consulting their preferences served small glasses of sherry before the meal. He bought wine at bargain prices and without much knowledge from a Corsican in Soho and depended on his own gift of words to make it seem drinkable. I would be deputed to wait till his guests were all present, than say something in praise of the sherry.

"You like it?" Louis would catch me up quickly and in case my mumbled lie had not been audible repeat loudly—"Rupert who knows Spain better than I do thinks this is good sherry. As a matter of fact it is not sherry at all!"

Sensation. Everyone waited.

"But Rupert's quite right. It's a wine from Montilla and

some of the best sherry is made from Montilla wine—hence Amontillado."

He would go on to describe the little Cordobese town and before he had finished Louis's guests believed they were drinking from the original cask in Poe's story, unless one of them happened to know a little about wine and such a one could usually be relied on to keep quiet. At dinner, swallowing a resinous tawny liquid Louis had bought from his Corsican, we would listen enthralled to a story of a nectar Louis had enjoyed with Sicilian goatherds or Greek monks, a story whose climax was inevitably—"And *this* is the wine!"

He usually had a newly-arrived middle European refugee as cook which gave him scope for bolder reminiscences of travel. Garnished with aubergines and pimentos, laced with red wine and reeking with garlic an honest stew became a rare Balkan dish called perhaps Djuvedje, or red with paprika it was an unusual goulash which Louis had discovered in one Hungarian village and eaten to gypsy music while a storm shook the inn. How between flashes of lightning he had obtained the recipe from a deaf mute cook against the wishes of the innkeeper's wife would hold us spellbound till the last mouthful was eaten. And if the young man serving became impatient with his temporary role of waiter and joined in the conversation, Louis was quick to recall the Wicked Right Hook with which he had demolished his opponent in the ring last week and everyone felt privileged to be waited on by such a doughty pugilist.

I enjoyed those dinner parties in the basement dining-room and I liked nearly all Louis's friends, particularly the members of the Owen family who long ago in Manchester had 'adopted' him when he was a small clever lonely boy from the poor Jewish section of the city. From his Manchester days also dated his friendship with Thomas Moult whom I met at this time, a man of considerable distinction in several worlds, not all of them literary. Twelve years before he had included a poem of mine in his annual anthology of poetry which had given me the best kind of encouragement. He had only written—so far as I know—one novel. It was called *Saturday Night* and I thought it first-rate. Editor, critic, anthologist, I feared when Louis told me I should meet him he would be someone formidable and perhaps overbearing but I found him a kind and unassertive man. I think he knew Louis and all his persuasive wiles and naïve pretensions, but had the amused affection for him which most of us felt. This is conjecture—I only met Moult once and he certainly never discussed his host. But there was a friendly humour in his expression which suggested that he was in no way fooled, yet found his old friend irresistible.

Another writer whom I came to know a little better and also met at this time at one of Louis's dinner parties was Richard Blaker. This was an unforgettable man and a novelist of considerable talent. A friend of Louis since Oxford, Dick Blaker wrote a series of good books without any great material success, as many other writers did in those years. There was distinction in each of them but for long they reached only a small and devoted public. Then, about this time or a little earlier, he produced a novel called *Here Lies a Most Beautiful Lady* which brought critical opinion to his heel, a superb piece of story-telling which ran through several editions and, with its sequel, gave him a new status. I suppose it is out of print now as so many fine books of the inter-war period are, in spite of the proliferation of paper-backs, but it will be read again.

Blaker himself was a charming man, somewhat retiring, at least in Louis's exuberant presence, with salty humour and stern criteria of taste and conduct. I respected and liked him and shared some of Louis's happiness when he married Louis's 'adopted sister' May Owen. I shared, too, some of Louis's distress when a year or two later Richard Blaker died suddenly in Hollywood, where a film of one of his books was being made. But just then Richard Blaker, newly married and a successful novelist after an uphill journey, was on top of the world. I remember driving Louis down to the village in Hertfordshire in which he and his wife had taken a cottage. We were all very cheerful people that year.

At Louis's home I also met Dennis Wheatley and took an instant dislike to that doubtless estimable man, a dislike which must have been reciprocated since a favourite joke of his was to refer to me as 'Rupert Croft-Cooke, pronounced Crook'. This, I was told, brought the suburban house down, but it did not prevent Wheatley sending me copies of my first editions to be signed and returned for his collection. I daresay he was pleasant enough but my prejudices at that time were highly personal, instantaneously formed and hard to shift.

Louis's attitude to others of his fellow writers was a revealing one. He was desperately anxious to be considered advanced in his work and opinions and had written a book about James Joyce to prove his literary alliances. He was almost obsequious in his attitude to young poets of the Left and reproved me for my hostility or indifference to them, affecting to find me subservient at heart to my father's political principles. My attitude to the Spanish Civil War he could respect—indeed he seemed relieved that I was not a Franquista—but that I should feel not even curiosity about much-lauded Left-Wing poets whom he knew shocked him.

On the other hand he encouraged me in the *enfant terrible* impudence with which I viewed the important literary figures of the time and added his own to the collection of disrespectful anecdotes I had made about Francis Brett-Young and Hugh Walpole. His story about Brett-Young was not very funny, not nearly so worth remembering as those I had already in my assortment, coming directly from Sheila Kaye-Smith and Norman Douglas's daughter-in-law and indirectly from Compton Mackenzie, but his account of how he had shown Hugh Walpole through the shadier depths of Berlin was unforgettable in its macabre climax, and when Walpole was knighted that year it had an impious topicality. Louis could be bitchy enough (as I suppose we all could) about characters like Cecil Roberts and Godfrey Winn, but he seemed a little fearful of ridiculing the more eminent and sometimes more truly comic members of our profession, though he egged me on to do so. "Tell the one about Morgan Forster at the boat-race!" he used to say, of 'about Jack Priestley at the charity matinee', or 'about Willy Maugham in the Turkish Baths'. I ought to have made a written anthology.

[3]

Louis had no conscience at all about telephoning a hostess, even one who had invited him to a formal dinner party, to ask if he might bring a friend with him, and I frequently found myself an embarrassment to some poor woman who had hoped that 'the author of *Magnolia Street*' would be prepared to hire a taxi and not ask for an extra place at table for someone who would drive him to the house.

This did not matter when it was a crush for cocktails but I remember once finding myself a last-minute thirteenth at a lavish dinner party given by Jewish friends of Louis who lived in a remote suburb, expensive of access by taxi. Louis had assured me that I was invited and his hostess who knew Louis better than I did and had taken in the situation as soon as my car appeared in her drive, lied bravely for him. She was famous for her dinner parties, a woman of considerable personality, an Ada Leverson *de nos jours*, and her friends were intellectual and artistic Jewish people.

Among these Louis was never at his best, treating them rather as though he was a member of their village community who had gone out successfully into the great world and was now back on a sentimental visit. This may have been accepted by the inhabitants of Magnolia Street itself but even I, who knew none of them, could see that the guests here were not prepared to lionize Louis unreservedly and that the evening might therefore be a difficult one.

The dinner was excellent and there was a really good claret served without pretentiousness or fuss, but Louis's enjoyment of it was disturbed by the conversation which was devoted, for a full twenty minutes, to a discussion of G. B. Stern's novels. There were present some relatives of hers and one, who had known the original character on whom she had based her play *The Matriarch*, held the table as no one could with impunity in Louis's presence. Seumas O'Sullivan, the Irish poet and editor was there, I remember, for he had married into one of the families, a handsome bearded man in his late fifties, and he seemed as deeply interested in *The Matriarch* as the rest of us. Louis sulked outrageously and not till a stage had been improvised in the drawing room in which he stood and rolled his eyes in imitation of Eddie Cantor and was applauded, did his good humour return.

Even then it was not for long. It was evidently a part of the tradition of these gatherings, along with a bout of charades, that Louis should tell a ghost story, and he had one ready, macabre, flesh-creeping, full of atmosphere which no one knew better how to exploit. The lights were lowered, the guests sat round expectantly and in his rich cultured voice Louis began to narrate.

Unfortunately he had chosen a story about a black cat whose gruesome appearances brought ghastly events with them, or which re-appeared, as if by chance, after every manifestation of horror.

"And there, under the table", said Louis describing the creature's first of three appearances in the story with dramatic awe, "was . . . *a black cat*!"

He paused for effect, when suddenly, incredibly, from a corner of the room occupied by a perky little bespectacled business-man, came a distinct "Miaou", followed by universal giggles.

Somewhat shaken, Louis proceeded. He had a long way to go yet, for the black cat would appear twice again. After a few moments he reached the second climax in which out of an empty coffin or through the window of a haunted house (I forget the details) once more appeared with all its dread significance the gruesome figure of . . . *the black cat*!

C*

"Miaou!"

This time there was laughter, only half-suppressed, throughout the room.

Louis was between tears and fury.

"If you do that again, Benny", he said, "I shall stop telling the story."

But he could not do that with the third and greatest climax still to come. He worked harder than ever, calling on all his resources as a raconteur. He used his voice as an actor might, and his sentences were beautifully manipulated. But he must have heard it coming—as of course it came.

"As he passed into unconsciousness", said Louis, "realizing that this was indeed the end, across his fading vision passed . . . *a black cat!*"

"MIAOU!"

Everyone was laughing now, even a little hysterically. The lights were switched on amid laughter, drinks were poured in merriment, Louis was thanked with streaming eyes. I was sorry for him, but angry with him too. Why couldn't he see that he *must* laugh with the rest? It was his only remedy. Anything else would be too undignified, too childish, too petulantly silly. But no—Louis was taking leave of his hostess, white with anger and pain and all the way home in the car I had to listen to a furious and half-tearful tirade in which were audible the frightened undertones of persecution mania echoing from his scarred boyhood. It was a *calculated* insult. They had *meant* to humiliate him. Didn't I understand how people *resented* his success? I had to check myself from uttering a last exasperated *miaou* which would have ended our friendship.

Literary cocktail parties, to several of which I went with Louis that year, were torture to me, as they are to this day, and it was distressing to Louis that the only available motor-car for getting to them without hiring a taxi belonged to someone who did not appreciate them. I felt desperately unliterary, out of it, shy and if not provincial at least rustic or even foreign. It was a milieu I did not understand and it made me defiant and

probably a little boorish. I longed to be back in the Smarden
Bell or in what for *that* matter (I reminded myself aggressively)
were the far less parochial gatherings I had known abroad. Nor
can I say now who gave those parties or where, but at one I
aroused the sympathy of Victor Gollancz with whom I talked
gratefully for half an hour, while at another I found myself
with three writers, Beatrice Kean Seymour, Rosalind Wade and
the husband of one of them who was later to become the husband
of the other. With Miss Wade I was relieved to find I had
something in common, each of us having depicted a school in
a book and been threatened with libel actions by the indignant
heads of similar institutions. But such moments were hardly
enough to tempt me to these covens.

Sometimes I rebelled. One evening when I was staying in
the house Louis told me winningly that he had arranged for
me to accompany him to a cocktail party given by the wife of
a Cabinet Minister, I think Lady Hoare, whose house was in
Rutland Gate. I should, Louis promised, me, meet a number of
important people. I refused and asked Louis what he, so
vociferously of the Left, would be doing in that galley. This
brought me despairing reproof. Was I really so *borné* that I
could not see the necessity for a writer in *his* position to be the
familiar of Cabinet Ministers of whatever party? Perhaps, I
conceded, but there was certainly no necessity in my case and
I did not want to go.

I could see that refusal would not be as easy as that. Louis's
face had the petulant, brooding expression it wore when he
was failing to get his own way.

"You see, old chap, I was rather counting on you to take me
there."

I told him I would run him over, if that was what he wanted.
It was only just across the Park. But it was not—at least, not
all he wanted.

"At these parties", he explained, "it doesn't really *do* to come
in a taxi. A footman calls for the various cars as people leave
and one really feels rather absurd if one's name can't be called

out. Besides, the press often rely on that to know who is there if they can't get a list of guests and are too lazy to see who goes in. You see what I mean?"

I saw, I was staggered to see, exactly what he meant.

"You want me to drive you over and wait to be called up to the door?"

"Oh, my dear old boy, I couldn't think of asking you to do that. It was just that your car looked so very smart, I thought, the other day . . . But naturally, it's out of the question. One doesn't ask one's friends. . . ."

"I'll take you over, Louis, and wait for you", I said, deeply amused.

And I did, giving myself an entertaining evening in the pub at the bottom of Rutland Gate with the chauffeurs of 'the Cliveden Set' and other politicians.

The chauffeurs of the great made a world of their own in those days. Meeting during functions they knew one another and a good deal more of the affairs of the country than many Members of Parliament. I did not test their security that evening however, for I found that they were keen dart players to a man and found myself in partnership with Anthony Eden's chauffeur against two stern-faced drivers who had put in a good deal of practice during all-night sessions. The games went one–one, and the final was never finished for a scout waiting outside heard the name of the employer of one of our competitors shouted from the steps of a house halfway up Rutland Gate. In due course came the summons "Mr Louis Golding!" on which I drove the old Lea Francis up to the steps and found Louis beaming with pleasure.

"Let's go and have some Chinese food", he said expansively.

A very different occasion was an 'authors' night' at Unity Theatre to which Louis had been invited. Unity Theatre was one of the projections of lively and intelligent Leftism which along with the Left Book Club and the *Daily Worker* gave young Londoners, in the years just before the war, a sense of belonging to a vital and growing movement which would combat 'die-hard Toryism' and 'sloppy Liberalism' in their own fields, something altogether different from the routine parliamentary socialism of today.

That visit to Unity Theatre was on a warm night in June or July, and I think in that year of 1937 though it may possibly have been in the following year. The production, at all events, was an American play called *Waiting for Lefty* and Paul Robeson was giving his performance in the name-part without payment. Whatever it was as propaganda, as drama the play was poor, but Robeson could carry anything and held the attention of a posse of authors, who had been asked to join in a debate later, as easily as he could hold a less pernickety audience by playing the Emperor Jones or singing *Ole Man River*.

In the interval we stood in a gravelled yard outside and Louis introduced me to Stephen Spender. He was, I think, a little overwhelmed by Louis's confident verbosity and gave me a shy, sidelong look as if in appeal for release, so I drew Louis off to meet someone else while Spender sidled politely away. I have never seen him again, He seemed, as Lawrence said of Mellors, 'a curious, quick, separate fellow, alone but sure of himself'.

The debate was a fiasco. I remember Louis being fruitily rational about Spain and Rodney Ackland passionately apocalyptic about Germany and someone else ecstatic about Russia. But it led nowhere.

[4]

His friends knew the danger of being enticed by Louis into voicing any criticism of his work. It was not merely a matter of flattering Louis—which any fool could do—for flattery was not enough; one had to read and discuss the stuff with an air of profound concern and what one felt was the right answer at the moment might turn out to be a gaffe in the long run.

I learnt my lesson when after *Magnolia Street* and its weighty sequel *Five Silver Daughters* Louis wrote a book called *The Camberwell Beauty* and sent me to bed one evening with a proof copy. I was tired and the light was bad, but I gathered that it contained a caricature of Aleister Crowley and was all about cockneys fighting black magic on a Mediterranean island.

Next morning Louis was in wait for me. It simply did not occur to him to doubt that I had sat up all night reading. He was rather surprised with himself for the honour he had paid me in showing me his book in proof.

I did my best. Brilliant, authentic idiom, gripping story, would outsell *Magnolia Street*. I was rather pleased with myself for sounding so convincing.

But it would not do. A month or two later when the book came out it not only received the critical blast which any novel following two best-sellers might expect, it also slumped commercially and the sales level which Gollancz had built up for Louis by clever exploitation of his previous books, dropped to almost pre-Magnolian depths.

Louis realized that it had been a mistake to publish it, 'at least at that point', and rounded furiously on me.

"Either you have no critical judgement at all", he said, "or you deliberately misled me. Why couldn't you tell me that this was too . . . light a book to bring out immediately after those two great sombre novels? I gave you the opportunity to do something really helpful. You might have had a valuable influence on my whole career. But I'm afraid you let me down."

I was never caught like that again.

[5]

One of Louis's more amiable traits was the way in which he magnified, in his own mind and in conversation, the virtues of his friends—or what seemed to him their virtues. My enthusiasm for darts and public bars and my at-homeness in their atmosphere were the only qualities in me he admired or envied. He was unable to adapt himself to this background appearing always alien, intellectual and a mite patronizing in spite of his best efforts to mix. (In fact, looking back on Louis I wonder if the most pathetic thing about him was not that he was never really at home in any milieu at all. He had left his first habitat far behind and even this, though he was born in a poor Jewish quarter of Manchester, had only been a place of refuge to which his parents had come in their thirties. Perhaps his real home, as one of his titles suggested, was ancient Babylon.)

But he had a healthy and understandable liking for publicity of the kind which made him appear interesting and many-sided. It was not so much as a novelist that he liked to figure in the public eye, for that, after *Magnolia Street*, could be taken for granted. But as an adventurous traveller, with undertones of exploration, as a collector of carved bambinos, as a gourmet, as a boxing enthusiast, as a wine-lover, he delighted in gossip paragraphs, press pictures and interviews. It was not surprising, then, that he saw possibilities in my addiction to darts and pubs and suggested that he should organize a darts competition between writers and boxers to be played off in one of the rooms of his house, converted into a 'darts parlour' for the occasion. There would be press photographers, he said, and plenty of paragraphs.

Not, he explained, that these could possibly be of any interest or advantage to him.

"I am delighted to do this for you", he told me with complete conviction. "It is just the sort of thing you need. It should not be only in reviews of your books that your name appears in print. You say *beer* is the right drink for a darts competition?"

But there was a fatality about things that Louis undertook—they were never failures but they never *quite* came off. The entertainments he gave, speeches he made, journeys he planned, his love-affairs, his friendships, even the books he wrote, all had a certain brilliance, a certain virtuosity, but lacked the ultimate triumph. He was constitutionally incapable of giving the last ounce. There was always something skimped, a compulsive strain of miserliness—emotional as well as economical—which robbed his efforts of effect. So now. His party took place and was publicized, there were 'names' heard and photographs published, but the occasion even within the limits of its purpose, was only half successful.

The 'names' were not good enough. Unable to find, or for one reason or another unwilling to invite half a dozen, say, of the writers of those days who were always willing to lend their names and presence to anything chronicled by the press, his team of four consisted of himself, me, a sports journalist and Bunny Austin, a tennis champion whose articles on his sport were held to qualify him. As boxers he had three of his young friends who had fought in professional matches at the Paddington Baths and Eddie Peirce, then the cruiser-weight champion of South Africa. He invited the press, supplied beer and hot sausages and depended on his own indefatigable bounce and persuasiveness to do the rest. I can still see him, beaming a little unctuously as he explained to a group of bored journalists the tie-up he wanted introduced between this and his last published book—*In the Steps of Moses the Law Giver*—a tie-up which to a less fertile mind than Louis's would have seemed impossible. It depended on a biblical reference to the Amalekites hurling darts against the Israelites. It was ingenious—a good example of Louisian tactics for the promotion of his career in which nothing was too trivial to be ignored—and it was taken up by the writer of at least one gossip column, that of the *Daily Sketch*.

Meanwhile, I richly enjoyed the evening. I was perfectly content to drink beer and play darts, and I certainly was not above taking pleasure in the resulting publicity. And I never, in those years, grew tired of watching with wonder, with amusement, with only the mildest touch of secret and friendly ridicule, the resourceful antics of Louis in action against the world's tendency to ignore him. It was of its kind superb.

CHAPTER SIX

Work and Freedom

[1]

FOR WEEKS ON END I did not leave my home for I was working on a new novel, writing dozens of articles, nipping away the side shoots of the tomato plants which were growing tall in the enormous greenhouse and pricking out perennials, all with enthusiasm. Dingo the yellow Alsatian, my constant companion now for four years, rarely left me whether I was writing, eating, sleeping, working in the greenhouse or playing darts at the Bell.

My first attempt at extrovert autobiography was published that year by Hodder and Stoughton. It was called *The World is Young*, a high-pitched title taken from a bad poem by Charles Kingsley, and it told the story of the two years I had spent in Argentina as a boy. (Its matter has been absorbed into an earlier book in this sequence.)

It brought me a thundering attack, which continued in headlines for several days, in a daily newspaper called the *Buenos Aires Herald*. The British colony in Buenos Aires in those years was so numerous and so financially powerful that two English daily papers were published, the *Standard*, a good old stager founded when the British first invested in, built and ran the railways, tramways, docks, electricity and telephone services of the country and settled in great numbers in the suburbs of Buenos Aires, and the *Herald*, a livelier newspaper, more slickly edited and written, which had the wider circulation. The *Herald's* leader-writer was a shrewd and fertile journalist called Goldflam who wrote a daily feature called *Round the Mulberry Bush* in a breezy, fairly professional manner. As a boy

77

I had read it keenly, envying Goldflam's self-confidence and sagacity and I had never forgotten the comment he made in his column on my own little weekly journal, 'It may suit you to see your name in print, but the game you have chosen rarely leads to the publication, in *The Times*, of your name in the only place worth while—under the heading Wills and Bequests'.

Now, however, the *Herald* was not making smart and patronizing comments, it was hitting out with indignation and vigour. In my book I had included a passage criticizing the insularity of the British community who behaved in those days much as their empire-building cousins did in the cantonments of India. Indeed, the parallel was close because both communities were made up of people who would have lacked significance at home and now found themselves in sunlit villas with servants to support their status, their self-importance expanding and their superiority to the 'natives' accepted by their fellows. It seemed incredible to me that people I thought to be the least estimable of the British in their homeland, the eagerly conformist lower middle classes, fearful of the Left for its threat to their harshly-won privileges and obsequious to both the highly born and the wealthy, should here strut about their clubs (British Only) talking of the Argentines, even of the most cultured and distinguished of them, as 'natives'. This was not imperialism, it was not in the least political—it was racial pretentiousness and a social inferiority complex which drove them to make themselves ridiculous in Argentine eyes. The climate and the cheapness of liquor had other unfortunate effects and in a city where the customer was handed the whisky or gin bottle at any bar or in any café so that he could pour as liberally as he wished, most of the men drank too much while the women, in contrast to the elegant Argentine girls, appeared, as I tactlessly wrote, 'scraggy and shapeless'.

When a copy of the book in which appeared these impolite and youthfully provocative comments reached the offices of the *Buenos Aires Herald*, that paper went into action with five column headlines across its front page. *Novelist Assails British Community.* "*Whisky Drinking Blonds.*" *Mr. Croft-Cooke's Tirade Against Anglo-Argentines.* "*Amphibious Monstrosities.*" Under these were several thousand words of text, mostly blind abuse without much sting in it. I wrote 'mediocre novels', other adventures by other young men would have made a more interesting book but remained unwritten; mine only appeared because I had a 'certain degree of literary skill', and so on. On the following day: *English Reputed Drunkards. Mr. Croft-Cooke Supported by Local Schoolmaster. An Overpainted Picture.* Three men who appeared in the book and had been interviewed gave their views—one saying that the excerpts quoted from the book were better written than the *Herald's* review. Correspondence began in which I was called 'an accursed son of Satan', 'a writer of tripe', 'not a homme de monde', 'a so-called school tie', while one Englishman claimed that I owed him 476 pesos and that during my two years in the country (as a boy of nineteen and twenty) he had scarcely seen me sober, while the only girls I ever went with were cabaret girls when I had money.

After that Goldflam gave me his column for two consecutive days, and under the heading 'Scraggy and shapeless' (it was that 'scraggy' that seems to have caused all the trouble) said I had 'probably only had experience with the charlady of the species', was a malpert (sic) and a worp, and that for a schoolmaster I must have done a lot of peeping, 'naughty, naughty!' On the second day he discovered that 'for every Croft-Cooke there are thousands of decent folk among us'.

I had wits enough not to make any retort to this abuse when I read it in my peaceful Wealden home, indeed I was flattered and delighted. One of my friends in Buenos Aires had ended his interview with the *Herald* by saying that I should 'laugh loud and long' over the attack since it would probably increase sales, and that was indeed my first reaction. But it interested me, too, to see what could appear in a newspaper beyond the strong arm of the law of libel. It was a small insight into methods quite common, I believe, in the American press but discouraged in England by Judges who award large damages to individuals libelled in newspapers.

It is nearly thirty years ago now and the young women whom I insulted so childishly are grandmothers, while the 'whisky-drinking blonds' are whisky-drinking greybeards or under the sod. The newspaper cuttings are yellowed by time and it was all a storm in a *bombilla*, but it gave me a fillip then. How I longed to be an *enfant terrible*!

[2]

I had more provocative opponents and better reasons for attack in the articles I wrote in those years for the Freedom Association.^e Here was full scope for my anarchism, here was an outlet for the anti-authoritarian, the extra-political classless rebel-for-the-sake-of-it, the character in which I saw myself with more determination as my contemporaries welcomed the disciplines of communism or fascism. Much that I wrote was trivial, much seems Canute-like today when forms of regimentation are calmly accepted which would have raised the hair of an individualist before the war, much was no more than Anti-Teetotalist propaganda, but there was, I am pleased to see now, a hard core of sense in some of the articles. *The Tyranny of Uniforms* was one in which I regretted the intimidation of unsophisticated people by 'inspectors' of various organizations and even rent-collectors tricked out in quasi-police

---

^e This was an institution which employed writers to turn out articles on any aspect of personal liberty but with an eye on the arbitrary licensing laws. These articles were sent out to local papers all over the country and their editors were invited to use them without payment, which, since the articles were often by eminent writers, they were glad to do. The whole thing was subsidized by the brewers and others who wanted propaganda against forms of regimentation. It was run by a Welsh solicitor named Ernest Williams and after his death, until it ceased to exist in 1946, by his son Brendan who became a friend of mine. For these articles the Freedom Association paid various fees from fifteen guineas to authors who earned big money down to eight guineas to me who felt lucky to be included in their list. Ernest Williams would invite a contribution two or three times a year and the subjects on which to write were innumerable, the aims of the Association things about which I could feel real enthusiasm.

uniform. *No Darts on Sunday* was another in which I railed against a piece of police arrogance of the time when publicans were visited by an inspector and told, on pain of having their licenses opposed, not to allow bar games, darts, skittles or shove-ha'penny on Sunday. Licensing hours, regulations arbitrarily ruling the lives of council house occupants, interference in all its (then less objectionable) forms, petty restrictions, conventions blown up to tyrannies, I attacked them as often as I was given the chance and trained myself to the parry and thrust of controversy against an unseen opponent. I would be attacking them still if I had not achieved a detached and flippant attitude with which to await that sudden day when men will stand no more of it from any damned party or religion, union, organization, demogague or system and a huge anarchic explosion generated by years of miserable conformity will destroy the whole bloody establishment. But I had not the vision, or the reason, or perhaps the divine irresponsibility to feel like that then and still scratched away with these trimensual protests.

My first book of short stories was published that year and a pretty mixed bag it was, some of the stories going back to my earliest efforts in 1925. The title story, *A Pharaoh with his Waggons*, however, was not bad and prophetically about gypsies. More important to me was the inclusion of my novel *Kingdom Come* in the Albatross Library. This, alas, is no more but in the years between the wars it was a powerful and benevolent institution, printing and selling continental editions of English books and paying the author a fair sum for his 'continental' rights. The idea had first occurred to Christian Bernhard, Freiheer von Tauchnitz, whose firm, Bernhard Tauchnitz, started a Library of English and American authors in 1841 and by 1929 had published 4800 titles. Oscar Brandsteller of Leipzig started the Albatross Edition in competition with Tauchnitz and produced more attractively printed books, taking over in 1934 the Tauchnitz Editions and continuing to print until the outbreak of war. Our own paperback editions, circulating freely on the Continent, eventually made these editions printed abroad uneconomical but in their time they were a boon to the author and the foreign student of English. Albatross had already included two earlier books of mine and of each they produced, according to their pleasant custom with all books, twelve copies on handmade paper, one of which bore the words 'This copy was printed for the author' and was bound in half morocco.

These were, I used to feel, the rewards of professionalism. More flattering but less profitable was the inclusion of three of my poems in R. K. Mégroz's *Treasury of Modern Poetry*, an anthology which had been published in the previous year and reached me now. It is interesting to compare it with Michael Roberts's *The Faber Book of Modern Verse* which appeared in the same year. Roberts had a narrow field deliberately omitting good poets who had not 'been compelled to make any notable development of poetic technique' and limiting his poets to little more than half the number included by Mégroz, but Mégroz had his standards and a few surprises. It is noteworthy that only six names are common to the two anthologies, Yeats, T. S. Eliot, Conrad Aiken, D. H. Lawrence, Edith Sitwell and Sacheverell Sitwell. Roberts had Gerard Manley Hopkins of the older poets and Spender, Auden, Day-Lewis and Dylan Thomas as his (then) moderns, while Mégroz starts with Alice Meynell and Francis Thompson and of this century has, besides many of the Georgian and *London Mercury* poets, Edmund Blunden, Roy Campbell, G. K. Chesterton, Richard Church, W. H. Davies, Walter de la Mare, Hugh MacDiarmid, Herbert Palmer and ironically Michael Roberts himself.

[3]

It was not only through Louis Golding that I met new and occasionally notable people and when I look back on that year's bag they seem an unlikely lot, and in retrospect few are more remarkable than my friends at the Smarden Bell.

Someone persuaded Walter Hutchinson to give a party for Franz Werfel the Austrian-Jewish poet and novelist who had somehow strayed into Jarrolds' list[d]. Werfel wrote intimidatingly long biblical romances with English titles like *The Forty Days*. He had recently come to England as a distinguished refugee. Walter Hutchinson had never been known to give a party for an author but this was a somewhat exceptional case and he not only hired one of the smaller party rooms at the Savoy but appeared in person among his authors, a unique and much-discussed occasion. I saw him across the room—the only time I ever set eyes on him.

I asked my friend Michael Harrison to come with me and our simple object was to consume as many of Hutchinson's martinis as time and decency allowed. Werfel talked ponderously about literature but Lord Dunsany, who had also been enticed into the Jarrolds list to do a book called *My Ireland*, sprawled on a settee, his fine bearded head noticeable among less picturesque faces, and took on all comers. Philip Youngman Carter, who in those days before he became editor of the *Tatler* designed book jackets for Hutchinson came, alas, without his wife Margery Allingham, the best of the women detective novelists, whom I wanted to meet. I remember some rather good talk in our corner after we had been formally introduced to Franz Werfel, but not to Hutchinson who had given orders that he was to meet no one and stood protected by members of his staff.

Another occasion that year which gave me some amusement was an evening when my old friend Roy Hardy, a bringer-together if ever there was one, a member of every club and society open to one in his profession of advertising, asked me to address one of the gatherings he organized and I found myself on the platform with a Methodist minister named Donald Soper[e] whose line was pacifism, good and strong. To my embarrassment he used the occasion (which was a meeting of advertising men who invited a couple of outsiders to put

---

[d] Jarrolds was the subsidiary company of Walter Hutchinson's organization which published my books.　　　　　[e] Now Lord Soper.

forward their lay point of view on advertising) for a non-stop harangue delivered without notes or pause or much entertainment on his favourite theme of pacifism.

In the bar afterwards I tried to nail him because this point of view seemed to me, as it still seems, not so much sinister or insane, over-intellectualized or anti-social as frankly silly.

"My position is a very simple one", Dr Soper said aggressively in answer to a mild question; "there are NO circumstances which I think justify force of arms."

I was not working the old raped sister oracle, but I suggested that perhaps causes like the preservation of Christianity, opposition to an absolute and philistine tyranny like Nazism if it could only be defeated by force, or the continued existence of mankind as more than a race of ants, might possibly, in certain extreme and unforeseeable circumstances, justify a little purely defensive action. Mightn't they? Just possibly?

Dr Soper sternly shook his head.

"No circumstances are conceivable in which force *could* be justified", he told me peremptorily and I began nervously to talk of the weather till he hurried off to deliver his discourse elsewhere. Evidently a dedicated man.

[4]

At Charles Lahr's bookshop in Red Lion Street new faces were to be seen, though the behaviour of visitors and of Charles himself had not changed from the days when *The New Coterie* was published here. Those who gathered to read copies of Left Wing newspapers and reviews which they could not find in public libraries seemed seedier and more hopeless than the ardent young writers I had known and the shop itself even less prosperous.

Frederick Carter, who used to correspond with D. H. Lawrence on occult and apocalyptic matters, was a very conven-

tional-looking magician with a ruddy face and a brusque forth-
right manner who had published a book, to me unintelligible
but to Lawrence exciting, called *The Dragon of the Apocalypse*.
Ernest George, an East End bookseller who had written a play,
came often and a number of sad and unsuccessful men who slept
in Sally Army Hostels came here to meet other unfortunates with
vociferous opinions. Charles was as enthusiastic as ever about
the writings of his friends and handed round esoteric publi-
cations in which they appeared. He still faked newspaper
posters, taking a word or two from one and gumming it carefully
on another so that one was led to suppose, if one did not
examine them closely, that the *Evening News* was featuring
Bishop Gallops Home or that in the *Evening Standard* one might
read of *Chamberlain Dismantled*.

No one was excluded from Charles Lahr's shop, though
Charles might move about muttering 'Christ!' and 'Get out!'
There was an unfortunate Australian-born Pole called Potocki
who, at first satisfied to call himself a Count, had now lost all
restraint and contact with reality and claimed to be heir to the
throne of Poland, and to prove it wore in the streets a full-
length cloak of moth-eaten red velvet and sometimes a stage-
jewelry crown. He had been addicted to such exhibitionism
when I had first seen him in Charles Lahr's shop in the 1920's but
a disgraceful injustice in 1932 had scattered what wits he had.
H. Montgomery Hyde in his *History of Pornography* describes it:

One case, however, must be briefly mentioned, since it
constituted an extended application of the ruling in the
Hicklin case in a most dangerous form, incidentally illus-
trating the fantastic lengths to which literary censorship
could go in the England of the nineteen-thirties. Here the
defendant was an eccentric poet, who styled himself Count
Geoffrey Wladislas Potocki of Montalk, dressed himself in a
wine-coloured cloak and leather sandals, and let his hair
grow so long that it came below his shoulders. Happening
to be with a friend one day outside the Old Bailey in London,
he asked a policeman if he could direct them to a typesetter

who would set up some 'spicy' poems, as he wished to have a few copies printed for distribution among his friends. 'The cop had a turn for practical joking', the Count later recalled, 'and sent us to an address which turned out to be that of the printers of the *Methodist Times*'. Not altogether surprisingly these printers were unable to oblige, and eventually Count Potocki found another printer who he thought might be more accommodating and left the manuscript of his verses with him. There were five poems in all, one being a translation of Rabelais and the others parodies or free translations of Verlaine, in all of which appeared what are colloquially known today as four-letter words. The printer immediately turned over the manuscript to the police and the unfortunate Count was arrested and thrown into Brixton Prison. Although he had only published the offending material in the technical sense of communicating it to the printer and had not done harm to anyone, Count Potocki was nevertheless found guilty in February 1932 of publishing an obscene libel and sentenced to six months' imprisonment by the Recorder of London, Sir Ernest Wild. 'A man must not say he is a poet and be filthy', the learned Judge remarked on this occasion. 'He has to obey the law just the same as ordinary citizens, and the sooner the highbrow school learns that, the better for the morality of the country.' The Court of Appeal agreed with the Recorder and confirmed the sentence, which a considerably more eminent poet than the Count, no less than W. B. Yeats, denounced at the time as 'criminally brutal'.

In his circle and among the habitués of Charles Lahr's shop, to be Left Wing was to conform with the crowd and to put himself in opposition Potocki printed a little broadsheet called the *Right Review*. He had been sent to prison more for wearing fancy dress and a toy crown in Court than for translating Rabelais and he continued to parade his costume with plaintive defiance. He and Prince Monolulu the tipster were the two most picturesquely garbed Londoners of that time.

As a contrast to Charles Lahr's shop the only commonplace-

looking man was John Brophy in his bowler hat. I used to go
to a pub in Fleet Street where writers conformed to another
pattern. Here Jack Squire, who had at last abandoned his
attempts to keep *London Mercury* alive, might still be seen sometimes, and here I met Ralph Straus who was then the fiction
reviewer of *The Sunday Times*. He was a pleasant man with a
mania for after-dinner speaking and the laboured wit and
portentous manner that go with it. He was on the board of
Chapman and Hall when the Registrar of Rochester threatened
to bring an action for libel against me and the publishers. He
had used the incident, he told me, in his book about writing
and publishing *A Whip for the Women*.

"Yes", he said complacently, "you will find yourself in that
book under the name of 'Mr Hooper'. It may amuse you."

"Then", I suggested facetiously, "why don't *I* bring an
action for libel against *you* for your libel in calling me a libeller?"

This did not amuse Ralph Straus at all and he quickly
invited me to dinner. He had a small ground-floor flat in his
brother's house and used to take one to an Italian restaurant
round the corner before returning to his fireside to show one,
rather purposefully, his collection of pornographic pictures. He
was a dull but kindly reviewer and a not very interesting
biographer. He never wrote a bad review nor even earned a
good one. How quickly and completely his name, once an
impressive and powerful one in English letters, has disappeared.

In the same pub was quite often J. B. Morton who as
Beachcomber in the *Daily Express* had lightened my days and
those of several million others for more than a decade. A short,
thickset man, he belonged to the Chesterton-Belloc school of
robust Catholic travellers, drinkers, talkers and professional
writers. I admired him immensely for having imposed what one
would have imagined was a highly individual form of humour
on the whole nation and I never met a writer who so fully
represented, in person and personality, what one would expect
from his work.

In very different bars, in over-decorated clubs with a ladylike improvising pianist, or behind the circle of the Palladium, I used to see James Agate who told the best dirty stories I have ever heard and showed a magnificent indifference to the whispers of jealousy. He used his splendid brain to get what he wanted from life, and did not care who saw him with a handsome guardsman. He knew his value to the papers for which he wrote and it made him immune to head-wagging about his somewhat raffish ways. As book critic of the *Daily Express* he was consistently generous to me for many years and I remember him with affection and admiration as a completely fulfilled, hard-living, hard-working human being, one of the few men I have known of truly independent spirit.

His story of the most sinister words he ever heard delights me still. They were spoken by a writer at the Café Royal who was passing through the swing doors to the kitchen with a tray of empty plates, and they were received with a nod by a waiter coming through the outward swing door with a laden one. The words were three—'he ate it'.

Who else, of any interest, did I meet? It must have been some years earlier, I think, that I found myself briefly cross-examined by Mrs Cecil Chesterton, a woman of purpose who dedicated her life to the reclaiming of erring sisters, a thankless task of doubtful service to the community. I would have liked to hear her talk of her late husband for it was said that G. K.'s brother was in many ways the more remarkable of the two, but she was too much concerned with fallen women for any reminiscences and understandably had no time for me. Another relative of a vanished man of genius who could not be induced to recall him was Hubert Cannan, a brother of Gilbert Cannan the novelist. Gilbert Cannan was not dead at this time though it was usually supposed that he was. He had been certified insane after the First World War and was kept in a private asylum till his death about ten years ago. As a young man I had read his novels with their avid sordidness and realism and thought him a bold and interesting rebel. He had been the co-respondent in J. M. Barrie's divorce which somehow added to his glamour, but by the time of which I am writing he seemed entirely forgotten and I could find no one to share my enthusiasm for his books. His brother Hubert was a big pink-cheeked rather effeminate man who dressed elaborately, went to first nights and wanted to talk about his titled acquaintance rather than recall his talented brother.

But A. F. Tschiffely when I met him that year would talk as much as I wanted of that one figure of the past who had in a sense brought us together. Tschiffely was himself an interesting man who had been, like me, a schoolmaster in Buenos Aires and had set off from there on horseback to ride to Washington ten thousand miles away. This he accomplished and wrote his book *From Southern Cross to Pole Star* recording the events of that marathon ride, a book which with Tschiffely's *Ride* and *The Tale of Two Horses* made a great appeal to a vast public in many countries. But less fortunate was his *Life* of Cunningham Graham which appeared that year.

Now Don Roberto had been a hero of mine since I found him still a legend in Buenos Aires when I arrived there in 1923. He was everything and did everything I thought fine, a Scottish laird who after being educated at Harrow ran wild on the Argentine *pampas*, explored dangerous places in Paraguay, Mexico and Morocco, talked Spanish as well as his Spanish grandmother, was imprisoned in England as a socialist rabble-rouser, looked like an hidalgo and wrote like God. He had died in the previous year and now too soon and not nearly good enough, was published *Don Roberto: R. B. Cunningham Graham* by A. F. Tschiffely.

I do not remember whether I asked to review this book or whether it was sent to me by coincidence by the three papers for which I most often reviewed, the *Yorkshire Post*, the *Tablet*, and the *British Weekly*, but reviews of mine appeared in all of these and in each I blasted poor Tschiffely till he must have wondered where the thing was going to stop. He immediately got in touch with me, not sending his seconds to call me out, but writing a cordial invitation to meet and talk about *Don*

Roberto at the Savage Club. I found him a grand fellow, completely unpretentious, down to earth yet still believing in the enchantments of life. Of his biography he explained—and it will stir the sympathy of most biographers in recent times—that his trouble was 'the family'. This must not be published nor that hinted at, these letters should be destroyed and those episodes forgotten. The families of great men seem concerned with everything but the truth. So Tschiffely had some excuse but I still think *Don Roberto* a poor book and Tschiffely's own accounts of his great ride splendid reading.

CHAPTER SEVEN

Ernst Thoma

[1]

IN SEPTEMBER I heard from my German friend Ernst Thoma that he was to be married in six weeks' time. He was working and living at Kassel and he asked me to come and stay until he went to Cologne for his wedding. I accepted at once. Though I did not think of him in these terms at the time, Ernst, in character and experience, was the best person to show me the reactions of young Germany to the portent of Nazism. A Rhinelander and a Catholic, he was a son of the middle classes, born in 1914, intelligent, state-educated, a young man of generous and rather noble instincts without fanaticism or any violent prejudice. In early childhood he had suffered from the shortages of the 1914–18 war and its aftermath, in adolescence from dead-end poverty and unemployment under the Weimar Republic, but with a cheerful and easy disposition he had never thought of himself as hard-done-by, or as one of a suffering generation, or anything of that sort. He was ambitious in an easy-going way, industrious, romantically-minded, perhaps rather sentimental, and, if there can be a 'typical' member of any race, a typical Rhinelander.

Nazism had come since we had last met and I did not know whether Ernst accepted any or all of it, but our friendship was a deep and intimate one and he was incapable of putting up a façade. What he felt and believed about Hitler (or about anything else) he would tell me without fear or reserve. I was curious about this but I did not go to visit him primarily to satisfy my curiosity. He was my friend, I had not seen him for a few years and wanted to be with him. I should see something

of the new Germany but had no subtle or literary motive in that.
It is only now that I see how valuable was that visit in helping
me to understand one of the most gruesome and misinterpreted
phenomena of our time, the gradual conversion of the people
of Germany to an odious ideology, their corruption by diabolic
propaganda, their mental enslavement and the disillusionment
that came too late to save them and the rest of the world from
abominations which are still multiplying. (Anyone who supposes that with the suicide of Hitler and the end of Nazism as
such mankind was freed from its effects, seems to me wilfully
blind. Those very policies of Hitler's which made us fight him
flourish as never before and the means he forced us to use, the
distorted morality, created by the war to expurge *his* distorted
morality, have become, in all their baseness, the accepted usages
of mankind.)

The way in which Nazism cynically exploited the willing
faith, the patriotism, the idealism of young Germans I could
observe in Ernst himself and did so without fully realizing it
at the time. I had met him first in 1930, he had stayed with
me that year in England and in 1931 in Switzerland. I was
meeting him now in September 1937, and should see and talk
with him again after a considerable change four months later,
and once more before the war in the winter of 1938. A week
before Hitler invaded Poland he wrote rather naïvely to say
that we should probably be unable to communicate for some
time but must get in touch once more as soon as it was possible.
We did so in 1946 and in 1949 he came from then very much
occupied Germany to stay with me in London, while I was
with him in Germany seven years later. So I saw, through his
eyes, the whole thing go full cycle.

This, I believe, has given me perceptions denied to those
English observers whose friends were among the first physical
victims of Nazism, Communists and Jews. For Jews there could
never be any doubt about the horror of it, and though the vast
majority of the six million people who had voted Communist
in the last free elections disappeared into the ranks of the Nazi

party the more prominent or obdurate were hauled off to forced labour or death, and it was such as these who seem to have made up the acquaintances of Isherwood and Lehmann, for example. This gave these writers considerable foresight at the time and they perceived the whole nature of the beast before I did, but it did not, I think, help them to understand the mass of Germans like Ernst who could not see Nazism in its full colours until it was too late to oppose it.

Not that Ernst ever became in thought or spirit a Nazi. But he was conscripted and fought fatalistically on the Russian front with a few million other young men, like them, like most of us in war, more concerned with surviving, with returning to a familiar life, than with victory or the destiny of nations. He was just a young German.

[2]

That autumn he was twenty-four years old, a handsome, athletic fellow but unlike the popular conception of a German in that he had dark hair and brooding dark eyes. He was deeply in love and this made him grateful to the New Order, to which, he believed, he owed the opportunity to work and earn sufficient for a home and marriage, in addition to the 'marriage subsidy' given to all young couples. This I learned in my first hour with him, but other aspects of the position were more intricate and took much longer to understand.

To reach him I drove to Dover, garaged my car for a week or two, crossed to Ostend and went by train to Cologne. That journey differed in nothing from others I had made in Germany before, till on Cologne station I saw the Hitler salute for the first time given by a party of recruits in uniform to their N.C.O. as they shouted a stern '*Heil Hitler!*' I had heard so many stories of Germany being an armed camp, a country of glassy-eyed automatons who resented the observation of foreigners, its

D

population, almost entirely in uniform, making stoical sacrifices in diet and comfort and displaying a humourless devotion to a cause, that I was almost surprised to see people apparently unchanged and going about their business with good-humour.

I was prepared for almost anything. My journey had seemed in anticipation surreptitious and daring, as though I were a secret agent making observation for a report to headquarters. To many of my friends in London, particularly Louis Golding who had spent long periods in Germany before Hitler, it was now a closed country which offered them, if they penetrated it, almost certain imprisonment on one pretext or another and probably, they believed, violent death. They spoke of it as the dark inferno it would become but certainly was not yet as far as one could see, hear or guess. Influenced by this and by reports in the press, I entered the country if not with trepidation at least with a certain awe, but within twelve hours it was almost as though I had come back to the village of Monschau in which I used to stay and found Frau Carl and 'Mr Saltcastle' and all the rest of the inhabitants their old selves.

Ernst was not changed. A little older, a little more solid and responsible, he had lost none of his placid, uncynical diffidence of manner or inward emotionalism. He met me at the station having taken an afternoon off from his employment as an accountant at Henschel's, the great locomotive works for which the town was famous. We went to a wide street called Admiral Scheerstrasse after that remarkable naval commander who led the *Hochseeflotte* at the battle of Jutland, a native of the town. Here Ernst had an attractive little flat, newly furnished for the reception of his bride.

We talked until the small hours that first night, having bought a couple of bottles of Rhine wine and a supply of *Kalter Aufschnitt*, the delicious porky *Delikatessen* then as now displayed with tempting profusion in the shop windows. Smoking once again those gold-tipped Balkan cigarettes which cost no more than Virginia cigarettes in England, we went on exchanging confidences till Ernst left himself only four hours' sleep before his early start for a ten-hour day. He told me of the change in Germany and in his own circumstances.

It must be remembered that at this point Hitler had not committed himself to the outrages of his later policy. Schacht remained Minister of Economic Affairs in a Cabinet which still, so far as most Germans knew, functioned. The Jews had been dismissed from government service in 1933 before Hitler was in power and the Nuremburg Laws had been passed but there had not been in cities like Cologne and Kassel any flagrant or visible acts of persecution and Jews, by paying a heavy and of course totally unjust tax on their capital, could leave the country with a proportion of it. Ernst simply could not believe things I told him which had been reported in the British press. Most Germans, he said, wished no ill to the Jews; they wanted them out of official positions, perhaps out of the country, but no one was going to ill-treat them. I could be sure of that.

Moreover, at this time when Hitler was attempting to soothe Europe by his peace front till his frantic re-armament programme would enable him to drop all pretences, there seemed evidence enough to convince the ordinary German that the Führer was a man of peace. His frequent protestations were given great prominence in the press and wishful thinking did the rest. Ernst believed that the regime was planning prosperity and prestige for Germany, not conquest. He pointed out that the Saar had returned to Germany only after plebiscite in which more than ninety per cent of the population had voted to do so, that although Hitler had re-militarized the Rhineland it was more to relieve Germany of the humiliation of Versailles than with any aggressive intention toward France, for Hitler had renounced all claim to Alsace-Lorraine. Then, last year there had been the 'gentleman's agreement' with Austria.

Put like this by my liberal-minded young friend in his apartment brightly furnished for a marriage subsidized by the Nazi Party, it all sounded very convincing. Ernst kept his sense of proportion and his sense of humour and still found many aspects of Hitlerism ridiculous while he never, thank God, throughout the whole epoch felt any personal affection or hero-worship of Hitler himself, recognizing at this time his achievements but remaining unenchanted by what he knew of his personality.

Nor was this attitude uncommon in Germany. The hoarse throats after a Nuremburg rally, the gruesome iconology which reproduced that silly visage with the mad eyes on every hoarding, the nauseating eulogies of the sycophants and the hysterical voice screaming for blood fooled no more than half the nation. A surprising number of Germans, while recognizing that unemployment had almost disappeared and poverty was relieved, while acknowledging that 'things were better' remained uncaptivated by Hitler himself, and while they examined pictures of him drooling over a small girl handing him a bouquet remembered the thuggery which had brought him to power. Ernst, for instance, who wanted to get on with his modest career, could not have been described as an opponent of Nazism at this time, but he was frankly bored by Hitler and told me so.

Walking about the countryside in the days that followed, we met groups of hikers, sometimes children, who gave the Nazi salute as though it were a challenge and Ernst could see the absurdity of this. But it seemed a small price for him to pay for that drop in unemployment from six million to less than two, for his subsidy, his work, his flat. When he had first become a qualified accountant before the Nazi accession to power he had worked on road-building because there was no clerical work obtainable and all the education which had cost his father so much self-sacrifice was wasted, an outrage to his German sense of order. Now hope and ambition were realities again. It would have been unnatural if he could not acknowledge that—at least with lip-service.

Just before we went to bed on that first night of my visit Ernst asked me a question which disturbed my peace of mind for years afterwards.

"Do you think", he said, "that if you were a German you would oppose the Party?"

Would I—at that point of time? Though I could safely say that I would not join it, that was only because of my private anarchic view of all parties, my hatred for mass thinking of any kind. Without that, if I had been German, I might easily have gone along with it, and many Englishmen, if they had faced that question honestly would have admitted no less. For Germans, in that year, it was all too logical and promising. They joined in their thousands, some with certain misgivings, some with a touch of cynicism or self-interest, but most because it seemed so right and at the same time so inspiring, because it gave them hope for the future and bread and circuses in the present. No one, perhaps not even Hitler himself, could foresee the nightmare horrors to come, for Hitler's madness was progressive and grew with both power and frustration, and I doubt if his sick imagination had as yet dared to conceive a gas-chamber. Some in Germany may have foreseen and even longed for war, but again the vast majority trusted Hitler's promise of peace.

As I recall that visit it seems to me important to remember that it was in those years, before the pogroms of November 1938, before the promises broken to Austria and shameless aggression in Czechoslovakia, before anything that decisively revealed the evil to come, that the Nazi Party in Germany gained the majority of its adherents. For me this was significant because Ernst, in a constrained way, was among them.

[3]

Every evening when Ernst came home from work we would walk round to the busy wine-shop. Many Germans seemed to buy their wine as part of the day's marketing, a bottle at a time, for although there was little unemployment, pay and price stabilization kept the standard of living of the people from rising and families lived from hand to mouth on just sufficient wages. But I wanted to learn about German wines and liked this daily studying of a catalogue and daily experiment. I learned the mysteries of nomenclature and labelling, the districts, the place names, the vineyards and how each type of grape is included in the name of the wine, Riesling, Sylvaner and the rest. I learned what was meant by *spatlese* and *auslese*, or *Kabinet* or *Originalabfüllung*. I found I preferred—on the whole and as a very rough generalization—Mosel wines in their long narrow blue-green bottles to Rhine wines in their brick-red ones of the same inviting shape. Ernst surprised me by his taste in wine and his considerable knowledge, acquired in his student days.

I bought our food each day and so learned something of prices and not very serious shortages. Goering had already made his guns-before-butter crack, but the butter remained plentiful and excellent as German butter has always been. I think there was some form of rationing for certain commodities but it was lax in application for as a foreigner I could buy all I wanted.

On Sunday, in the German manner, we set out for a day's walking and climbed to the Wilhelmshöhe, the large rococo palace of the Princes of Hesse which was Jerome Bonaparte's home during his short inglorious reign as King of Westphalia, Napoleon III's prison in 1870 and Hindenburg's headquarters in 1918.

I felt no admiration for that ornate but Teutonic pile of masonry but was more interested in the hunting-lodge concealed in the pinewoods. The very name *Jagdhaus* had a ring of old Germany and the Austrian Empire and the secret affairs of Eastern European royalty, for much history seems to have been made in hunting-lodges. Germany has always kept a good deal of nineteenth-century atmosphere—to me sometimes overpowering. With a small effort of imagination one can feel oneself back at the quaint little courts of small principalities, one can imagine a visit of Kaiser Wilhelm to a provincial town, see the peasant costume the elaborate brightly-coloured uniforms, the plumes, the helmets, the highly-trained moustaches. One can hear brass bands and shouted choruses, visit beer-halls and see gatherings of university students in their coloured

peaked caps, the Gretel plaits of the girls, the great meerschaum
pipes of bespectacled professors—all that in my childhood I had
imagined of the German scene. In less obvious, less cinemato-
graphical terms it was never far below the surface and the
Nazis did nothing to discourage that sentimental traditionalism.
What they wanted to wipe out was the Germany in which
Hitler had felt hungry and humiliated, the mad, Liberal, bankrupt Germany of the years after 1918. They had already
dropped all pretence of Socialism or even Radicalism and
supported the great industrial empires with a respectful salute
to the imperial past.

So when Ernst and I tramped over the hills above Kassel
and met parties of hikers, the girls with flaxen plaits and the
boys in leather shorts, who greeted us with a smiling *Heil
Hitler*, I did not see them as deluded unfortunates who would
have to be bombed and bombarded into surrender before a
decade was past, but as children of an older Germany who,
tired of curtseying to a royal hunting party in the forest but
bred to reverence authority, now acclaimed a megalomaniac
house-painter of whom they made a god.

Ernst could of course see the ludicrous side of all this and I
mocked him without mercy when in a shame-faced and half-
hearted way he had to return those greetings and gestures.

"Why?" he asked. "It's only a little salute."

Perhaps that was all it was in 1937, but there were people
in Germany who died, heroically but quite uselessly rather
than give it, circumstances of squalor and secrecy being imposed to deprive their bravery of all panache. There were
others who lost their virility and self-respect by submitting.
Ernst belonged to neither of these but with the great majority
of Germans saw it at that time as 'only a little salute', something
rather silly but quite innocuous, more an expression of that
nebulous ideal of comradeship which Germans have always
sought than an obeisance to the man it hailed.

[4]

At this very time Mussolini was making his state visit to Hitler in Berlin and public opinion was being led by Goebbels to accept the Duce as a kind of inferior Mediterranean Führer, longer-established but without the messianic qualities which the Germans attributed to Hitler. It was still possible, indeed healthy, to laugh at the two dictators, undersized pop-eyed clowns giving one another the Roman salute, but very few people as yet saw them as a pair of maniacal gangsters who would cause a score of million deaths before their preposterous antics were done, or dreamed that the pasty-faced neurotic Hitler, with his hysterical oratory and jack-in-the-box movements, would have as great an influence on the destiny of mankind as any individual in history.

George Orwell wrote in 1941: 'The people who say that Hitler is Antichrist, or alternatively the Holy Ghost, are nearer an understanding of the truth than the intellectuals who for ten dreadful years have kept it up that he is merely a figure out of comic opera, not worth taking seriously.' The truth surely was more painful than either of Orwell's alternatives, for Hitler was *both*—buffoon and Mephistopheles, barn-stormer and genocide. Mussolini had not the satanic will to evil of his fellow hoodlum, and was the better actor of the two. But how could we, seeing on newsreels their meeting that autumn and splitting our sides with laughter at the pair of them, have failed to order another thousand fighter planes as we compared their outshot hands, their overfed figures and popping eyes?

The German press was full of pictures of the two together in their comedy uniforms, each trying to out-do the other in chin-thrusting and the adoption of facial mannerisms. But neither Ernst nor I saw anything very significant in this new piece of buddy-buddyism between them, or guessed that the precious pair were playing a mad game of Monopoly together to carve up Europe. 'All right, you have Austria, but I want Nice.'

'Good, then I'll take Czechoslovakia while you occupy Albania.'
We could not even see Hitler's immediate object in the meeting
—to persuade Mussolini to accept the German–Austrian
Anschluss which the Italian had so far opposed. (It will be
remembered that Hitler marched into Austria less than six
months later.) No, we had both lived through times of so many
handshakes between statesman, so many conferences, pacts,
meetings of the League of Nations, state visits, 'better under-
standings', informal talks, exchanges or view, conventions and
consultations, each of which had appeared in press and news-
reel as a promise of peace, that I, at least, had long since ceased
to expect anything whatever, good or bad, to come of them.

There was a comic echo of the meeting in Kassel while I was
there. The Italian film industry had discovered a boy actor
called Bruno Somebody, a clever little monkey who in films
appeared to be about twelve years old but may have been an
undersized sixteen. They had made a propaganda picture in
which Bruno, heroically opposing his dirty, lowdown Liberal
schoolfellows, takes part in the march on Rome and so on.
This film was being shown in Germany while Mussolini made
his state visit and with the film travelled its protagonist, the boy
Bruno. I went to see it in Kassel and sat through its cheers and
salutes and oratory till it ended with—I think—the martyrdom
of the boy at the hands of Marxists. There then appeared on the
stage a man in evening dress who made a bright speech. "We
know the Duce is with our beloved Führer", he said. "We
would like to see him here in Kassel but we know that is
impossible. Instead we have here OUR LITTLE BRUNO!"

Wild applause as the small boy, dressed in the uniform of
the Fascist youth organization stepped forward alone and gave
the Roman salute. Very spruce and soigné he appeared and his
movements were sharp and military. That was the sort of
propaganda which brought lumps to Fascist throats all over
Europe before the war.

D*

[5]

There was something melancholy in the atmosphere of Kassel. It may have been the desolation of autumn which always seems sadder in Germany than elsewhere, with its red leaves and dripping trees, and last despairing rays of sunlight in the windswept rainy streets. The architecture of the town was gloomy, too, dull red brickwork and nineteenth-century pomposity. But it was not only this. There was, or there seemed to me to be, a hollowness somewhere, a falsity and emptiness in the very occasions of joy. In the beer-halls, at night, in cabarets and cafés, the *gemütlichkeit* was shrill enough but it lacked the wholeheartedness which I had known in the Rhineland eight years before. Places of entertainment were noisy, there was plenty of raucous laughter, conversations all took an optimistic turn, but it was not convincing. Ernst himself had always been pensive and whimsical rather than jovial and I did not see much difference in him. But when parties of gaily-clad young people came round selling Winter Help Fund badges and jollied me into buying one of each type, I felt there was far less genuine exhilaration among them than in the ragged and uproarious beggars I remembered in Republican days, singing, clowning and hungry.

This, I realize now, but was very far from understanding at the time, was an interim period in the history of the Nazi movement. The violence, the intimidation, the reckless flouting not only of law but of all the hardly-evolved decencies of civilization by which the Party had come to power were no longer necessary. Opposition in every form had been suppressed almost out of existence. As far back as the summer of 1933 Hitler had realized that the excesses of his followers had done their work and become superfluous. He had made a great show of calling them off, and persecution, which still continued of course, was out of sight and out of the knowledge of ordinary Germans. It was a period, in other words, of false promises, false security and false hopes.

If I had been in Berlin when Hitler came to power and seen the means he employed, I might have seen Germany in 1937 for what it was, a country bull-dozed and hypnotized into belief that Hitler would give it a glorious future without war. But I had not and had read of the Nazis' murderous tactics as mere street fighting between followers of Hitler and equally unpleasant Communists. I was not entirely fooled by Hitler's peace offensive, but I felt a certain sympathy with Ernst in his future.

[6]

I travelled with Ernst to Cologne and met Clemens, the pretty blonde girl he was to marry. But I could not wait for the wedding. When I left Cologne I had no idea that before Christmas I should return in unusual, and at that time incredible circumstances.

CHAPTER EIGHT

The Circus Has No Home

[1]

WITHIN A WEEK of my return to Smarden I had an experience which changed my life for the next three years—and in some ways for the rest of my span. It was not an experience that would be thought profound or soul-stirring. It was not religious, philosophical, literary or political. In basic terms it was simply that I went to the circus.

To explain the significance of that I must go back to a Sunday three years earlier when I lived in the Cotswolds, and to an episode that I have purposely left unrecounted till now.

There was staying with me for that week-end in 1934 a man named Richard Fletcher or Fleckheimer, a very odd character whom I had first known as a 'press agent', in which capacity he worked to secure gossip paragraphs in the evenings press for ambitious hostesses and, it was said, was not above mild social blackmail. He was born in America but that could not be guessed from the tone of his voice or his enunciation which were impeccably English and cultured. He was then in his fifties, tall, handsome, well-dressed, a ruthless social climber and, in a rather grand way, a sponger. I liked the old charlatan and his stories of high queerdom before the First World War.

He had lately become a Catholic and with all the ardour of the recently converted made his first questions, on arriving at my cottage in Gloucestershire, concern his distance from a church and the times of Mass. On the Sunday morning Eric drove him to Stow-on-the-Wold and he came back in a state of excitement.

"A circus!" he said. "I saw their waggons and horses and

two elephants. I stopped and asked them where they are showing tomorrow—it's at Shipton-under-Wychwood. We can go over and see them."

A circus meant nothing to me. I had seen only one, a rather tragic affair with raw-boned horses in a suburb of Buenos Aires ten years earlier. There seemed to be a cult of 'the sawdust ring' at that time—Laura Knight, Lady Eleanor Smith and a big snob attendance for the Opening at Olympia each winter when Bertram Mills was there. I suspected this cult of being intellectual and artistic, but I agreed to take Richard on Monday.

That early summer afternoon in the Cotswolds in 1934 remained vividly in my memory at the time of which I am writing and is scarcely less vivid today. I remember the fruit blossom in my orchard as I drove away from the house and the drifts of white cloud in a windless sky. I remember Richard in an expensive grey suit indulging in the eccentricity of white socks and a white beret. We found the circus tent among buttercups and daisies in a field outside Shipton, then scarcely more than a sleepy village, and a straggle of children chattering their way to the field. We arrived before the show was due to begin and one of the tent-men, rising from sleep, showed us a tent where two elephants were munching hay, impassive enough but for the expression in their fierce, ugly little eyes. The group of circus waggons and tents seemed almost a natural part of the landscape in the placid warmth of the afternoon.

When the perfomance began there were not more than fifty people on the hard wooden seats and it was all so homely that one could smell the fresh grass of the ringside. The succession of clever acts seemed to me competent and varied— bareback riders, the elephants, a wire-walker, acrobats—but not in itself a revelation or a startling new experience. Perhaps the atmosphere was too intimate; certainly I was not conscious of 'the glamour of the sawdust ring' or anything of the sort. The children in the audience cheered and laughed and the performers smiled back to them. It was a happy friendly rather than a brilliant or startling occasion.

When it was over Richard Fletcher, with more brazen courage than I possessed, made himself known to the family who owned the circus and soon we were sitting in one of the living-waggons to which we had been invited for tea, though by what clever cajolery my friend had broken the forced defences which circus people have had to raise against such inquisitiveness as ours, I do not now remember.

I remember the mother of them all who, following the circus tradition of assuming a title ('Lord' John Sanger, 'Sir' Robert Fossett), was known as the 'Countess' Rosaire. She was sitting near the stove handing us tea, talking, and introducing each of her eight children. For there were four boys and four girls, all of whom performed in the circus, and all of whom came into the cosy mahogany-lined waggon while we were there. I remember, without being able to distinguish them from a later knowledge, the handsome dark daughters with quick lively eyes, and bright teeth and friendly smiles. The eldest son had not taken off his clown's make-up, and one brother, whom I recognized as the wire-walker, sat next to me, and the youngest of all, who was then only sixteen, ran in for a moment and was off again, carrying some food, as soon as he had greeted us. With his long hair, merry black eyes and powerful build he looked more foreign even than the rest of the family who all had an exotic look. It was not that they were un-English—the 'Countess' seemed in many respects very much a North Country women— but undomesticated, of some quite extraneous tradition and habit which I could not at first analyse, knowing only that they were unlike anyone I had met, escaping all familiar categories, of class, of intellect, of background, of profession. They were sitting in a small, mobile home, with nothing between them and the stars but a half-inch of roofing, on a ground that they would leave tomorrow, in a village to which they were strangers and which they might never see again. They had no reason to suppose that any man's hand was not against them, and their whole manner of life was precarious. Yet they had the superb confidence in themselves which is only given to the strongest, who have been able, or who have wished, to rise above the eternal inter-dependence of people in more gregarious ways of life. Let the heavens fall, they seemed to say, let famine, blood-shed, pestilence, war, strike the earth, and we shall survive. We are prepared for every emergency. We are not intellectual, we are not in the narrow sense cultured. But we depend on no man, and our acquaintance with Providence is remote. There was nothing arrogant in this, nothing self-assertive, even. They were modest to the point of diffidence, they were good-natured and friendly. But they could not hide it.

The 'Countess' heard from Richard that I was a writer.

"There have been lots of books written about the circus", she said, "but writers seem to study a show like Bertram Mills and forget the smaller circus—like ours. You ought to come and travel with us for a time. Our boys are performers, but they work fourteen hours a day. We build up our own tent every morning, fix up all the seating, and take it down at night, then travel to a new place the next morning. A tenting-show like ours has a life of its own, quite different from a big circus which stays three days in a place. Yes, you should come along with us for a time. . . ."

I meant to go. I am sure now that I really meant to pack up and go. It was the sort of escapist dream that was always disturbing my will to be a householder in those days. I would close up my house, buy a trailer-caravan for my car, and see England from a series of circus-sites. I would travel with this glorious family for the whole summer, without an address for letters or a tie with everyday life. I would go at once, the very next day. Why not? What was there to stop me? Didn't I boast of having planned my whole life so that I could take ad-vantage of such impulses? I asked them where they would be tomorrow, and they gave me their route for the rest of that week.

Richard, who was wise and more experienced than I, said nothing as we drove home. He had gone as deep as he wished—he was perhaps able to time and limit his enquiries precisely to give him the maximum interest. With less balanced knowledge of the world I had first veered away from the whole thing, and was now preparing to plunge more deeply. I was determined to 'go off with the circus' next day.

Of course I did not. Back at home the commonplace became real, and the vision remote. Books, pets, people, work . . . these were what mattered again. Such a summer as I had caught sight of—dew on the circus field and ring horses grazing—was a fiction lovely but absurd. I forget now what excuse I found for myself, a contract, or lack of money, but the days of that week began to pass and I was back at my job, and the circus moved nothward. Until at last it was Saturday, and I knew no more of their route, and could not have found them, I said to myself, even if I wished to do so. With their horses and elephants and blue and yellow waggons they had gone, and with relief that was not without regret I remained at home to write yet another novel. Although occasionally I remembered the scene in that warm waggon, and the people I had liked and wondered at, the experience was soon merged with others into the past.

But what I had not realized was that a circus, like a chance acqaintance in the street, may be wholly lost. It arrives in your village before you are up in the morning, from heaven knows where. At noon you see its canvas city as strong and settled, it would seem, as your own parish church. In the evening you watch the performance, and next day there is nothing but a sodden paper bag or two and a torn poster on the field gate to remind you that it had existed. It is already a dozen miles away, and in a week's time it is lost somewhere in the patchwork of the counties.

Knowing nothing then of such organization as exists for the dozen or more circuses travelling England, I had no means of re-discovering my friends. Only once, a couple of years later, motoring in Scotland, I saw one of their bills on a gate-post, and found that they had been there a week before. For a few days I chased them through the Highland villages, but lost the trail again near Dingwall, and with my own time pressing I had to turn southwards without having seen their tents.

[2]

Now home from Kassel, I came on their fly-bills and small posters stuck illegally on telegraph posts and house-sides, or covering other posters as the bills of small circuses habitually did in those less penalty-imposing days of decent and inexcitable country policemen and a general attitude of live-and-let-live. So I knew they were in the district.

I had not been to a circus since I had seen theirs, or read circus books, or felt the least curiosity about riders and clowns. I had not, and should never become a circus 'fan', and it was my hour in the Rosaires' living-waggon which I remembered far more clearly than their show. But when I found that they were at Tenterden, that little fresh-looking red-brick town with its long, wide, central street and prosperous shops, I resolved, of course, to go over.

It was a Saturday afternoon and the whole of the younger population of Tenterden seemed to be making for the circus, which had been built up on the football ground.

In the pay-box was the mother of the family, selling tickets with a speed and accuracy which would have served as a lesson to railway booking-clerks. I reminded her rather dubiously of my previous visit, three and a half years before, scarcely hoping for recognition from someone who must pass a good many thousand people in review every week of her life. But she knew me.

"You were coming tenting with us, weren't you?" she asked "Why have you never been to see us again in all this time?" I had to stutter some sort of reply.

But when she had finished dispensing tickets she came to sit beside me, just inside the big tent.

She was then in her fifties and one knew she had been pretty as a girl and was still a handsome woman. She had blonde hair touched only lightly with grey, and a face which showed no guile or bitterness but suggested something of the long struggle her life has been, a struggle which could not damage the essential kindliness of her nature. Her eyes were pale and humorous; she was neither tall nor slim, but looked, as she was, a mother who had fought successfully for her own and had attained prosperity after many hardships.

I have said that the Rosaires seemed to escape all categories. This is most true of the Countess, from whose 'title' I shall now drop the inverted commas. She was, and wished to be thought, no other than 'circus'. Her life had been spent in the living-waggons, moving over the country for thirty years without more than a winter's rest. Yet she had a culture, a knowledge of men and things, a sense of proportion and criticism, out of keeping with her origins. I have known her at an exhibition of pictures in a London gallery as shrewdly critical as those whose custom it was to see and criticize new pictures, I have heard her discuss books and music with acumen, and it was not long before I learned to respect her gift of narrative. I can see her now, putting someone in his place, cooking one of the dishes on which she had brought up her family and discussing plans with the advance agent at the same time, enjoying the ease and pleasure which a long and uphill journey had brought her, sitting in a smart new car to drive on to 'the next place', or setting out for a day's amusements on Sunday, competent, sometimes caustic but friendly in disposition and very much mistress of her own and her family's destiny.

That afternoon seems in retrospect to have proceeded with a sort of gathering momentum to a happy climax. First I was alone with the Countess, then one by one the Rosaires came to us and I made or re-made the acquaintance of each of them, until, at a memorable moment when the show was over, we were all together in one place.

First came Vivienne, the third daughter, who was not performing that day, as she had been away and had only rejoined the family an hour earlier. Her ring name, 'La Petite Vivienne', was well chosen. Petite indeed, she was the most exquisite of them all in person and performance. Slim, trim, beautiful, she had the dark burning eyes of her father and brothers. She gave an effect of perfection—figure, complexion, movement—like some-one created a little more carefully than other human beings. She had composure of a kind which could bring her to rest suddenly and completely in a graceful but unconscious pose. She joined us, professed politely to remember my visit at Shipton-under-Wychwood, and said happily that on Monday she would be riding again, thank heaven. She told me where she had been staying, but to me then and thereafter, the life of any of the Rosaires away from the show which was their home, seemed unreal. It had grown and changed immensely since I had seen it last and was now highly professional, brilliant, rather grand, much more than an intimate family circus. Yet the essentials remained: Salt and Saucy, the two elephants who played cricket and football; Aubrey, the eldest of the Rosaire brothers, clowning (and wearing for it, I was happy to notice, an Old Tonbridgian blazer), Freddie, the 'little fellow', whose minute figure and stentorian voice delighted the children; Dennis, the second son on the wire.

It was Dennis who approached us next, as soon as his act was over. He had strolled up and down the tight-rope, lain on it, knelt on it, danced on it, balanced on one hand on it, passed through a small hoop without leaving it, and he had come straight round to us, not even out of breath. He wore a decora-tive version of a bull-fighter's costume, which suited his thick black ringlets. He remembered my visit of more than three years before and proved it by using my Christian name.

"I knew you when you came in", he said. "Didn't you see me grin across to you when I was on the wire?"

A small brass band on a dais near the ring entrance beat out tunes which soon I was to know too well and the crowded tent was responding warmly, the children flushed and enraptured, their elders laughing, applauding, wondering at the small coloured figures in the ring.

"My other two boys now", the Countess said. "You remem-ber them—Ivor and Derrick. Well, Derrick would only have been about sixteen when you saw him. He's twenty now. Here they come. . . ."

There was a curious sound from the audience as Ivor and Derrick walked out to do their act on the rings, and at future performances I became accustomed to hearing it from other audiences. It was something like a gasp, a sort of wordless exclamation. Stripped to the waist, wearing pale blue trousers with a gold stripe from waist to heel and blue shoes, the two brothers showed the sort of muscular development that appears in those photographs which are voluntarily contributed by enthusiasts in Sweden or Ceylon to physical culture magazines. They were good-looking young men, too—Ivor chestnut-haired and tall, Derrick with the dark ringlets of his family, the black quick eyes and intelligent square face. With them was their sister Zena, slim and straight like all of them, looking too young and slender in her ring clothes to be the mother of a five-year-old girl.

"Isn't there *one* member of your family who is a cripple?" I asked the Countess despairingly.

She smiled.

"It's funny you should say that", she began. "For our Derrick might have been once." (They had the pleasant North Country habit of referring to each of the sons and daughters as '*our* Dennis', '*our* Ida'.) "He had an operation in his back which I believe is almost unique. He was four months in hospital over it, and there will always be a little gold pin in his spine, they tell me."

I watched Derrick go through his whirling convolutions on the rings, letting go and catching them again in mid-air, turning a back somersault from mid-air to the ground, and coming to rest, it seemed, as surely as a bird alighting.

"In his spine?"

"Yes", said the Countess calmly. "They said he'd never walk again, of course, and as for performing, it was quite out of the question. He doesn't look much the worse for it now, though, does he?"

He certainly did not. But I own I was half sceptical until long afterwards when I saw the surgeon's neat scar, six inches long it looked, at the base of that mighty and flexible spine.

Act after act—it was a long and generous programme. I watched the children who squatted noisily on the narrow forms before the ring fence and one child is still vivid to me. He was not more than four years old, and there were no parents visibly with him, only a cluster of slightly older brothers and sisters. He was watching the ring, his small face flushed with rapture, fixed in an expression of such happiness that the smile seemed a part of him. His hands were clapping, slowly and gently, moving apart and together in a rhythm out of his own consciousness. He had forgotten he was clapping, forgotten his brothers and sisters and the other children, forgotten his existence. Only his eyes waited greedily in pursuit of more colour, more movement, more comedy.

Then came the trapeze act—the traditional swinging bar and figures looking small and elegant so near to the overhead lights.

"This is my youngest", said the Countess, for it was Ida up there with Dennis on the ground below her.

Ida was eighteen or nineteen at that time; she looked sleek and lithe but untamed and I used to think that her quiet voice had the threatening purr of a feline in readiness to spring. She was handsome like her sisters, but as Vivienne was exquisite Ida had a more indolent beauty, as Vivienne was vivacious Ida was reserved. On the trapeze her movements were graceful and her assurance and professional smiles made her act seem less perilous than in fact it was.

Only one member of the family was not with them that day— the second daughter, Cissy, who had married since I had visited the show before.

"You remember Cissy", the Countess said. "She was in the waggon that afternoon. She and Derrick are the most alike. She married back in the winter. Her husband has a show of his own."

At last, then, I had that astonishing family sorted out in my mind—first Aubrey, the clown, who was then about thirty-three years old and whose wife travelled with them. Then Zena, whom I had seen on the rings with Ivor and Derrick, whose husband Ted, the show's electrician, I was to meet tomorrow. Then Dennis, the young wirewalker, who was still in his twenties and looked even younger. Then Ivor, the taller of the two whose muscles had brought that despairing gasp from the audience. Cissy came next, and it was a long time before I met her again, then Vivienne, who was beside us now. Derrick, the shortest of the men looking as broad as he was tall, and the survivor of the operation described by the Countess, was next, and finally there was Ida.

But I still had not met the Count, the father of the eight Rosaires.

"He's in the town with Ruth," explained the Countess. "Do you know Ruth Manning-Sanders? She's a writer, too."

No, I did not. I knew her name but it was not a very welcome one at that moment. I had no literary plans in connection with the circus, but I do not think any writer, already enchanted with this family and its remarkable little show, would have been pleased to know that another writer was already established with it. Besides, as I have explained, it was very much my position (I still do not want to call it a pose) at that time to be ill-at-ease with my own profession, to avoid being in any sense a 'literary man', to disassociate myself from anything highbrow or intellectual.

It says all that I can say now for Ruth Manning-Sanders that her tact and sweetness killed all that nonsense in me at once, that within twenty-four hours I was glad she was with the circus, and within a week or two could scarcely think of it without her. Wholly unpretentious and unliterary, she insisted on justifying her presence with the show by selling programmes or chocolates from a tray slung over her shoulders, and wandered round the seats casually and happily, a gentle auburn-haired woman in her earliest forties, with a quiet friendly voice

and kindly eyes, walking with a chocolate-tray before her among
the children and soldiers and workers in the Rosaires' audience.

She and the Count arrived together, from some expedition
undertaken in Ruth's car. I shook hands with the progenitor
of the family which I had only just then got sorted out in my
mind.

The Count was nearing sixty, but looked younger by a
dozen years, and in character was the youngest and most
enthusiastic of them all. With a nature as volatile as the
English climate which had been a vital factor in his nomadic
life, he was at once the happiest and most downcast of men—
at times openly proud of his family and their achievements, at
others gloomily foreboding. He had the quickest, keenest, most
humorous black eyes and retained, in the tradition of music-
hall chairmen, ringmasters and showmen, a spruce wax-tipped
moustache. Growing a little stouter than of old, he was still a
quick powerful man.

Sanguine—that, now I come to think of it, was the word for
Count Rosaire. In appearance, in character, in outlook sanguine,
his energy and loquacity never failed.

[3]

Not far from the circus ground—I had not yet learned to
call it the *tober*—was a pub called The Cellars. It has this name
because at some time in its history shortage of space, perhaps,
or a stroke of originality on the part of a landlord had caused
the cellars of the house to be opened as a bar and one descended
by narrow stone staircase to a low room in which white whisky,
unmatured or uncoloured whisky, was sold. This made a somewhat incongruous background for a memorable scene.

During the two hours between the afternoon and evening
shows that afternoon the whole Rosaire family came here for
a drink. Naturally enough the habitual customers of the bar

watched them with curiosity, neither friendly nor unfriendly, but sidelong and tentative. The Rosaires came in, some of them with their make-up still on, with coats pulled over their costumes looking strangely alien. There was a nonchalance in the bearing of the young brothers which was almost a challenge and the girls seemed deliberately unaware of their surroundings and of the strangers who watched them. It may be (though they always denied it indignantly) that their father from whom thay inherited their jet-eyed brilliance had Romani blood, or perhaps there had been an upsurge of some Latin inheritance—it is always difficult to guess with the English. So far as the Count knew he was a Yorkshireman, Frederick Ross, and it is certain that he was born at Saddleworth on the Lancashire border in 1877 and his wife was from Staffordshire. No one, in a sense, could be more English than this family, none of whom at that time had been abroad. Yet seeing them in The Cellars that afternoon, the merry-eyed Count himself and his almost unnaturally vivid and lively children, one could think of no English class, or clan or type, or tradition to which they could belong.

So far as I was aware at the time, I felt nothing more significant or fundamental than interest in their life and work and an immediate affection for every one of them. But now, with hindsight, I see that it was much more than this. Standing among these exciting, extraneous people, gazed at with curiosity (which could easily have been hostility) by the settled inhabitants of a country town, I was identifying myself, in secret unconscious pride, with nomads whom I saw as outcasts. I was 'one of the people from the circus', and delighted in it.

This was a rebellion against my conventional upbringing, I think, and I can find traces of it throughout my life till then, while in later years it became dominant. From childhood I had sought minorities for their own sake in great and little things, and been in my mind and sometimes openly a champion of unpopular gang-leaders at school, of first the frowned-on High Churchmen and then the Catholic Church, of Bosie Douglas and Roger Casement, of the last pirate buses on the streets of London when they opposed the monopoly, of Irish nationalities, of almost any man, any cause, any fraternity which was anti-Establishment. Later this dedication to more or less disreputable minorities was to give me sympathy with gypsies, soldiers and finally criminals, to bring pattern to the whole of my later life. That afternoon I exulted secretly in it and believed myself in love, not with a person but with a family.

I sat alone and saw the show through that night—item by item, from Ida's riding act with which it opened to the performance of Salt and Saucy, the elephants. I invited the whole family to visit my home next day and drove home intensely aware that something had happened at last, that I had broken restricting bonds, that life could not be the same again.

CHAPTER NINE

Tenting

[1]

ON THE FOLLOWING MORNING Louis Golding came down to spend a few days and was delighted to hear what had happened. But his reaction, as usual, was one which I could not possibly have anticipated and failed at first to understand.

"Of course", he said when I had told him enthusiastically about the Rosaires and prepared him for their visit that afternoon, "I shall regard this as *yours*."

He saw that I was puzzled.

"I mean, as a thing to write about", he went on. "I certainly should not take advantage of my meeting these people through you to exploit all their *immense* possibilities from the writer's point of view."

I had not got as far as this. I felt, that week-end, as though I were under some potent drug or enchantment and had no conception of the Rosaires as 'copy', a word which, to do him justice, Louis never used. But Louis's quick mind worked differently and it is noteworthy that he afterwards respected the undertaking he had spontaneously given.

At four o'clock the Rosaires arrived, but not from Tenterden, for in the meantime they had moved on to Rye. That is one of the odd if obvious things about circus people, one rarely sees them twice in the same background. A conversation begun in Warwickshire is continued in Worcester, an invitation to a nearby house brings them sixty miles away. But they came, two car-loads of them, arriving in Smarden that Sunday afternoon in a very different guise—for this was the only day of the week on which they could escape for a time from their work and their waggons. The Countess came, and Ruth Manning-Sanders, Vivienne and Ida, Aubrey, whom I saw for the first time without a clown's make-up, and his smiling amiable wife Helen, Dennis, Ivor and Derrick.

I saw that Louis was instantly and with only a touch of amusement accepted by them. He laid himself out to be interesting and succeeded. Realists all, for whom classes and categories had little meaning, they did not see Louis as exotic or find his showy intellectualism in any way incongruous. To the family he became 'Lou' at once as I was already Rupert and it brought out the best in him. This was stranger and to me more noteworthy than it would appear from the simple recalling of it. Louis did not always realize how frankly bizarre he seemed to conventional and unintelligent people. It took him months to earn familiarity from his boxers. He could not talk their language and when he tried to do so the results were embarrassing. He would carefully learn their slang but always pronounced it in parentheses. Eventually, by using his lively intelligence and by calculated expense, he would achieve a status of his own among them and liked them to call him Uncle Lou. But he could never make them feel he was one of them and remained mysterious to them.

The Rosaires, themselves nomads, a conscious minority, free of categories and affiliations, accepted him at once at his face value. To them he was a brilliant and charming man who was interested in them and in their show. If they perceived his egotism it did not offend them—he was a fellow-performer and they were all egotists in a sense. If he liked to hold forth in his rich voice, using his large vocabulary and all his persuasive gifts as a talker, they were happy to listen to him, for their turn to show off—in the ring—would come tomorrow. He was a success with them and it gratified him, and increased his efforts. That Sunday afternoon began to pass with animation, with growing intimacy all round as though everyone was intent on knowing and liking everyone else.

I do not know what we talked about. I remember Helen,

Aubrey's wife, and at that time the only daughter-in-law, leaning back comfortably in an arm-chair with Ivor and Derrick sitting each on one arm of it, and Aubrey opposite.

"What do you think of *our* wife?" Ivor asked.

Helen came from a big family of Scottish show-people, and she and Aubrey had only been married a few months. Aubrey who, as the eldest son, had had to start working earliest and perhaps had the hardest fight of all, lacked now the weight and robustness of his brothers, though he was as tough as any of them. A little sallow and dyspeptic-looking, he had the pale frank eyes of his mother, and much of his father's impulsive enthusiasm. His nose had been broken in booth-boxing many years before. There was nothing in his appearance to connect him with the white-and-pink-faced pantaloon who had exchanged the florid humour of the ring with Little Freddy and Charlie Austin the evening before.

We went to the Bell Inn, we played darts, we returned to the house to eat and the evening went by leaving no sense of the passage of time. Nobody asked me if I was coming to see the show at Rye tomorrow—it was simply assumed that I should do so, and continue to follow the progress of the circus in the days after that. I had no thought of doing anything else. My life at Smarden, my work, my household—all these were left in suspense. I had already joined them, as though I had a job in the show. My contract with Hutchinson, my garden, my series of articles all dropped out of consideration. I said I should drive down to Rye in the morning whereupon Ivor and Derrick announced their intention of staying the night.

[2]

It was a fresh sunlit morning when we crossed the Weald, and drove through Tenterden to Rye. The two brothers claimed to be pleased because they would escape the morning's work of building up, but when we reached the circus field, on the 'Salts' outside the old city gates, and actually saw that the big top was already up, they seemed a little shocked to find that they had missed so much of the day's routine.

Louis and I wandered about the field, Louis watching keenly each detail of the operation of preparing the tent and I feeling a little shame-faced at being idle among so much activity.

An idea came to Louis.

"Do you know that E. F. Benson is the Mayor of Rye? He lives at Lamb House in which Henry James lived for years. We will go and ask him to come down for the show."

"You know him?"

"Oh yes. I've met him several times. It's not as a writer we want him, though, but as Mayor."

Louis explained his purpose to the Count who was optimistic and encouraging about it and in a moment the news was across the field—Louis knew the Mayor and was going to bring him to the show.

I drove him up to Lamb House which was known to me not as Benson's home but from a letter written by Rupert Brooke describing a call there in 1912. Edward Marsh had printed this letter in his *Memoir*, a piece of prose which as a boy I knew almost by heart. "James (his companion on a walking tour, James Strachey) and I have been out this evening to call on Mr. Henry James at 9.0. We found—at length—the house. It was immensely rich, and brilliantly lighted at every window on the ground floor. The upper floors were deserted: one black window open. The house is straight on the street. We nearly fainted with fear of a company. At length I pressed the bell of the Great Door—there was a smaller door further along, the servants' door we were told. No answer. I pressed again. At length a slow dragging step was heard within. It stopped inside the door. We shuffled. Then, very slowly, very loudly, immense numbers of chains and bolts were drawn within. There was a pause again. Further rattling within. Then the steps seemed to be heard retreating. There was silence. We waited in a wild agonising stupefaction. The house was dead silent. At length there was a shuffling noise from the servants' door. We thought someone was about to emerge from there to greet us. We slid down towards it—nothing happened. We drew back and observed the house. A low whistle came from it. Then nothing for two minutes. Suddenly a shadow passed quickly across the light in the window nearest the door. Again nothing happened. James and I, sick with surmise, stole down the street. We thought we heard another whistle, as we departed. We came back here shaking—we didn't know at what. If the evening paper, as you get this, tells of the murder of Mr. Henry James—you'll know."

The little scene had appealed to me and stuck in my memory, and I thought of it again as Louis rang the bell of Lamb House.

A neat parlour-maid appeared. Louis sent in his card and we were shown into a small room near the front door where we waited five minutes.

The maid returned.

"Mr. Benson is sorry he is working this morning", she said in a polite but businesslike way.

I rose to leave. It seemed to me a very understandable situation. Why should the old gentleman be disturbed? But as we walked back to the car I became aware of volcanic emotions in Louis. His face was grey-white and set in lines of rage.

His first words were spoken impressively.

"This", he said, "*must never be known.*"

Then for five minutes he let go a furious and vituperative tirade. Benson had always been known as a conceited empty man, the failure among the three Benson brothers, a social climber, a snob, an unsuccessful writer, a secret homosexual, a literary *arriviste*. That he should have *dared* not to be at home to Louis! Benson's was the meanest exhibition of jealousy because he could never forgive another writer for big sales and must have *writhed* over *Magnolia Street*.

"But if he was *working*, Louis . . ." I tried to reason.

"Working! Do you think *I* would refuse to see another writer whether I was working or not? Dont't you *see* it is the *most* appalling discourtesy? He knows my name perfectly well. We have met several times. It's quite unforgivable. I shall write and tell him so when I am back in London."

Then suddenly Louis's manner changed and became guarded, almost secretive.

"When we get back to the circus we will say simply that he was not there and you must *never* tell anyone what has happened this morning."

"Why, Louis?" I asked annoyingly. "If you think he has behaved so badly why shouldn't it be known?"

"Don't be obtuse", he said. "Surely you can see what this means to someone in *my* position?"

So I have kept the secret for just on thirty years, which is long enough for any secret.

[3]

When we returned to the *tober* we found the seating was being unloaded from its lorry and fixed into position in the tent. For this work an army of small boys had been recruited, and laboured bravely in carrying the planks.

I asked Ivor, who was swinging a great iron mallet, driving in stakes with precision and speed as though he enjoyed the rhythmic movement, whether this voluntary labour was usual.

"Good Lord yes", he said. "We get hundreds of them where-ever we go. They love being given a job. Well, wouldn't you have, when a circus came to your town when you were a kid? They'll work all the morning if we let them. Chinese labour, we call it".

The whole field was crowded, as though a fair was actually going on. The tent-men were still busy with stakes and pulleys round the wallings, while in the tent, where the seating was now in position, red felt was being spread over the more expensive seats, and the band platform was draped with flags. Townspeople strolled about watching the work of construction, commenting and gossiping. Round the living-waggons there was evidence that lunch was being prepared. From the big waggon in which the Count and Countess lived, Vivienne came, neither the spruce and spangled Vivienne of the ring, nor the neat and sophisticated Vivienne of yesterday afternoon, but a busy brisk Vivienne, with sleeves rolled to the elbow, a scarf round her hair, and a giant saucepan in her hands. Dennis, after a long morning's work was stretched at full length on the ground—for he had, like all of them, a great capacity for sudden and complete relaxation, and could lie down and sleep for just so long at almost any moment of the day.

"But this is nothing", he said when I had made some remark about the work of building up. "We've done no journey this morning. You see, it's Monday, and we travelled to this place from Tenterden on Sunday morning. Usually we're up at five or six, starting the lorries and driving on to the next *tober* before breakfast."

He rolled over on his stomach with his face in the crook of his arm, so that his black ringlets fell forward and touched the grass.

Blue and gold were the circus colours, and it was a blue and gold windy noon. The waggons, painted in blue and yellow, stood round, forming a rough outer circle to the big tent. There was a pale blue sky, and though the seashore was a mile away across the marshes there was a salt tang in the air. The tent-men were singing as they worked; a wireless set was audible in one of the waggons.

Louis and I lunched in the town and he saw the afternoon show, but he wanted to leave for London in the morning so we drove back to Smarden. That evening the Maidstone paper, the *Kent Messenger*, sent a reporter to interview us and I find a souvenir of that week-end in an old press-cutting book—*Two Spell-Bound Authors*: A Strange Half-hour with Louis Golding and Rupert Croft-Cooke: *They had Smelt the Sawdust.*

[4]

The circus moved on Tuesday morning to New Romney and here I joined the family to remain with them for the rest of their tenting season, bringing Dingo with me and leaving Eric alone in my house. I must have arranged that at an hour's notice—I wish I could make moves like that today.

From New Romney we went to Dymchurch, and from there to Hythe. I began to understand a little what made the Rosaires so different from the house-dwellers before whom they performed. All the eight children had been born and brought up on the road and the clean outdoor and vigorous routine they had followed from childhood had given to each of them a splendid physique while the changes and chances of their life had inspired them with an alert, enquiring view of humanity, unreserved humour, and an entirely amiable and natural vanity. Without having left England they were cosmopolitan. With little routine education they were sophisticated. Their characters were full of contradictions—crude yet in some respects polished, self-sufficient yet curious, arrogant but modest.

I had feared at first that writers and artists were making a cult of the circus and that self-conscious organizations like the Circus Fans Association would end by patronizing it out of existence. There may have been some substance in this for in those years it attracted devotees like the *aficionados* of the bull-ring and I myself, after the war, collaborated in several books about it. But then, and while Rosaires' circus existed as a unit, my passionate interest was not in the tradition of the circus—which as it is understood now is a parvenu affair no older than the last century—but in the Rosaires themselves, who seemed to me to belong to something much older, the long genealogy of jugglers, acrobats, animal-tamers and clowns who have travelled the roads of Europe from Roman times, or earlier. Whether or not the Count Rosaire was in fact the offspring of a family of such people, the life, the art, the character of him

E

and his children showed their motley and archaic descent. That enchanted me far more than the Dickensian tradition of the circus itself.

So that my appreciation of them was on two levels. First I had a philosophical and romantic view of them as rebels against conformity and descendants of the *jongleurs,* the aristocrats of the road, blandly indifferent to householders who loved them for the colour and gaiety they brought with them, anachronistic, of an immemorial heritage, heroic and humorous. As such I would one day try to put them in a book for with no interest in the matter at all they had inflamed my imagination.

But on another level all this was forgotten in a strong and healthy love for them all as glorious human beings, in my physical enjoyment of the life I shared with them, the joy of passing day after day from waking to midnight with never-flagging gusto, taking pleasure in the small incidents and chances of their existence, being among them, being one with them. On this level each of them was very much an individual and their grandiose Christian names, Aubrey, Vivienne, Zena and the rest stood not for *them,* the Rosaires collectively, but for one or another being of strong character, each of whom was becoming a friend.

They accepted me, almost as one of themselves. There was never any fuss about this; nothing that I can remember was said. Overnight I had become one of a score of people who travelled together. This gave me a sense of privilege and a certain pride. I felt that in abandoning the life of a householder, even for these few autumn weeks, I had achieved something positive in that search for experience which was my life.

I began to learn more of the practical, even the technical details of circus life. I learned how to drive in a tent stake, and what elephants eat; I began to learn the language of the circus, and, already knew what a *tober* was, and what *vada* meant. At eleven o'clock at night, when the folk in the villages we visited had been asleep this half-hour or more, I watched the tent hands and Rosaires 'pulling down', till the vast spread of canvas had become a few bundles on one lorry while seating for five hundred had been packed in piles on another. I slept in the Barracks.

The Barracks was a bus, a single-decker, which had been converted into living quarters for the unmarried sons and daughters of the family. It was in three compartments, one of which Vivienne and Ida shared, one contained two double bunks, one above the other, for the boys, while between them was the living-room. It was into this central compartment that we used to crowd at night—Ruth Manning-Sanders, Vivienne, Ida, Dennis, Ivor, Derrick and I. That would seem impossible enough, but while we stood or crouched or sat in whatever small space we could appropriate, Vivenne would be cooking the boys' supper, and making tea for us all.

At first there would only be three or four of us, for the work of 'pulling down' would still be going on outside, and shouts would be audible from across the field. When the doors opened you could smell the salt air of the Romney Marshes, and our own clouded atmosphere of simmering supper and cigarette smoke would be dispelled. Then one after another each of the boys would arrive as his particular part of the work of pulling down was completed. Now and again one of them would be late if some village beauty had persuaded him to take her home, for nearly nightly a group would wait in hope of being noticed by the men they had seen perform. But at last they would all be in, and their supper eaten heaven knows how, with a plate balanced skilfully on the knees or the crowded eaters standing beside a chest of drawers. The windows would be clouded to opaqueness by the atmophere within, two or three of us would be straphanging, for the bars still remained above us from the former life of the Barracks, and the wireless set in the boys' compartment would be beating out dance-music. Thus we would squat and talk till long past midnight, and someone would open the door to show the field almost in darkness, every other waggon having long since turned out its lights, and the wind-swept moon showing the lorries laden and ready for the morning's journey. Some nights we could hear the sea beyond the marshes, on others, when the night air was still, there was audible the steady munching of the ring-horses put out to graze.

From Hythe we went to Ashford, from Ashford to Wye, from Wye to Chilham, and still I made no effort to return to my home and responsibilities. I had learnt how Johnny Swallow had once had a circus of his own, how Little Freddy had worked on the music halls and in pantomime, and certain dim suggestions of the story of the Rosaires themselves which, I was promised, I should hear fully 'in good time'. My circus vocabulary was improving— I knew what *mangiari* meant and *kushti* and *pallone*. I had seen every one rise at five or six or seven, according to the distance to be covered, and after a quick cup of strong sweet tea set out for the next place. Ivor, Dennis, Derrick and Aubrey would each swing the starting-handle of one of the lorries they drove, while Vivienne drove her mother and Ida in the saloon car. An hour after waking they would all be on the road.

But earlier still, before I or most of those who drove lorries were awake, two parties would have left the field. First the elephant man with Salt and Saucy, who walked at a solemn and even pace to the next *tober*, and after them the Count, with the horses. The Count used to say that this was the best part of his day. Accustomed to horses before his show had been moved by petrol he was jealously attached to this one horse task left, and sitting on the box of the little monkey-waggon, with his hat down over his eyes, he would crack his whip and set off with a cavalcade of ponies following him. He was happy then, for he liked to see the sun come up, he said, and he liked to be out on the road while other folks were sleeping.

Then I watched the whole process of building up, from the time the position of the big tent on the new ground had been marked out by the tent-master, till the moment when its huge shape was complete and a flag flying on its king-pole. The tent-men and the Rosaire boys would knock off for an hour to have their breakfasts, but the work of building up lasted them till midday or more, and then Ivor and Derrick would advertise the show by riding through the town on the elephants. After lunch there would be a new pony to be practised, or a change in one of the acts, or a little veterinary work to be done, or a piece of the ring fence to repair, and the afternoon show at four o'clock would start before anyone realized that the day was half gone. Between afternoon and evening show there was a bare hour, and each of the family was in the ring three or four times at both performances, so that by the time it came to the two hours' task of 'pulling down' they were pretty weary. How after that they could find the energy or even the civility to talk to us in the Barracks, was hard to understand.

But the girls had no less of it. They cooked their brothers' meals, drove into the town for supplies, probably worked at making a new costume, cleaned out the Barracks, washed up vast quantities of crockery, practised riding and themselves performed in the ring. At a low estimate there were fourteen hours of solid work in the day of each of the family.

With this routine I had become familiar before we reached Lenham. But from Lenham we went to West Malling, from there to Borough Green and so to Sevenoaks.

At last the tenting season came to its close. Already the audiences were leaving the afternoon show to find darkness outside the tent, and at Borough Green the wind and rain were so violent that it had been doubtful whether the big top would stand the strain, or a show be given. The wind rattled the wallings at every performance, and rain found the weak points in the canvas. The family was preparing to turn in for the winter, and their route was taking them each day nearer to Woolwich Ferry, over which they would pass to their winter quarters in Essex. I had never been made so conscious of winter's approach as I was when the circus moved towards home.

In those weeks I learned something of the character of each of them. I knew that Derrick, the quietest and most unbookish of all, had a reputation for drollery, for a dry and devastating retort; that Dennis was considered 'deep', given to reading books at odd moments of the day as he balanced himself on an upturned box or squatted on the floor; that the waggon occupied by Aubrey and Helen was a hospitable place where the tent-men were given a cup of tea, and Helen amiably looked up from a wash-tub to welcome anyone in; that Ivor was the greatest showman of them all.

I had learnt, too what was indicated by *parlari* and *chat*, what it was to do a John Audley, and that *col* is the commonest word in use from one circus *omy* to another. I knew that we had reached the 'back-end' of the season, and that this winter would be spent in preparing for the next.

It was not until the circus reached Woolwich itself, having left the small red towns of Kent and gone into the dreary suburbs of London that I finally brought myself to leave it. Then it was with the promise and intention of joining it again next year, when, the Count said, I should hear its whole story from the time he met the Countess until now. With that promise I reluctantly drove away from the dismal patch of waste land near Woolwich on which their waggons stood, and returned to attack my neglected work.

CHAPTER TEN

The Man in Europe Street

I FOUND IT IMPOSSIBLE to settle down at Smarden, however. The routine and order of my life had been irreparably smashed and I was in revolt against the very things that had meant so much to me during the last five years of householding. My faith in myself and in my destiny as a writer did not weaken but I sickened at the idea of writing novels one after another in fulfilment of an oppressive contract. My nights in pubs and weekly articles on darts no longer seemed worthwhile and my friends at the Bell who had once been such 'characters' were now no more than kindly stay-at-homes. I was tired of house-keeping though it had absorbed much of my daily energy for a long and pleasurable period, and the garden, with its Conference pears which failed that year and the big greenhouse full of tomato plants became almost tedious. As for the bookshop—I had not visited it for a month and did not feel like doing so again.

The truth was that those few weeks of tenting with the Rosaires had made my life seem homespun and inadequate and domesticity a bore. I had seen one form of Englash nomadic life and realized, as I had never done before, its intrinsic, its quite startling difference from the more or less settled existence most of us followed.

I did not yet know much of the people of the roads or realize that they were of four distinct categories—circus people who were the nobility among nomads, fairground people who were of a very different tradition, gypsies of all kinds from the few remaining Romanies to the lowest *didakai*, and tramps, milestone inspectors as they were called, the unfortunates who walked from workhouse to workhouse. During the following years I dedicated much of myself to a study of all these, and came to know them well, but just then I was feeling the first shock of discovery and it blew my sense of proportion to hell. I was not going to suffer again the fret and tedium of trying to maintain a kind of existence I could not afford and no longer wanted.

There was no circus to travel with till next year but in the meantime I determined to go abroad. I had to find some pretext which would attract a publisher for I had no money and whatever journey I made would need to be subsidized. For several days I could think of nothing which would meet the case, then in the small hours of a November morning I had an idea and instantly decided that it was an inspiration.

It was this. War was threatening and books were being written (and avidly read) about the probability of its outbreak next year or the year after. Writers and star reporters were hurrying about Europe interviewing all the statesman and those in their confidence, Hitler, Goebbels, Goering, Mussolini, Stalin, and nothing they published seemed to help anyone to make a guess at the future. So why not interview the man in the street and see what *he* thought about it?

The plan was of course naïve, for the day when the man in the street had any say in the matter at all (if he ever had) was long past. He was the merest cypher, in no concrete sense existing except as a convenient cliché. One might in a three months' journey talk to a few score people, even a hundred or two, and what they said would depend wholly on the chances which selected them. But this sort of survey was in the air, for in that year Tom Harrisson and Charles Madge had set up their *Mass Observation* and the scheme I put forward would not be seen at once as adventitious and irrational. It would enable me to travel about Europe for a time and that was primarily what I wanted.

I drove up to London to seek advice from Louis Golding as

I did on so many issues in those years. He was at his best as a consultant, wise and generous with his time and attention. He saw the whole thing at once in all its strength and weakness and gave the book a title—*The Man in Europe Street*. What was more, he suggested a publisher for it—the firm of Rich and Cowan who had come into publishing with a considerable flourish and were said to be enterprizing and generous. Characteristically wanting to follow a suggestion of his at once, he phoned the firm and arranged an appointment for me that afternoon. Before I returned to Smarden, therefore, within twenty hours of the notion's first occurring to me, a verbal agreement had been made which became in time and after much discussion a signed contract. I was to receive an advance of £200 and out of this to pay my own travel expenses, a fair enough arrangement by the standards of those days, and I was delighted with the terms.

But I was not satisfied with the scheme itself. It would enable me to travel—but how? By car or train? When I thought of my last weeks' tenting with the Rosaires all travel except with a circus seemed tame. From this realization I evolved a bolder scheme. Why not *with* the Rosaires, or with any of them who would come? A small living-waggon and all the resourcefulness of people who had spent their lives in wayfaring under hard conditions would get me round Europe.

It would be a fulfilment of nearly all my ambitions and many of my ideals: my new-found love of the circus and of this circus family; my passion for travel for its own sake which had already taken me to a dozen countries; my determination as a writer to live among and know 'ordinary people'; my belief in 'experience' as something to be gained at all costs, almost as a commodity stocked by the writer; my confidence in myself as one who knew the under-dog better than the intellectuals who claimed to join his struggle—all the good absurd tenets of my youthful philosophy. But there was something more than this. Dearest and most secret of my ambitions was to be a man of action, to pit my hardihood and resolution against violent adverse

E*

circumstances, to fight something powerful for my own survival, the spirit, I suppose, which had made other men deliberately seek expensive dangers and become mountaineers or explorers. I felt I had never been tested and I wanted, in down-to-earth terms, to do something that needed courage and physical toughness in addition to intelligence. It is the oldest dream of the man condemned to a desk and few of us find the means to satisfy it. But here, it seemed to me, was the possibility.

An old living-waggon with an uncertain engine (for I could scarcely hope for better), a number of frontiers to cross in a Europe tense with the prospect of war, snow, rough and ice-covered roads, barely enough money to cover the expenses of travel, a strong chance of being arrested on some charge or other, daily small hardships and a large element of unknown danger—surely this could fairly be called adventure.

I saw it all and drove at once to the winter quarters of the Rosaires at Billericay. I put my case squarely to the family and asked if any of them would join me. At once, without asking questions which were then unanswerable or making conditions of any kind, Ivor and Derrick, the two younger brothers, volunteered to do so.

[2]

The next two weeks were hectic. We had not got a vehicle and if it had not been for the circus grape-vine we might never have found one, but the Rosaires heard of an old Morris Commercial which had done six years' service as a bus on the hilly roads of Wales.

I remember the black and stormy evening when we went to see this in a yard at Sidcup. It belonged to a showman named Botton and we sat in his trailer drinking tea which his chatty half-gypsy wife had made for us, discussing the deal. I think Botton would have been disappointed if there had not been some haggling—a life time on the roads had taught him that no price should be named and paid without it. In the end he agreed to sell the bus as it stood for £50.

When I first saw the thing, by lantern light, the whole project suddenly seemed far-fetched. The bus looked enormous in the dark shed, its wings were battered and its headlamps broken while its paintwork was deplorable. Its interior was empty and dirty and smelt of oil.

Ivor Rosaire eyed it with satisfaction—he was proud of his find.

"The stove could go there and the chimney there", he said.

I had known vaguely that the bus would be warmed by a coal stove, and when it was brought home to me by a casual indication of this sort it sounded forlorn and improbable. How could one drive into Vienna or Milan with a chimney smoking?

Moreover I had not got £50. The sum which Rich and Cowan were advancing had not yet been paid and would be just sufficient, I calculated, to see us over the route, allowing nothing for the purchase of the bus or fitting it up.

"We shall want a folding bed which will be a settee in the daytime and a wireless set", Ivor went on.

Suddenly the difficulties seemed insuperable. Even if I could find a way of buying the bus, there were necessary repairs to make, new tyres to be bought, lighting to be fixed, the settee-bed and curtains to make, cooking utensils, bedding, dozens of necessary pieces of equipment to be obtained somehow. Then there were passports to be got for Ivor and Derrick, documents for the car, a booking on the ferry . . . and time was pressing because we should have to be back before April when the circus would start its tenting season. For the first—and I believe the last—time I thought of all the disasters which might overtake us, breakdowns involving the purchase of new parts beyond my means, road accidents, difficulties with police or Customs officials, possible enmity towards us, even the outbreak of hostilities somewhere on the route. It seemed the most desperately hare-brained project.

"Well, are you going to buy it or not?" asked Botton, who was growing impatient.

"Give me forty-eight hours", I said and to this he agreed.

As we drove down to Smarden for the night Ivor and Derrick discussed it all with complete confidence and their faith was infectious. I realized that in everything that appertained to the bus and the difficulties of travel they had no doubt of themselves. The circus had known not just bad or difficult times but situations which would have meant for any other family a dead end. Penury, even hunger, they had known and days when the show was all but derelict, but somehow they had gone on. Nothing that could happen to us on the road was beyond their resource. In this they trusted themselves absolutely and in all else, all that had to do with money, documents, foreign parts, foreign languages, they trusted me no less. It was a somewhat disconcerting realization. If I failed in my side of the undertaking, to raise enough money, to obtain necessary documents, to plan the route, they would be doubly disillusioned and contemptuous, for in all this they had no doubt of me. I should have to find the means.

That night, going over my dilemma, I remembered a conversation of some months ago with that imperious figure of my boyhood, John Bayley. In *The Drums of Morning* I described him as a great man and showed him dominating the extraordinary school he had created.[f] He was in several ways unique— perhaps the only Englishman to make a large fortune out of education, though this in his long life was not his most remarkable achievement. I had kept in touch with him, finding him in retirement even more astonishing than when he had his school for I had come to see other qualities in him, his sense of humour, his delight in good living, his knowledge of wine and cigars, his boyish taste in music and literature. He was now an octogenarian who lived in a large house by the sea at Ramsgate, still played golf and motored about the country to speak in public.

[f] Wellington College, Shropshire, now Wrekin College.

I had lunched with him at his somewhat over-spendid home which had been built by one of the Wills (tobacco) family and was so much panelled that one felt as though one were sitting in a large cigar box. Afterwards he had said, quite unexpectedly —"If you ever need financial help in your profession, Rupert, you can come to me. I know yours is a hard life, me boy."

I decided that this was the sort of crisis he had visualized and drove down next day. He agreed at once to buy the bus for me and pay for its fittings, and wrote me a cheque for £75, but insisted on seeing Ivor and Derrick who gave him an impromptu exhibition of acrobatics in the hall of his house.

"I could do that when I was a lad", he said and it was probably the truth. He was a miner's son and as strong as a horse.

Gradually the other difficulties were surmounted. After a consultation with amused and helpful officials at the A.A. headquarters a detailed route was drawn up which covered five thousand miles and led me through the nine countries I wanted most to visit—Belgium, Holland, Germany, Czechoslovakia, Austria, Hungary, Yugoslavia, Italy and France— while all the documents necessary for taking the car across ten frontiers were made ready. Ivor and Derrick took the bus to their winter quarters where, with the help of Ted (Zena's husband), it was fitted out as a living waggon while the girls made curtains for it. A stove was put in with a chimney protruding through the roof and the settee-bed was made. Passports for Ivor and Derrick were obtained after they had spent a difficult day obtaining their birth-certificates. A booking was made for the Dover–Ostend crossing for a day in December— the 14th I think it was—and Count Rosaire took charge of Dingo, while Eric returned to his home in Gloucestershire and Bob Parker, the ex-mariner squatter of the Bell Inn, moved into my house as caretaker. We were all set to leave.

[3]

I had never till then had such a sense of 'setting forth', even when I had sailed for South America as a boy. When I saw the bus in the orchard fully equipped for the journey, I felt as cocky and expectant as an old-time ship's captain with his little barque victualled and armed for a voyage to the New World. I had no more doubts of the bus or of myself and certainly none of my companions.

We had to be on the quay at Dover at half past eight in the morning since the Ostend ferry sailed at ten. This meant rising at five that day and we left my house in darkness. When we reached the docks we found John Bayley, wrapped in an immense fur-coat, encouraging and very cheerful, though he himself must have risen early and driven twenty miles to see us off. He was, I realize now, though nothing would have convinced me of it at the time, in his eighty-sixth year. To those who remember him only as the fierce autocrat of school days, this benevolent Santa Claus who had given me the means to make my journey and stood there in the cold morning air, pink with health and energy, cracking jokes about the journey, will be an almost incredible figure. But there he was.

There was no runway on to the ferry-boat in those days and the bus, with all our furniture and cooking pots, wireless set and stove, was swung unceremoniously from dock to deck, while we anxiously watched it in mid-air. The other motorists, with smart saloon cars that had skis strapped to them, watched too, but with amused curiosity. What seemed to astonish them, and the stevedores and the Belgian stewards, was that we should be going in winter.

"I shouldn't care for it just *now*", volunteered an English-women in a fur coat, as she shivered deliberately.

We were told by one of the stewards that Queen Elisabeth of the Belgians was on board, and before other passengers disembarked at Ostend she was escorted to the waiting train.

She looked pale and rather tired, but bowed swiftly to the people who had been waiting for her. She moved beautifully, a perfect compromise between hurrying to the train in consideration of the waiting passengers, and acknowledging the crowd. To see the score of porters who had been drawn up to the barriers to receive the Queen Mother, one would have supposed that one was back in the nineteenth-century Europe, when kings and queens sat on thrones and wore crowns, or moved eternally through aisles of their cheering subjects. The porters stood with their caps clasped to their breasts in an age-old attitude of homage, with bowed heads. That brave and greatly loved Queen, whose devotion to Belgium's troops in the First World War was still remembered, had probably been doing her Christmas shopping at Fortnum and Mason's.

It seemed a long time before the bus was ashore and all the formalities settled, and we were ready at last to start. It had grown cold now and Ostend looked rather cheerless. But we had an amusing send-off from the station, for our high chimney seemed to make it impossible for us to follow the usual way from the docks, and there was much Flemish advice and suggestion from the crowd which had gathered to see us leave. Other gates must be opened, the onlookers said, for a bridge under which we had to pass here was quite evidently too low for us. The Rosaires however, had an instant solution. We were all three inside, and Derrick was in the driving seat, when Ivor went up to the stove and lifting the metal chimney off its socket on the stove-top he pulled it right into the waggon. It must have looked very odd to the porters who saw only the chimney disappear from sight for a moment as the bus went forward. There was a roar of laughter, which developed into a mild cheer, and we set off for the centre of the town.

Pulled up in the Grand Place, with the interior of the bus brightly lit and the wireless competing with the *carillon*, we were relieved to find that we attracted little attention. It would be tiresome, we thought, if wherever we went we gathered a crowd. That evening, and thereafter throughout the trip, we were rarely without a few inquisitive people who tried—usually in vain—to glimpse the interior of the bus, a few children who brought out a word or two of textbook English, and one or two individual visitors who had their own reasons for knocking at our door. But we were not often or seriously molested by the inquisitive.

We were soon away from the lights. Derrick found no difficulty in keeping to the right of the road, but the special cycle track which ran beside it caused some confusion at night, for oncoming lights seemed to be on the wrong side of us.

Had we realized, as we did in the following weeks, how pleasantly elastic were the parking regulations abroad, we should have stayed the night in the Grand Place at Bruges. But fresh from England we were doubtful whether we should be allowed to leave the waggon there even while we dined at the Pannier D'Or, and certainly never supposed that we could have slept peacefully in the shadow of the belfry. So at nine o'clock or more, rather wearily, we moved off again on the road to Ghent, in search of what the Rosaires described as a '*tober*'.

The Belgian Fascists, or Rexists as they called themselves, led by Léon Degrelle, were at their most vociferous and powerful that year. They had promoted themselves by making a pact with the Flemish Nationalists and it was not until 1938 that this pact was broken and the Rexists well defeated in the municipal elections. That evening as we drove towards Ghent our headlights illumined on every roadside tree the word 'Rex' in white letters and this continued for several miles. It seemed to give us a dubious welcome to Europe.

CHAPTER ELEVEN

Belgium and Holland

[1]

IN RECALLING THAT eventful journey through a snow-bound
Europe on the eve of war, it is not my intention to reproduce
the many conversations in different countries from which I drew
the material for the book I wrote after my return, *The Man in
Europe Street*. They may, though even this I doubt, have had
some significance at the time and the book was quite widely
read in England and America, but they have little interest now,
even as period pieces. Yet the story of the trip itself may have
a certain, perhaps somewhat morbid interest, for it was made
with intense enjoyment and optimism through countries which
would soon be devastated, among people about to be wiped out,
in a Europe which has disappeared for ever.

All eyes were on Hitler, but few with much discernment.
Who could believe that Satan had his habitation in that mean
and shallow being with his macaronic personality, his hysterical tirades, his commonplace features, his second-hand prag-
matism? All eyes were on Hitler, some already with fear, some
with no more than anxiety, some with hope but most still with
grim amusement or contempt. In fact, what I really learned in
those conversations was not what various people felt and
thought, but what they felt and thought about Hitler, and that
was not worth learning because Hitler was still anyone's guess,
even perhaps his own.

I had no remarkable percipience and returned from that
journey still unconvinced that war was inevitable. Military
'lines' were being openly constructed, the K-W Line in Belgium,
as well as the Maginot and Siegfried Lines. Re-armament had

been undertaken frantically almost everywhere and Fascist parties were thriving under one name or another, Degrelle's Rexists in Belgium, Mussert's N.S.B. in Holland, Henlein's Sudeten Party in Czechoslovakia, Seyss-Inquart's Nazis in Austria, the Arrow Cross in Hungary, as well as the two main parties in Germany and Italy. Many of Europe's young men were already in uniform. Yet people, perhaps the majority of people, managed to believe that there would be no war. Frontiers were easier to cross then than now, officials less suspicious, security slacker and the general attitude far less jittery. It is not pleasant to realize that a journey like mine by the eccentric means I had chosen, which met no serious opposition or interference in any country eighteen months before war broke out, would be quite impossible today.

[2]

From the very first we found that the kind of people we wanted to meet were friendly and communicative. We were so well received in Ghent that we might have been 'I and Joris and he' bringing the good news. In Antwerp ("*An*' you're a twirp!" said Derrick Rosaire on hearing the name), we spent the evening teaching the patrons of a café to play darts on the board we carried. At a village just beyond Antwerp we were invited to his home by a Flemish foreman docker, a massive bull-necked man, who had spent five years in Manchester during and after the 1914–18 war and was pleased to show off his English.

The ugly little sitting-room in which we sat with him while his wife gave us tea and he pressed cigars on us, was typical, I thought of the new proletarian homes of those years. The cottage rooms into which I had been taken in boyhood, the peasant interiors of France and Germany I had seen only ten years before were gradually disappearing. They had been bare with plain wooden chairs and a few inherited pieces of cottage furniture, and in England were stuffy with tight-closed windows whose light was blocked by geraniums. They had bare brick floors as often as not an old wooden clock which ticked wheezily. Horsehair, Spanish mahogany and an enlarged photograph of a wildly staring bridal couple in Sunday best were almost always in evidence while the single sitting-room of continental country homes was a kitchen too and had solid oak furniture and a *batterie de cuisine*.

For good or ill, that was gone and we sat on new upright chairs threatened by barbarously coloured wallpaper, staring at the yellow surface of a mass-produced dining-table. There was a meagre sideboard with chromium handles, there was a geo-metrically patterned carpet of shoddy material and the curtains had an artificial sheen. It was all scrupulously clean, modern and uncomfortable and the kindly Flemish couple who had invited us to it were so proud of it that we would have been tactless not to admire it. I saw it again in other countries, or something very like it and over Western Europe it is being reproduced today in all its synthetic pretentiousness, and the only change in these last thirty years has been the addition of a television set.

We pulled the bus into a farmer's yard for our last night in Belgium. He was a Flamand of another, more picturesque, type, a tall lurching young fellow with an intelligent narrow face, who had inherited his acres from his father and made the most of them. In fact it was scarcely five o'clock next morning when we were awakened, and the Rosaires got up to move the bus because the farmer wanted to get his donkey-cart out. It was pleasant, however, to wake to a farmyard smell which came through the greyness of the morning, pleasant to hear the cattle, and feel that sort of comfort and reassurance which a farm always gives one, even in war-time. There is something in the perennial continuation of farmwork, its dependence on the seasons rather than on the events recorded in newspapers, which restores one's confidence in the placid continuation of life as we know it. Such confidence may be false, but after an evening spent in talk of the future, of wars and rumours of wars it was good to see the donkey-cart led out and the cows driven in.

The farmer was friendly, and sold us milk and eggs and wished us *bon voyage*, which pleased Ivor. Derrick was sceptical, not of the farmer's good will, but of his brothers' comprehension of anything the man had said.

"That was a nice fellow", Ivor reflected as we set off.

"How do *you* know?" asked Derrick sharply.

To which it seemed there was no possible reply.

[3]

I have the pleasantest recollections of Dordrecht, our first Dutch stopping place. We drove into the narrow streets of that old town at dusk, our chimney smoking and our appetites raw. We found ourselves in a maze of one-way directions and to manoeuvre the bus over bridges and between the overhanging walls of houses was not easy. We were even thinking of leaving the town when a solemn Dutch policeman stopped us.

"Where do you want to go?" he asked in English.

"We want to stop for a bit."

"Then drive over there to that space by the river."

"But . . . it says 'no entry'!"

"Never mind. I will come with you."

He came and directed us to a cobbled square in front of a large building.

"Drive right up to the steps", he said.

"What is that building?"

"The town hall."

"Then surely we can't park right in front of it?"

"Why not? You can stay there all night if you wish."

The Rosaires were frankly incredulous. Years of driving their circus waggons through the English counties had taught them to expect a very different attitude from the police.

"Well, if you say so", we agreed doubtfully.

"Over there is the police station. If you need anything, come and ask", said our friend, who had never dropped his grim solemnity. He saluted without smiling and disappeared.

It was a crisp evening, and the little town was brightly lit. From where we sat in the waggon we could hear the river rippling by in darkness and the noise of clogs and the voices of children who were staring at our bus. Our lamps were lit, the stove heaped up, and Ivor set about peeling potatoes for our evening meal.

I can see the interior very clearly as it was just then. The table was laid, and in those early days there was clean linen and plenty of unbroken crockery. I was sitting on the couch, which would later become a bed, writing the few notes I kept as a journal each day of the tour, in a book which the Rosaires called a diarrhoea. Ivor, in a pair of Dutch corduroy trousers which he had bought that day, a pullover and a beret, was helping Derrick who had undertaken the cooking and catering for the trip. Derrick's thick dark hair hung in ringlets round his forehead, and he was intent and silent, frying steak and onions over a primus ring. Dance-music came from the radio and the air was deliciously thick with the smell of cooking. I smoked contentedly, warmed by the blazing stove.

From our chimney the smoke rose and the smell of our onions must have been carried into the mayoral nostrils so near us in the town hall. The food was good, with a bottle of rather sweet wine and black coffee and Dutch cigars after it. When Ivor needed water to wash up, he recalled the policeman's invitation and went across to the station for it. While he was there he was given more coffee and told which was the best cinema to visit, and came back grinning at the amiability of the Dutch police.

[4]

Eight years earlier in Germany I had met two young Dutchmen on a camping holiday, with a tent pitched beside the river at Monschau. One of them, Franz Dupont, wanted to be an artist and gave me several of his early drawings. My habit of keeping in touch with friends made casually abroad served me well here, for Franz, married now and a successful film photographer, invited me to his home at Blaricum, outside Amsterdam, and we pulled the bus into his garden and settled down for a few days.

There was nothing of the traditionally heavy Dutchman about Franz who had a gay and volatile nature. His small pretty wife looked dark beside him and both had a gift of intelligent chatter which made for ease and confidence. Their home was fresh and light—a very happy house. It had been built to Franz's own design about the big studio-gymnasium, which he used for film work and photography. There was a bright little sitting-room, the colour of daffodils, and an *eetkeuken*, a dining-room-kitchen, which he said, was an institution in most middle-class Dutch homes. There were vast windows everywhere; the whole house was beautifully light, although it stood deep in the woods.

These woods and the open country beyond them, it seemed, were a hiding-place just then for a number of foreign refugees, many of them made dangerous by despair.

"We have a great number of Jews in Holland who have escaped over the frontier", my friend said. "The best of them have adapted themselves to Dutch life. But there are others, more desperate, or perhaps more wretched, who have no papers and no means of livelihood."

Their existence round Blaricum led to a significant little incident on our first evening there. Ivor and Derrick wanted to go to the cinema and set out from the studio to find their way through a maze of woodland lanes to the bus-stop. Needing

directions they asked a man at the wheel of a stationary car, but
to their surprise he started his engine and shot off down the
road without answering. They next approached a pedestrian
who shrugged and turned in at a nearby gate which he had
already passed. A cyclist approached, but when they spoke to
him he pedalled away as hard as he could.

Baffled and irritated, they decided that the next passer-by
should answer, and when it turned out to be another cyclist,
one of them took the precaution of holding his handle-bars
while they inquired the way. He, however, spoke English, and
offered to accompany them to the bus-stop. When they told
him what had happened he laughed and explained.

"Your foreign clothes and accent were enough", he said,
"they took you for some of the 'roughs' who have been round
these woods lately. There have been quite a number of hold-ups,
you know, and all that is agreed about them is that the men
speak German among themselves."

The Rosaires were tickled at being mistaken for refugee stick-
up men, and walked home after the pictures talking their few
words of German as loudly as possible, and jingling coins, in the
hope of either being mistaken for the 'roughs' again, or of
being attacked by them. Either of these, they explained, might
have led to an incident which would be useful for "the book".
But they reached the studio without interruption.

This was the first time I had heard more than rumours of
the great hosts of displaced persons and refugees who were
beginning to move to and fro across Europe in desperation and
hunger, and have continued, homeless and hopeless, till this day.
As yet they were numerically not very formidable and came
almost exclusively from Germany and Russia and their tragedy
was only beginning, for they were not yet hunted out and
rounded up to be sent to forced labour or mass-murder camps.
We were to come on traces or hear stories of them in almost
every country, including Germany itself, but I for one failed to
see in them a portent of horrors to come, for a refugee to my
generation had meant either one of the thousands of Belgians

who were received and cared for in Britain during the First World War, or the usually well-to-do Jews who had found the means to reach London since Hitler came to power in Germany and were for the most part useful citizens of the professional classes. No one could yet forsee the uprooted millions of people born and bred to security who would lose that, and everything else, and move this way or that across frontiers till they could no longer even look for asylum and died from sheer despair.

[5]

Holland gave me the impression—it could be no more than that—of a sleek, hospitable country, a middle-class Eden in which everyone from the comfy-looking Queen on her bicycle to the well-fed workers was content to let things continue as they were.

Amsterdam seemed a most beautiful and impressive city in those crisp winter days, and we came to know its waterways and fine Renaissance buildings quite well. Its restaurants seemed always full of hard-eating people, and the population in the streets looked solid and serious. The men in their warm high-buttoning overcoats and queer thick hats balanced squarely on their head-tops, avoided all rakishness, all flippancy, and marched stolidly along the pavements, the women were plump and respectable. "We are the most bourgeois race in the world", said a man I met in a café, "and I am the most bourgeois member of it. Have some beer?"

"Yet you have produced more artists to the square mile than any other country."

He laughed.

"But were they not bourgeois artists?" he said.

On Sunday afternoon Franz Dupont took us across the Gooi, a windswept heath stretching down to the Ysselmeer to see the unbelievable village of Huizen. This was a Calvinist stronghold and when we entered it at about three o'clock, the church bells were sounding for the third or fourth time that day, and every man and woman in the village who was not actually bedridden was going to church.

The women wore the Puritan costume of the seventeenth century, and their white coiffes were spotless, their aprons stiff and clean. The men walked solemnly with them. Not a laugh could be heard, not a smile touched their faces. There was no traffic—for even the bicycle, so universally used in Holland, was forbidden by common will in Huizen on Sunday. The effect on that grey December afternoon was macabre. It really was as though one had gone back to Puritan times, for this sombre and solemn procession was no pageant, no rehearsed or artificial display but, to those who took part in it, commonplace and to the onlooker, wholly real. We could not take photographs because, said Franz, if they saw us doing so they might smash our camera and not long before some boys who tried to cycle through the village on a Sunday were stoned. The gloom was too intense and positive to be depressing, the houses ugly with tightly-closed windows, the streets colourless, the silence after the church bells ceased unbroken. The atmosphere was suffocating and we were glad to leave Huizen and find sharp contrast in the neighbouring village of Laren.

The contrast, in fact, seemed to be stressed by the inhabitants of Laren. The population was predominantly Catholic and there was a colony of artists here. Franz took us to a hotel owned by an art patron named Jan Hamdorff where there was a cheerful *thé-dansant*. The guests were such as could be found in a cinema café in any English provincial town, but when I pointed this out to Franz he smiled.

"But this", he said, "is our *haute monde*. These people have come from the Hague in motor-cars. I assure you that this is what is known in Holland as 'Society'. So you see that your stout friend was right. We really *are* a bourgeois people."

There is about that long-ago Sunday both vividness and unreality—itself a Dutch landscape. The figures in the foreground are radiantly painted, each feature exact and clear, and the background lies under a lucent winter sky. But it is all somewhat other-worldly, no part of the life I have known. We went to another, less pretentious hotel where a different kind of dance was in progress for young farm workers had crowded in, the crimson-brown skin of their faces shining with perspiration, their large hands carefully cleaned but having the rough flat-nailed appearance which marked the hands of all farm workers, their Sunday suits stiff and uncomfortable on their big-boned bodies, and their mouths a-grin with pleasure. Then to what Franz called the Montmartre of Laren, for a fifteenth-century farmhouse had been turned into a pub, and the long cowshed which stands so close to all Dutch farms that you may pass straight from the kitchen into it, had been converted into a simple theatre. This, if a little self-conscious in decoration, with its walls stencilled by local artists and its light supplied by candles stuck in bottles, yet succeeded in having an air of some authenticity. It was empty when we saw it, since this was Sunday, but once a week in winter, my friend told me, a show was put on by the organizing genius of the place, Edwin Gubbins Doorenbos, an erratic creature who stayed in Laren only until spring, when he disappeared with his guitar to make a living on the roads throughout the warm months, returning to hibernate.

Perhaps if I had visited Holland since then the outlines in recollection would be less stark and the places and people less memorable. But it happens that I have never returned and the country lives for me in those wintry vistas. Nothing could have been less like a nation on the eve of war. I see it still as not so much complacent as frankly delighted with itself. There seemed to be no real poverty or anxiety and even the artists flourished. A benign country of beautiful cities, its sufferings under the Nazis were to be as great as those of any western country and nowhere was the brute philistinism of Hitler and his thugs more obvious than in their wanton destruction of Rotterdam, no-where was their barbarity more savage than in the enslavement, starvation, mass-assassination and deception of the Dutch people. Yet there it was in December 1937 placid, assured of its immunity, enjoying its ponderous pleasures, a garden unprotected from a herd of swine that would root and trample its congenial symmetry.

Franz and his wife survived the German occupation, for he remains my friend, but most of the young people we saw that day were its victims.

CHAPTER TWELVE

Germany

[1]

WE DROVE UP TO the German frontier on a misty afternoon just a fortnight after crossing the Channel. The Customs officers, who looked like soldiers, were intensely curious but not in the least hostile. It was obvious that they were trying to find an explanation for the sudden appearance at their post of this unlikely vehicle. It was with relief that they discovered from the Rosaires' passports their normal occupation and told one another that these were *Cirkus Menschen*.

We came at nightfall to Emmerich and all I knew of it then was its Roman origins and the fact that it had been a town of the Hanseatic League. It was brilliantly illuminated, festive, and crowded with Christmas shoppers. Children wrapped to the ears in warm clothing, women in bright colours, laughter, the chime of bells, tinsel in the shop windows, piles of food on show—everything was set for a German Christmas and everyone seemed determined to enjoy it. The next time I should hear the town's name was as an RAF target, 'oil tanks, refineries and marshalling yards at Emmerich' seemed to lie on the route of every bomber and I never heard them mentioned without remembering those jolly Christmas crowds. How war twists our thinking. I would not have spared the people of Emmerich one raid that served our purpose, for all my happy recollections of them. Nor do I forget that the children of Coventry were doing their Christmas shopping that same evening. But when I heard of those raids on Emmerich I saw the bombs destroying the very crowd I had watched, scattering them panic-stricken from the bright shop-windows. I never

felt like that about Cologne or Kassel or places I knew far
better when their turn came. Vistas, snapshots, impressions
are what have influenced my life, more than emotions and
deep-rooted memories. A child I saw that night pointing a
woollen-gloved finger at something in a toyshop window became in my mind all children everywhere in Europe, and these
wartime thoughts reached their maddest whirlpool of illogi-
cality when I felt shame at that child's death, or mutilation
or even her sick terror, for no better reason than that it was
our men, our bombers, our righteous cause which brought it
about.

But that was far away as we drove through the busy centre
of the town looking for a place to park because we were hungry.
We drove into a side street and pulled up under a street light
to cook and eat and drink.

How I enjoyed those rough, evening meals in the waggon
during the earlier parts of our tour—for later we grew lazy and
depended more and more on restaurants. The evening was
before us, and we had a bottle or two of wine. The trip would
seem an Odyssey as we sat there, pleased with one another, and
with the people we had met that day. The 'fug' would be as
thick as I remembered it in the study at school, and outside in
the street there would be a few dawdlers trying to peep between
our curtains. There was no hurry—that was the grace of it—
no need to move from the settee, to rush off to an appointment,
to think of tomorrow's work. I had weeks of idleness before me,
idleness made delightful by perpetually changing sights, and
new contacts.

But on that evening, our first in Germany, our after-dinner
peace was disturbed by a steadily increasing hum of voices
around the waggon, and the sound of many boots on the road.
We looked out to find that we were completely surrounded by
Brownshirts. Had they been paying any particular attention to
us this might have been disconcerting, but most of them had
their backs to us, and although now and again a group would
glance curiously our way, it was obvious that they were there

for a purpose which had no connection with us. We had, it soon appeared, chosen the Brownshirt headquarters as a building opposite which to stop for dinner. Our bus must have caused them some inconvenience in the narrow road, but they did not trouble to ask us to go away. An officer appeared and issued a command, at which they formed two lines.

"*Heil Hitler!*" the officer snapped.

"*Heil Hitler!*" they replied, their deep voices chorusing the greeting as a matter of course. They moved into their Headquarters without more fuss.

We dawdled next day because I did not want to reach Cologne before Christmas eve, when Ernst would arrive there. We spent a night in the village of Praest where we had a friendly welcome and drank a lot of beer—since for me there has never been better beer than Münchener from a stone mug. I drank it first on a German ship coming home from Buenos Aires in 1925 and nowadays I want no other beer at all and drink none except in Germany.

I decided to stop some days in Duisberg for in no other place on our route would we be so entirely among factories and factory-hands, and I hoped to get some insight into their feelings. It was ugly country through which we passed to reach Duisberg, and the outskirts of the town were rather squalid and grey. Here at last, I thought, there would be some signs lingering of that grimly determined Communism which had flourished before 1933. Though I could not expect to glimpse even a flicker of its old fire, I might at least perceive some passivity which could be thought to cloak it, some hint of indifference to current enthusiasms, or some self-consciousness in their manifestation, which would be all that was left of the clenched fist I remembered.

I left the Rosaires for long periods and explored the drabbest quarters of the city. I went into workman's bars in the colourless suburbs, the sort of places which once were the very cells of Communism. There would be groups of men, rather savage-looking as the town workers in Germany often were, drinking and gossiping. There would be van-drivers, postmen, machinists, lolling easily at tables, or absorbed in talk. Everywhere the familiar '*Heil Hitler*' was spoken in greeting as one entered or left, not rhetorically, not grudgingly, but as though no other form of greeting, *Guten Tag* or *Guten Abend*, had ever been heard here. The speakers seemed to assume that Nazism was a natural and permanent form of government. They spoke of the earnings of the police or the skilled machinist as compared with those of the land-worker, as a matter which could be if necessary adjusted, but not as if all wage-scales were a part of some grossly unjust system forced on them by a mysterious power. They spoke of other nations from the same standpoint. They assumed that each man in their group regarded Russia as a potential enemy, but they were as drearily conformist as the Russians themselves.

I was left wondering, as others were, what had happened to those six million Communist voters in the last free elections when I was answered, not fully but somewhat dramatically, by a small event on our last night in Duisberg.

We were about to leave the town. We had taken on coal and water, milk and bread, and the engine had been started, when two young men lounged up to the door of the bus and said good evening. The Rosaires, accustomed to inquisitive visitors to their circus waggons, were more tolerant than I, and when the strangers asked if they could see the interior, they asked them in. The two sat, drinking some Advocaat we had brought from Holland, and one of them, the taller and elder of the two, talked easily.

He was, he said, a Nazi. He had joined the Movement after reading *Mein Kampf*, and foresaw a great future both for Germany and for his own class under the regime. He hoped we would take back a good impression of the country. Didn't we think it had improved? Didn't people seem happier?

The younger, a little dark fellow, scarcely spoke. Once or twice he seemed to be watching us with more than ordinary interest, as though he wanted to study our reaction to his companion's enthusiasm. But even when they got up to leave us, he said little more than good-bye, and *Gute reise*.

We left Duisberg on our way to Düsseldorf, and saw no more then or thereafter of our visitors. But when Ivor was converting the settee into a bed that night he came on something concealed under the cushions on which the little dark fellow had sat.

"What's this?" he asked and handed me a German newspaper.

I looked at the thing and was puzzled. For it was a copy, printed a year previously, of *Die Rote Fahne* (the red flag) the secret organ of the German Communist party.

It was one of the strangest papers I have seen. Octavo in size it was printed on paper as thin as a five pound note, in type so small that one would—literally—require a magnifying glass to read it. There was no indication, of course, of where it was printed, but it was founded, it said, by Karl Liebknecht and Rosa Luxemburg. One of its articles was headed with the name Ernst Thalmann and its sub-heading said that the fight for his freedom was the fight for the freedom of Germany. Another was entitled *Hitler faschismus und Trotzkismus*. There was something very clandestine in its appearance, something pathetic in its limp leaves which had cost so much in risk and labour, and something heroic, too, in it.

How it got into the waggon we never knew for certain. None of us had seen our visitors put it there, and yet no one else had visited us that day.

I have no explanation or theory. It is just possible that our two visitors had nothing to do with its presence under that cushion, for the waggon had stood untenanted in the street more than once. Again, the talkative one may have been a genuine enthusiast, the other an enemy of the regime. Or they may both have been of the secret opposition, anxious to show visitors that it still existed. Or even, and this was the theory which Ivor and Derrick favoured, *agents provocateurs* who intended to have our waggon searched if we had stayed in Duisburg. I do not know. But there it was, and it made good reading after the complacency of opinions we had heard.

[2]

Düsseldorf, two days before Christmas, was brilliant, the windows of the food-shops were piled lavishly with all the luscious cooked foods and salads and *Wurst* which I remembered eating in Germany when I lived there seven years earlier, and the air of festivity and plenty was as noticeable as in England. There was butter and dairy produce in abundance, and though the usual bread supply was rather heavy and coarse, a whiter bread was obtainable. Nor did I find anybody who had suffered from food shortage or even restriction since the first months of the National Socialist regime. Düsseldorf was overflowing with good things and as in Emmerich there were crowds of happy-looking people on its pavements.

There was an officious man in charge of the car park, however, who plainly disliked having our shabby waggon, with its homely chimney, among his neat and polished cars. He moved us irritably from one place to another, and when the Rosaires got out he made some bad-tempered and incomprehensible protest. But they had an effective way of dealing with this. Derrick stared solemnly at the man while he was speaking, and then answered him by doing a quick back-flip in front of his eyes. This caused the spectators to giggle, and the attendant to turn angrily to Ivor, with a gabble of words. Ivor in turn waited until he had finished, then did a neat hand-spring. The man grew openly furious. The Rosaires proceeded to more elaborate convolutions. He shouted at them. They spun in the air. People began to gather. Each time the man spoke one of the boys, as though startled by a gun-shot, left the ground, and twisting high in the air, landed with irritating security on his feet still staring respectfully at the attendant. Finally, as though realizing that it was useless to rave at two over-sprung jack-in-the-boxes who did not understand a word he said, he made an appeal to the spectators. When this was met with laughter he turned sulkily away and left us in peace.

F

We went through the streets, enviously examining the bright winter sports clothes in outfitters' windows, and buying what we wanted in food-shops. Then reaching a big café which had an orchestra playing, we went in and ordered tea and rum. Uniforms were everywhere about us—the smart grey-green with silver braid of army officers, Brownshirts, Blackshirts, Luftwaffe men and a few naval officers on leave. The orchestra began to play a Christmas fantasy, with impersonations and a soft rendering of *Heilige Nacht*, and everyone seemed overcome with good will. This was what Prince Albert had brought to England almost a century earlier, and the Anglo-German conception of Christmas with a decorated tree, presents, greeting cards and over-eating had long been a symbol for those romantically-minded people in both countries who saw in an emotional as well as military friendship between England and Germany the main hope for Europe and—in those days—for the world. *Stille Nacht, Heilige Nacht* crooned emotionally in a Düsseldorf café full of men in uniform seemed to have some significance, some warm, tender, nostalgic appeal which I could not grasp. Perhaps it was Christianity.

[3]

We stayed a night at a village called Dormund, once again enjoying ourselves in the local inn, *Zum Stern*. Looking back I think that in spite of Queen Victoria and Thomas Carlyle and arguments about consanguinity, the most real and vital thing that the English and Germans have in common is their love for inn-fires and beer, their understanding of what the inn means to the community. In none of the countries which we call Latin does this exist for the cafés of France or Spain or Italy have a wholly different atmosphere. In watching the Rosaires in German inns I realized this, for they were at home.

[4]

I had come to Cologne seven years earlier to stay in Ernst Thoma's parental home, but that had been in another Germany, the needy chaotic country of the Weimar Republic, and we had been very different young men, Ernst a student and I consciously at the beginning of a writer's career with my first novel just published. That visit had been made only four years after the end of the British Occupation of Cologne following the First World War, and the visit I was making now was four and a half years before the great British air-raid of May 30th, 1942 when in ninety minutes 1130 planes all but destroyed the city, though the cathedral was left standing amid ruins. I remember these dates because I find it remarkable that my friendship with Ernst, one of the firmest in a life of friendships, should have begun and persisted through these events, that we have deliberately maintained it untouched by international relationships however searing, with a break of only six years while we were fighting on opposing sides in the Second World War.

During the first visit of all in 1930 I was invited by his father and mother to their modest tenement flat in the suburb of Lindenthal. I remember very well the rather forbidding building of dark red brick overlooking some public gardens. Ernst's father was a clerk earning just sufficient to keep his wife and three sons. He was a quiet unassuming man who worshipped routine and order, whose days seemed to vary from one another not at all. He set out for his office after a noisy family breakfast and returned at precisely the same hour each evening to sit by the stove smoking a large hooked pipe and reading the evening paper till just ten o'clock when he went to bed. Ernst's mother, a warm-natured kindly *hausfrau*, portly and grey-haired with a round unwrinkled face, worked from dawn till bed-time to feed and care for her four males and was deeply loved by all of them. Ernst's younger brothers were then schoolboys, and I shared the room in which the three of them slept.

Now we rattled into Cologne on the afternoon of December 23, and found that same dull red building in Lindenthal. (It was to be destroyed with most of Durenerstrasse in which it stood in 1942). Ernst and his wife would arrive from Kassel tomorrow for Christmas and I found his young brothers, now almost grown to manhood. The elder was a talkative scatter-brained youth of nineteen who had vague anti-Nazi sentiments so that his indiscretions worried his mother. The younger had been a member of the Hitler Jugend and was more scholarly and stable in character. Both were to be killed on the Russian Front five years later.

Ernst's father obtained permission for us to put the bus into a yard beside the block of flats and we drove in at nightfall. This yard belonged to a tradesman and seems to me, as I remember it, very truly German. It was perhaps a hundred yards long and thirty wide, and it stretched back from the houses in a busy street. On one side were shelters for carts and cars and there were stables there, and a manure heap. On the other side a dozen hungry chickens scratched in a small run, and a water-tap hissed incessantly. It was clean and neat, but rather gloomy, in spite of the dove-cote in which the shop-keeper's young son bred pigeons. It was an obstinate survival of the country, set among dull urban buildings.

Next morning I had an opportunity of seeing the Rosaires in action, for the bus caught fire. The cause must be traced to the occasion, a few miles back, when we had run out of paraffin.

"What do you call it in German?" asked Derrick, who did most of the shopping.

"The same, I suppose," I told him. "Wait a minute and I'll look it up. Yes. '*Das Paraffin.*' "

So he went off with the can to buy some.

"It's expensive in Germany", he said when he had returned later. "Four marks, this cost."

It was not until he was filling the lamp that evening that he found he had bought thick prepared medicinal paraffin, useless for our purpose, and as we had come thirty miles from the shop it was no good complaining.

Here in Cologne, however, the son of the hospitable shop-keeper, in whose yard we stood, explained.

"You want petroleum", he said, and went off to fetch it.

"The Germans are crackers", sighed Derrick, "they call paraffin 'petroleum', and petrol 'benzine'."

Next morning he set about cleaning the sticky oil from the lamp and lamp-wicks. To do this he needed "real petrol" and, pulling the rubber tube from our windscreen-wiper, he sucked it up from the tank of the bus and started to let it siphon out. Now the tank in our Morris-Commercial was on the right flank of the body, and Derrick had set the lamp he was cleaning on the ground nearby. As it later appeared, the extinguisher of the lamp, made to get rid of the flame from ordinary paraffin, had allowed the wick under it to smoulder gently all night and as soon as the petrol dropped on it there was a column of flame.

Derrick acted quickly. He pulled the tube sharply from the petrol tank, but in doing so spattered the side of the bus with petrol, and this of course was soon ablaze, together with the lamp on the ground, the rags which were being used for cleaning, and the rubber tube. He got the top screwed on the tank, however, while Ivor jumped into the driving seat and backed the bus away from the fire. In a moment the flames rising from the paintwork of the car were extinguished, and later those of the offending lamp itself.

Throughout the whole crisis the brothers never exchanged a word, each knowing exactly what had to be done and what the other would do. They lived largely by instinct; their insight was far more acute than the average man's, and they could foresee one another's movements. Their nerves, of course, were iron. Derrick, whose brain in such a moment could take in every possibility, knew exactly the risk he ran in approaching the tank to screw the lid on while flames were dancing near it.

Ivor had no illusions about the danger of jumping into the bus to run it back.

"Afraid one of the towels is spoilt", remarked Derrick.

That was all. But they knew, as I did, how near we had been to losing rather more than the rest of our trip.

[5]

The atmosphere of Christmas grew almost oppressive. But during the feast days Nazism took a second place, which was pleasant. Hitler managed to identify himself with many German things but a Christian festival defeated him.

I went alone into the city to do some shopping, and later to meet Ernst and his wife who would be arriving from Kassel at six or seven o'clock. The streets had become one ceaseless parade of chattering people, and the shops were so crowded that one had to wait everywhere to be served. But I had not anticipated the sudden emptiness and silence which fell over the city towards six o'clock for no one had told me that it was on Christmas Eve not Christmas Day that German families celebrated the feast.

Everywhere, for days now, we had seen Christmas trees, in cafés, bars, shops, homes, hung with the customary glittering decorations and crowned with a silver star. We had seen a workman cycling home with a small tree across his handle-bars, and watched children lugging a larger one through the streets. We had heard everywhere of *Weihnachten*, seen pictures of the three kings, watched presents being bought. But even then I was unprepared for the emotionalism of it in Ernst's home, for the singing and toasting, the childish warmth of it all, the approach to the little crib, the feigned surprise, the excited laughter, the noisy happiness. It was the tradition of the pre-War Christmas cards 'printed in Germany', with their sparkling trees and absurd pink-faced fairies and abundance of snow and hoar frost. It revived in my mind stories of how on the first Christmas Day of World War One the soldiers of both sides had come out of their trenches to meet and greet in No Man's Land and how all the High Commands had sternly forbidden this in subsequent years. It might have stopped the war.

I set off with Ernst and Clemens his wife to the Cathedral for Midnight Mass. Though I was taken to task afterwards by a haughty reviewer with architectural pretensions for saying so, I have always found the massive and splendidly proportioned building of Cologne Cathedral with its aspiring twin towers, one of the noblest works of man. ("This muddy rhapsody would not, one feels have been written had Mr. Croft-Cooke taken the trouble to inform himself that the greater part of Cologne Cathedral is a mid-nineteenth century product and well recognised to be an audacious piece of Gothic faking by those qualified to judge." *Truth*) I loved 'those qualified to judge'.

Inside the vast floor space of the nave was already crowded, and the aisles were filling as the Mass began. Before the Gospel the whole Cathedral was thick with people, and those entering had difficulty in finding a place to stand. Conspicuous every-where were the uniforms of soldiers, S.S. and S.A. men— indeed, it seemed that there were more men in uniform than not. With profuse lights blazing under those cloudy arches, and the organ booming sternly to the motionless packed crowd, the Mass began. Five or six thousand people heard it, and filed slowly into the chilly small hours afterwards to meet as many thousands on their way home from other churches. There was as yet little interference with the Church and persecution, which grew in the war years, was secret.

But there was no secrecy about Hitler's mad anti-Semiticism. He had proclaimed it as a doctrine from the start and though he still kept knowledge of the excesses of his thugs from the general public, he was furtively increasing the tempo of victimization to the point when he could unleash the great pogrom of the Kristall-Nacht, November 9th–10th, 1938. That evening, for instance, we found a shop, on a street corner not a hundred yards from the Cathedral, which had had its windows broken and scrawled over with Jewish characters in some white paste which could only be removed from the glass by hours of work. But someone it seemed, had blundered, for over the characters and cracks were stuck printed notices which announced that the proprietor of this shop was not a Jew, had no Jewish blood or even Jewish customers, and that the perpetrator of this outrage had already been arrested and fined one hundred marks. So there would be business as usual.

On Christmas day I had lunch with the Rosaires at a huge crowded restaurant in the city. We ate roast turkey, carved in the coarse and unfamiliar way which the Germans have with poultry, and served with cranberry sauce. We drank champagne and thoroughly enjoyed ourselves, to the delight of our waiter who had been in England and knew, as he said, that for us today was the real feast day. Afterwards we went to the Burghof Varieté, a beer-hall theatre with tables round a dance floor and a stage on which variety turns were given, one by a circus acquaintance of the Rosaires. Beer and wine were cheap and great mugs or long thin bottles stood on all the tables. But the comedians, playing to an audience of starchy officers of the regular army, had not the bawdiness and abandon of the clowns I remembered in beer-halls a few years earlier.

[6]

I was to see Ernst again at Kassel, when his Christmas, holiday would be over, and he would be back at his flat there, and at work.

When we left Cologne next morning we entered on a new phase of our journey. Hitherto the Morris-Commercial had had nothing but level roads to cover, and since crossing the frontier into Holland there had been excellent surfaces. But Boxing Day afternoon saw us climbing the steep hills of the Sauerland, and finding them snow-covered. Till now the engine had plugged away without interruption, but had stood no unusual test.

The snow was thick round Hilchenbach, and we had no skid-chains. We decided that we must get some at the first garage. But the bus found her way through the drifts without difficulty, and after a long day's driving we were too tired to bother about buying chains. For the next three weeks or more we never saw the road surface—travelling continually over snow. For days we continued to say that we must buy chains as soon as possible, but as we went on without a skid and without being caught in a drift we began to forget them, and in the end, we finished the whole journey, including the Alps, without using them.

That first afternoon, before we had an experience of the bus's behaviour in snow, travelling was anxious work. Derrick took over from me, I remember, and had the worst of the journey as we crested the hills near Erndtebruck. He never tried to rush a drift, but kept the bus moving steadily forward, while Ivor banked up our stove and we watched the slow miles of white downland pass.

Once we paused and left the waggon to look out across the lonely hills, with their pinewoods stiff and black, and their scarce, untidy villages. A fox crossed the road ahead of us and trotted gently down the slope to our right, and a giant kestrel hawk hovered low. But we saw scarcely a human being that afternoon and met only one oncoming car.

We stayed at Erndtebruck, finding in the inn there just such a circle as I remembered on a Sunday in Monschau—all the comfortable old men of the village seated about one large table, drinking beer, laughing a great deal, talking contentedly, their flushed and honest faces, their best clothes and ponderous watch-chains over rounded paunches, were all in the German tradition, and they turned to greet us when we entered. In nearly all such places there was conversation which I con-scientiously reported in my book.

F*

I had to do a week's writing in Kassel and stayed in Ernst's flat but the disposal of the bus for a whole week was again something of a problem. For the first night Ernst got permission for the Rosaires to run it into the yard of the local fire-station, and sleep there. This was hospitable and friendly of the firemen especially when they woke Ivor and Derrick at dawn with hot coffee and an invitation to use their shower-baths. But when the Chief of the station found on the third day that they made no attempt to leave, he became concerned. Had he turned his yard into a permanent camping site for Englishmen? Were Ivor and Derrick even then wiring to other circus people that here was an ideal *tober*, with free baths and coffee?

He was embarrassed, too, by his inability to speak English, and the complete incomprehension of German displayed by the Rosaires whenever he hinted at their departure. Being a courteous man, he could not bear to do more than suggest delicately that they should move. But on the fourth day he grew desperate, and after referring to a German–English dictionary he brought out the three words most appropriate for the situation.

"Three o'clock—out!" he said, pointing to the gateway. Then to soften the matter he smiled, and shook hands warmly, and wished them *gute Reise*.

So the brothers found themselves in the street, and there for a night they stayed. Parking regulations, as elsewhere abroad but not then in England sensibly provided for the extinction of lights on a car if that car was standing near enough to a street lamp for its number to be read. So that in one of the main thoroughfares of Kassel the bus stood undisturbed all night, with Ivor and Derrick asleep in it.

For the next night, seeking to avoid the disturbances of passing traffic, they drove the bus on to the snowbound cobbles of a deserted market square. This would have been most satisfactory if the morrow had not happened to be market-day. They were awakened at five o'clock in the morning by indignant voices around them, and looked out of the window to find themselves completely surrounded by stalls. They stood, it seemed, on a spot consecrated to the use of one of these, for its owners were banging impatiently on the waggon door while the framework of their stall awaited construction and their competitors were already at work. Finally a policemen approached and told the brothers curtly to move off.

They were accustomed to impatient policemen however, and not much impressed. They dressed slowly, while sounds which they took to be abuse rose from the crowd and the policeman, who had lived in England it appeared, attempted to hasten them with brisk instructions.

When at last Derrick got out to swing the starting-handle the policeman made one disgusted comment.

"Fish and chips!" he said, eyeing our road-soiled bus.

As they drove away, the stalls, so the boys told me afterwards, closed in like water over the spot where they had been, so that before they reached the road there was no gap in the market.

On our last night in Kassel they slept again in the street and this produced an incident which, they assured me rightly, was 'one for the book'.

That evening, it seemed, they had been much annoyed by crowds of boys round the waggon who did everything to irritate them, from knocking on the door to throwing snowballs. By methods which were not explained they got rid of the mob, leaving only one survivor, a boy of eleven or twelve, who refused to take flight with the rest. He had shouted, thrown snow, and peered in, and in answer to their efforts to rid themselves of him had grinned.

Derrick then waited until he approached, and threw a cup of water in his face. The child laughed, ran to a safe distance . . . and then returned. He was abused, pelted with snow, and pursued. But he came back. Growing really angry, Derrick crouched in readiness for him with a bucket of water, and next time he came to knock on the waggon door this was thrown right over him. It seemed to strike him as particularly funny. He came near once more.

This time Ivor and Derrick were more impressed than angry. Derrick went to the waggon door and beckoned him in. He immediately climbed into the bus.

"Hanged if I should have", said Derrick telling the story. "I should have thought it was a trap."

But the boy entered, and was soon sitting over the stove drying his clothes, and bringing out the little English he knew. He was already popular with Ivor and Derrick, who liked people with guts. He was cheerful and unembarrassed. Only once in their conversation did he show any sign of distress, and that was when ski-ing was mentioned.

"Do you ski?" asked Ivor.

"I used to", the boy said quietly, and was thoughtful for some minutes.

Next day he took Ivor and Derrick out shopping and to see a cowboy film. He was immensely proud of being able to translate the shopkeepers' German with his few words of English, and to understand the two Englishmen. They enjoyed it.

But that evening in the street they met him with his mother. She stopped them at once, and speaking excellent English thanked them for all they had done.

"My little boy has been so glad of it", she said. "He has been lonely and unhappy lately. You see . . . we're Jews."

Ivor and Derrick, who did not fully understand the implications of this, nodded.

"My husband had a big practice here", she went on. "But we're leaving for America in ten days' time. We shall lose everything, but we feel that even so, it is worth it—for the boy's sake. It is not good for a boy to feel that there is some difference between him and others. So, though it means that we shall start again with nothing, we are leaving."

Ivor and Derrick wished her luck.

"You asked him about ski-ing, didn't you?" she said, "That's rather a sore point, I'm afraid. He was so fond of it— and so good at it, too. But now that we are leaving and could not take them with us we have sold his skis."

She thanked them again, shook hands, and left them.

After that the Rosaires, whose reactions were always direct and not complicated or distorted by newspaper-reading or theorizing, suspected German amiability, even that of Ernst, and detested Nazism.

[7]

There was, I think a subtle change in Ernst since I had stayed with him four months earlier. He had come as near as he ever came to being a victim of propaganda. I remember walking with him and his wife in some public gardens during that Christmas holiday and seeing a couple with two children walking towards us in a lonely part of the park.

"Jews", said Clemens unemotionally.

"Yes, Jews", said Ernst with no particular intonation.

I stopped short while the couple passed out of hearing and said angrily and loudly, "*So what?*"

Ernst and Clemens exchanged rather shamefaced glances and Ernst said at once, as though recollecting himself— "Exactly. So what?"

But their comment, their finding cause to comment, had been spontaneous. That the kind and idealistic boy I had known should have made this invidious remark, however casually, distressed me and I suspected that behind it was more than Ernst would admit. My suspicions, I believe, were unfair, but I could scarcely be blamed for them.

When we discuss that epoch today and Ernst at fifty-odd tries to remember exactly how he felt and to tell me of it, we are baulked by hindsight. Ernst (and by Ernst I mean a few million deluded young Germans), knowing what came of it all, finds it difficult to believe that he was carried along with the tide. He remembers the crisis of 1931, the seven million unemployed which vanished under Hitler, the air of optimism which lifted German morale before 1938. He joined the S.A.

because he could not take his final exams without doing so. He was more bored by it than in revolt—for he wanted to study and practise sport. He managed to be 'ill' on the night of November 9th, 1938. Two things Hitler gave him and his fellows which seemed worth while, enough to live on and a sense of comradeship.

The argument that he *ought* to have known what would come, that Hitler's sick prejudices were fully proclaimed in his book, never seems to me a valid one. Did *we* foresee the future from that farrago? Was it to be expected of my young friend—who was not specially perceptive politically—that having read *Mein Kampf* he should have proclaimed himself in opposition to the tidal wave of general enthusiasm that was sweeping the whole nation along? If there had been any opposition as he grew to an age of judgment he would almost certainly have joined it. But the opposition in Germany had vanished utterly and had become something maintained by prominent intellectuals and socialists who could afford to go abroad. The most Ernst had to give was a measure of open indifference and passivity (he was three times reprimanded for lack of enthusiasm) and a certain secret distaste.

He has told me recently that he remembers that walk and my irritated 'So what?' perfectly well. But it needed, he says, someone from abroad, from outside the range of propaganda, to pull him up with that simple question. He never forgot it and recognized it as the voice of sanity. Four words of dialogue spoken thirty years ago—but they were not for us without a certain sombre significance.

[8]

We left Kassel on New Year's Eve and came that night to the pleasant little town of Kreuzburg. We had motored all the afternoon through the snow, and when we saw the *schloss* on the hills, and the neat town in the valley, with an open space in which to park for the night and the hotel *Zum 'Sonne* throwing its lights over the crisp whiteness of the square, we felt that we need go no farther. There was a dance in the town to which we went and the Rosaires decided to do some acrobatics and found themselves the embarrassed recipients of a public collection. At midnight we were all shaking hands and drinking and shouting *"Prosit Neujahr,"* in complete accord. After a few hours' sleep we were shouting *"Prosit Neujahr!"* again, for at the hotel *Zum 'Sonne* at nine o'clock next morning we found a New Year's hot rum party in full swing, and were invited by the landlord to join him in a glass to bring in 1938.

We passed through Thuringen without incident, the old Morris-Commercial still finding her way confidently through the snow. So far we had not had a moment's delay through a fault of the bus and we felt that even if she broke down now she would have shown her mettle. But she did not break down. Day after day, mile after mile, she continued to throb happily, through Jena and Gera to Donneburg, and then into Saxony, where we spent our last night in Germany and, we considered, our best.

The Rosaires always looked in every stopping-place for a dance and when we found there was to be one in a little town called Geyer, not far from the frontier, we halted. It was a crisp, light evening, and soon around our waggon were half a dozen young ski-ers, boys and girls of seventeen, dressed in flashing colours, with flushed cheeks and that peculiar sparkle which brightens young people who take pleasure in a snow-covered world. They with their skis and we with our Morris-Commercial were the only users of the snow-bound, hilly road that evening, and they stood long at our door gossiping cheerfully, and promised finally to join us later at the dance.

They did, and half the village, it seemed, with them. They were alive with happiness. Talking, dancing, fooling—the air was dizzy with a kind of irresponsible and irrepressible gaiety. Perhaps it was the thick white snow and clear starlit sky outside the dance hall, perhaps it was the Rhine wine which we were drinking for the last time, or perhaps it was our jolly young hosts. For the rest of our trip Geyer was a byword, and when I met Ivor and Derrick afterwards it had become a legend.

CHAPTER THIRTEEN

Czechoslovakia

[1]

IT WAS NOT MERELY the scenery which was different as we drove into Czechoslovakia; there was a clearly perceptible change in the atmosphere, and I use the word in no meteorological sense. From the moment we came into the little town of Weipert and talked to the German-speaking people there we were made conscious that there was constraint and suspicion in the air. It was not only the outward signs of these, and the inconvenience they caused us, but the odd *sense* of tension which predominated. An hotelier at Weipert who came to our table and began to talk amiably enough of our trip, was suddenly checked by a question of mine about the change-over from Austrian to Czech rule in this place.

"We have had twenty years of it", he snapped, "long enough to grow accustomed to the change."

He rose from the table and left us.

This was scarcely to be wondered at in Sudetenland nine months before Munich, but it was impossible not to feel that we had come from a festive optimistic country into a grim and watchful one. Even the bank cashier with whom I changed money seemed jittery. "We are German", he said, "and there are three and a half million of us. Do you think we like . . ." Someone entered behind me and he became suddenly concerned with the correct counting of my notes.

We did not like this frontier town, and decided to attempt the climb to Presnitz. "Try not the pass, the old man said", but our excelsior was curt and determined, for already the police had been to our waggon to inspect our papers, though

173

we had shown them at the frontier a hundred yards away. It was impossible, we were told, to make the climb from the town without skid-chains, and difficult with them. Unpleasant predictions followed us out of the town—that we should be held up by the snow and forced to spend a night if not a week on the bare hillside, or that we should lose our way since the road was too deep under snow to be distinguished.

It was, in fact, a difficult climb. There were times when the bus had to attack drifts as high as her bonnet, and times when she skidded alarmingly. Also it was a dark night, with snow falling and our own headlights dulled by its clinging to their glass. All the way up to Presnitz we met only one other vehicle, a horse-drawn sleigh returning to the light and shelter of the town below. We were axle-deep most of the time, and the gradient was as steep as one in six. There were branches of wayside trees weighted to hang so low that the body of the bus knocked their burden from them. A group of ski-ers, the only human beings we met, stared incredulously at the phenomenon of a foreign bus with its chimney smoking, coughing its way up-hill. But we reached Presnitz before eight o'clock, and drove to the large, deserted market-square.

That town was almost dead, it seemed. In one lugubrious hotel, with a vast lounge and no customers, we drank without enthusiasm, and were told by the waiter that the only amusement in the town that night was a film shown in a concert hall next door. We were a little cheeerd by the Slavonic twist given to the names of film stars, and noted that we should that evening see Edna May Olliverova. But this was soon damped by a visit from the police to our waggon while we were enjoying an evening meal.

"Your papers please", said the official, who had fought his way through the snow to reach us. He kept us with an open door letting in the icy cold for ten minutes while he made a thorough examination of out passports.

In a little *wirtschaft*, which I visited while Ivor and Derrick were changing, was a loquacious drunk from Weipert, who addressed me at once. He spoke of politics as though they were conspiracy, and when he got up to go raised his arm uncertainly.

"*Heil Hitler*", he said then turned to me. "You know we mustn't say that, don't you?" he giggled. "Well, we mustn't. It's forbidden. Mind you, I say it if I want to. I'll say it again. *Heil Hitler*. But it's forbidden." He lurched into the snow.

Presnitz seemed more oppressive as the evening went on. The cinema was half empty and the film badly shown. The streets remained deserted and the few shops were closed. We were glad to get to bed.

But we did not sleep undisturbed. At some time in the small hours of the morning there was a violent knocking on the door of the bus.

"—— off", shouted Derrick from the darkness.

But the knocking continued. We turned over and resolved to ignore it. The waggon was cold and in darkness. Whoever it was would have to knock unanswered.

There were shouts from outside. The knocking grew violent. Someone tried the door.

"What the hell do you want?" called Ivor.

In the long and peremptory answer I caught the word *polizei*.

"Come back later", I shouted in German, but this only brought us a string of commands, to answer, to open the door, to produce our papers.

"But we've done that once", I said, and turned over again.

More knocking. Our visitors began going round the waggon, banging in new places—on the windows, on the door at the back, on the paintwork. Finally Ivor pulled on some clothes found our three passports and handed them out to the two men who stood in the snow. He would not be questioned however. "*Nichts verstehen*", he said brusquely each time the policeman opened his mouth. So that after the passports had been once more examined by electric torchlight, we were left in peace again.

But not for long. We had barely sat down to breakfast at about eight o'clock that morning when two young men in plain clothes arrived. They were civil, even amiable in manner, but their first request was to see our papers.

"Look here", I protested, "we showed our passports at the frontier yesterday and an hour later in Weipert. We were asked for them again last night soon after we reached this place. At dawn this morning we were disturbed by another policeman and showed them to him, and now you come along. Just where is this going to stop? Are we to produce our passports every hour all the time we're in Czechoslovakia?"

The young men were smiling with an air of someone who is only waiting till a tirade is finished in order to deliver a crushing retort.

"Ah!" one of them explained, "but we are *stadt* police—quite a different thing."

Rather sulkily I pulled out the passports again, and once more they were scrutinized.

"Thank you. All in order." They raised their hands to their little furry hats and marched off.

"Come on", said Derrick disgustedly. "Let's get out of this."

So we bolted our breakfast and fled from Presnitz before any other police organization should send their representatives.

[2]

In Prague our spirits rose again. The river was frozen and the whole city deep in snow. The people told us that it was the coldest week they could remember—and we could well believe it. But with its lights streaming brilliantly over white roofs and the soiled snow of the roads, with its cafés steam-heated and its air of hurried abandon, with its hospitality, its ubiquitous orchestras, its friendly people, its freedom and gaiety, it was still "the beautiful city of Prague". We were caught up at once by its movement, we found it hard to leave it a few days later.

We had some difficulty in finding a *tober*, a place to stop for the night. When we approached the city it was already dark and we saw its lights spread out beneath us as though it were a vast illuminated arena. We made for what we supposed would be the centre of the town, and found ourselves parked beside the station, the Bahnhof Wilson. (The American President who helped to give the Czechs their independence was remembered in a street-name.) But we were somewhat puzzled. Several of the people from whom we sought directions as we entered had not spoken German and I knew no Czech.

However, the owner of a car parked next to us helped us. He came to examine the waggon, and volunteered to go with me as interpreter to the nearest police station to ask where we might park for a night or two. I told him of our experiences with the Czech police and said that from these it would seem doubtful if we should get much of a welcome. He brushed that objection aside.

"That is the old Austrian police tradition, persisting in parts of the country where Austrian influence was strongest. You will find them very different here."

He was right, for his inquiry at the police station on our behalf led to a long and solemn discussion. The official in charge was willing enough to help us, it seemed, but Prague was not well provided with camping-sites for Englishmen who arrived in converted buses in the depth of winter—which, I had to admit, was not astonishing. However, after a time the tone of their deliberations seemed to go into a more hopeful key, as the word "Karlin" was repeated. Finally the official took up his telephone.

So serious had been the talk that I only whispered my inquiry to the man who was helping us. "What is he doing?" I asked.

"He is 'phoning to the police of the Karlin area", I was told.

"What is the Karlin?"

"An open square on which the soldiers drill."

Presently the telephone conversation was finished and our interpreter explained: "You can go to the Karlin square for tonight", he said. "The superintendent has obtained permission from the Karlin police."

"Good. And thank you so very much."

But he had not finished yet. He found a youth in the street outside who agreed for a small tip to guide us to the Karlin. So by nine o'clock we were settled there, in a sheltered corner of a big barrack square over which the icy wind carried drifts of fine snow and the sentries looked like figures in a film version of Napoleon's retreat from Moscow.

I had an introduction to a Czech writer named Vincy Schwarz. He was an immensely kind and hospitable man and readily gave up his time to showing me Prague. I have rarely met anyone whose life was so filled with gusto. He talked, ate, sang, and moved as though driven by it. He was a big untidy fellow with hair tumbling about on a large head. His cheeks were crimson and his eyes merry. Life was the most enjoyable joke to him—every minute of it.

That afternoon he marched me round the city, into the offices of Karel Čapek's newspaper which was running a novel of mine as a serial, down to the frozen river, into cafés, talking and laughing volubly. When evening came, and he had collected a few friends, we started to explore more cafés and restaurants, and to talk. Our whole party went to a *weinstube* where there was a typical Slovak orchestra, and settled round a large table to drink dry light wine and gossip. The orchestra wore its national costume and when we entered it was playing a stirring folk song.

The orchestra was remarkable. Its six or eight musicians had stolid, happy faces—they were from one remote village in the Slovak hills, and though they played their own music most vividly they had no musical education. With their embroidered shirts and boots, with the faces of men born to a land-working tradition, they used their instruments delicately, but they looked bovine.

"This is a peasant dance they are playing", said Vincy Schwarz, "I think they will dance."

Soon some young people rose and facing one another started the intricate steps of a country dance. There was a soldier in uniform among them, enjoying himself immensely.

"You see", said Vincy Schwarz, "that our democracy is more than a word. The man at the next table is a colonel."

The atmosphere grew more lively. The orchestra was challenging the dancers to greater activity.

"It's very like Hungarian music, isn't it?"

"Yes. But more sentimental usually. If you compare the themes of our folk songs with theirs you will find that ours are concerned with love and friendship, memory and regrets, while the Hungarians sing more often of heroism and warfare."

"It's fine."

"You must tell the leader of the orchestra that", said Vincy Schwarz, and when the dance ended he called him over. Slovakia was his home, it appeared, a fine rugged old fellow, with the voice and physique of a young man, though he was well into his sixties. He was pleased with a foreigner's enthusiasm and when I remarked on the beautiful embroidery of his shirt he insisted that he should give me one which he had at home. It arrived next morning at the waggon, with a message saying that not only had it been embroidered by his daughter—the work of several months—but that its linen had been hand-woven by her. It was an enviable possession.

We moved on from that *weinstube* to a little pub in a poorer quarter of Prague. Under a vaulted ceiling, like that of an ancient wine-cellar, we sat at bare wooden tables which had been scrubbed to whiteness and listened to another orchestra, this time led by a gypsy youth of sixteen. There were old mural paintings—the usual design of wine-press and flowing beer-mugs, jolly old crimson faces and white beards. The floor was bare, and the other customers were working-men and women with a soldier or two and a group of students. The building, so Vincy Schwarz told me, was of the thirteenth or fourteenth century, and it had been an inn, he believed, ever since it was built. It seemed to me characteristic of this city—an air of old Bohemia overlarded with the Austrian paintings, and now crowded with festive Czechs. We ordered food and some more of the country's good white wine, and they brought us *kebbab* which we ate pretty readily.

Vincy Schwarz, always in high spirits, was irrepressible. He was singing with the orchestra, releasing a big baritone voice to its full, and pausing only to eat with as much vigour as he did everything else. A big Rabelaisian type he looked as he ate, and sang, and drank, and laughed. The boy who led the orchestra came and played his violin into our ears, and smiled with dignified ingratiation. That was his father, he told us presently, who played the second violin. Why was he the leader and not his father? Because he was a better musician, of course. As he answered our questions he continued to play mechanically and smile.

The whole atmosphere of the stone-walled room was exciting. The smell of our rich food, the carafes of good cheap wine, the grinning, slightly perspiring dancers, the passionate music, and Vincy Schwarz bellowing melodiously to the ceiling. When the dance-music became modern, Ivor and Derrick rose and took the girls from our party out on the stone floor.

"The *csardas* itself is Slovak in origin", said Vincy Schwarz. "The Slovaks have a great tradition, you know. Few of you in Western Europe have bothered much about those people. But they're very interesting. Their civilization is older than yours or the German", he added.

[3]

Next day we went by taxi across the river, and climbed to the Hof and saw the old Hapsburg palace in which the President lived, and stood for nearly half an hour looking out over that splendid city. It was in this very spot that nine months later

Hitler stood as we did looking at the lights stretched out beneath him. "I never knew that Prague could be so beautiful", he was unctuously reported to have said.

Descending, we found a restaurant where we ate enormously of roast venison—at six o'clock in the evening of a day in which we had had no time for lunch. Then we spent two cheerful days shopping, eating, dancing, talking, exploring, before we realized that we had to move on.

We left early one morning—but not too early for Vincy Schwarz who came to see us off. He brought to the waggon an immense ham, cured in the inimitable Prague way. It was the finest ham I have ever tasted and it lasted us right through Austria and into Hungary. He brought, too, with great pride, a bottle each of Merunkovice and Slivovice, the fiery Vodka-like liqueurs of the country, and told us how there were peasant songs that celebrated them: "Drink a glass of Slivovice, the best medicine", and so on. While he stood by the waggon talking, there was a scuffle and three small boys appeared. Their faces were roughly and patchily blackened with burnt cork, and they wore paper crowns on their heads.

"The Three Kings!" explained Vincy Schwarz. "On this day every year the children go round the city in this disguise and sing their carol."

He spoke to them, and standing by the bus they piped in chorus, with a little acting, their song. They were not in the least shy, even of the foreigners who listened to them. But they must have been cold, for the chill in the air was keener that morning and we were glad to return to our heaped-up coal stove as we climbed in to move away.

Vincy Schwarz and his wife waited till we actually started to move so that they could wave us good-bye. That was the last I saw of them for, Jews and Liberals, they perished, after fearful humiliations and privations, in extermination camps.

I salute their memory, to which I have dedicated this book. For me they stand for the six million, among whom were many thousands of gypsies, who died with them. It is futile to write of

that now or to try to conceive the proportions of that crime—
like trying to imagine eternity or an unending universe. But I
had as a friend for five days, a generous and great-hearted
friend, one man at least whom I *know* to have suffered that fate,
and only through the one or two he knew can a man's mind
begin to encompass the whole tragedy. That six million people
were deliberately massacred in or out of death camps must
necessarily, by the mere fact that I can calmly pronounce the
words, convey very little of its dreadful meaning. That my
friend Vincy Schwarz and his wife and six million of their
fellows so died begins to have some vestiges of reality. Enough,
almost, for me to desire the same fate for those cretins, publicity-
seekers or criminals who dare to speak of neo-Nazism. Enough
certainly for me to hope that mankind, till the end of time, will
keep a mouthful of spittle for the memory of Hitler and his
minions who were directly, personally responsible for it.

[4]

That night we stayed at Nemecký Brod, which looked like
a Russian village with snow-covered minarets. This was
Bohemia as I had always pictured it. The snow lay more thickly
here than in any other town we had visited and the windows of
houses seemed to be peering out from a white wall. There was
little sign of motor traffic—a sleigh or two, a few ski-ers and
a snow-plough were all we had passed for the last ten miles.

But this place, was more cheerful than German-speaking
Czechoslovakia had been, the bars were crowded, the shops
attractive and busy and a pleasant Kavarna where we had tea
was not unlike an English provincial café on a weekday afternoon—cake-munching women and a good deal of busy talking.

Next morning there was sunlight over the snow, and the
little town as we left it looked brilliant and rather beautiful.
Our road from there was lonely, with only an occasional small

village to break the dazzling white of the bare hillsides. We saw wild deer, and disturbed a covey of partridges, which made the brothers curse for the twentieth time at the impossibility of carrying guns.

Our last evening in Czechoslovakia was the saddest. We stayed at a village called Pohorelice. The inhabitants, who were quite friendly and talkative, groaned openly at their poverty and the poverty of this area. The pub was almost empty, the few customers drank poor wine at less than a penny a glass.

"A farm worker round here is lucky if he earns six kronen a day", they said. When the Rosaires asked whether there was anything to do in the village they were surprised at the question.

"What money we had was spent at Christmas. People here must stay in their houses at night for a month or two before they can afford to amuse themselves again."

One old fellow was pointed out to me as "a rich man", but as soon as he got me alone for a moment he tried to sell me his gold watch. It was all rather depressing, and when a young Czech officer appeared and asked through a German-speaking policeman to see our passports, and made the usual inquiries about our destination and last stopping place, we were conscious of a certain constraint in the room, and were glad to go back to the waggon and turn in.

[5]

I treasure the memory of those ten days in Czechoslovakia for I recognize as I look back that I was hearing the last gasp of a nation created and destroyed within my life-time. The miserable alien thing that Stalin made of the country, the slave state of the 1940's and 1950's, may one day give birth to a free people and that indestructible portent, the national character, may be roused from its torpid acquiescence under totalitarianism. But probably not in my lifetime, and I am grateful for the mere glimpse I caught of the country before its long night set in.

CHAPTER FOURTEEN

Austria

[1]

NOWHERE WAS THE futility of my scheme to 'interview the man in the street' more obvious than in Austria. For this was a country of café politics where everyone had his solution to political problems and was quite willing to state it. In order to gain any sort of balance of opinion I ought to have heard from Social Democrats, Christian Socialists, Royalists and Nazis, all equally articulate and convinced. Even this would have produced nothing cogent. I see from the book I wrote at the time that I was very wise about the people's expectations of Hitler's coming, but this was written after the event for almost as we drove out of Austria Hitler entered.ᵍ

But if I learned nothing to add to anyone's political knowledge of Europe, I gained personal impressions which are fresh today, I saw something of the tragic city of Vienna to which I have never returned, I was intensely interested, as I was in most places, but here with more feeling and sense of doom than elsewhere on my route.

A. J. P. Taylor, whose book *The Habsburg Monarchy* is something of a classic, has said two very enlightening things about the *Anschluss* which was about to come. "It seems to have been Hitler's original intention merely to establish a Nazi government in Austria . . . but once on Austrian soil Hitler was intoxicated by the general enthusiasm and proclaimed the union with Germany. A plebiscite on April 10, held throughout 'greater Germany', recorded a vote of more than 99 per cent in favour of Hitler. It would be an error to dismiss this vote as meaningless

ᵍ More accurately five weeks later on March 12th, 1938.

or forced. Though many Austrians were not yet nazis they welcomed incorporation into Germany almost unanimously. Even the Socialist Renner, then living in retirement, welcomed the anschluss." Of that general enthusiasm there cannot be much doubt. It was Hitler's one annexation which pleased the vast majority of the people annexed. The other thing said by Taylor is: "When World War II came, many observers in the west who had previously admired either traditional Austria or Austrian social democracy looked to Austria for a heroic resistance. Nothing of the sort occurred. The Austrian Germans were if anything more loyal to Hitler than even the Germans of the old reich, and many of the worst nazi atrocities were committed by S.S. (*Schutz Staffel*) divisions from Austria. This was especially true in the Balkans, where Austrians resumed, under different auspices, the civilizing mission of terror and persecution which they had once exercised under the Habsburgs."

This seems only too likely, for that unhappy people, left by the Treaty of Versailles without a means of livelihood, believed that Hitler came as a saviour to relieve them from years of hunger and misery, of political oppression and desperate unemployment. When they in turn felt disillusionment it was too late to withdraw.

But all this is in retrospect. I came to Austria in that January of 1938 very ignorant of the country's recent history. I doubt if I knew why Dollfuss had been murdered or what Schuschnigg represented. After *White Horse Inn* and all that I was sick of the notion of Vienna as the dizzy home of waltzes, elaborate uniforms, court gaiety and curtseying peasants and did not expect many relics of these to survive. But I was not prepared to find only the miserable empty shell of a great capital with a population of human rats frolicking wildly in its gutters.

[2]

We crossed into Austria with a blinding snow-storm. There was a Czech officer at the frontier post wearing one of those immense fur hats such as one sees in films of Czarist Russia.

"Smashing titfor", Derrick remarked, and I wanted to take a photograph of it. But the officer became very excited when I produced my camera, and pointed out that we were in a military zone. So we set out on the long climb to Poysdorf.

That was one of the most difficult stretches of roads which the bus had to negotiate. There was a steep ascent and drifts in places were several feet deep. When we came on a number of cars already stuck in the snow near the crest of one hill, and saw a horse-drawn snow-plough advancing from the other direction, it really looked for a time as though we should have to spend the next few days there. We were well-provisioned, of course, and had an adequate coal supply, so that even that prospect was not too scarifying.

But we got through. Ivor and Derrick went to the assistance of the cars ahead and appeared to lift them bodily out of their troubles. This is not so far-fetched as it sounds, for it was always their custom if a locked car impeded our exit from a close-packed parking place to lift its rear by the buffer and move it gently aside. That morning the two of them, assisted by the half-dozen men in charge of the snow-plough and the motorists themselves, with a good deal of unintelligible shouting at one another, cleared the way, and we got through to Poysdorf.

In that pleasant village there was a horse fair in progress and the inn was crowded. There were gypsies and dealers, and we were glad to be among so much noise and activity after the lonely gloom of our last days in Czechoslovakia. Indeed, so pleasing did we find this that although we had originally intended to leave for Vienna that afternoon, we made a splendid lunch of *schnitzel* and decided to stay the night. We did not regret it. For that evening there was a cellar party.

Poysdorf, it appeared, was the centre of a vine-growing district, and scarcely an inhabitant of the place was without his cellar. Some of them are as large as cathedral crypts, others hold only a barrel or two, but each is sufficient to provide a living of some sort for its owner. The one we visited belonged to Frau Flora Wild, who presided cheerfully over the scene in its brightly lit interior. There was a score of us, perhaps, and by a glass siphoning device we were enabled to taste most of her wines right down to the raw 1937-er. It was all very hilarious, and it was late when we left it to walk back through the snow to the café, and to the vast covered yard or cattle-shed in which our waggon was to stand for the night.

[3]

Next day we drove into Vienna and for the ten days which followed I am distrustful, for the first time in writing these books, of the accuracy of my own memory. Not in factual details—I know what I did well enough, where I went, whom I met—but in the all-over picture I have of the place and my recollection of the atmosphere which prevailed. I cannot believe that it was such a necropolis as I see in retrospect, or that such violent contrast can have existed between the vast imperial state buildings and the miles of dreary tenements, between the few rich and greasy citizens one met in the places of amusement which still flourished and the hordes of shivering but insanely cheerful rag-pickers from the doss-houses and sleeping-dens of the city. Nor can I believe that such dense and icy gloom and empty silence could settle on its cavernous half-lit streets. If the picture I see is only half true, however, it gives explanation enough for the tumultuous acclamation of Hitler five weeks later. If the Devil himself had promised these people bread and work they would have fallen at his feet.

But whether distorted or not I prefer the picture in my

memory now to the account I wrote of Vienna a few weeks after my visit when I was already aware of the *Anschluss*, and I find the conversations reported then—accurately enough, I daresay —irrelevant and insignificant.

I spent several days in sightseeing, driving by taxi to the incredible Ringstrasse and gaping at the elaborate Renaissance buildings raised by the Habsburgs. The Ringstrasse itself, two miles in length and 150 feet wide, was so opulent, so monstrously grand that it reminded me of the American's remark on seeing Randolph Hearst's home at Santa Barbara—"Think what God could have done if He'd had the money!"

I remember clearly visiting the vast ornate Opera House built in a vulgar French early Renaissance style and seeing what is perhaps the world's most pretentious staircase. Naturally the place was empty for I went in the morning but it made me feel that it had been empty since Franz Josef descended those stairs attended by over-dressed courtiers and would be empty —at least of the kind of people for whom it was built—for the rest of time. Everywhere this monumental grandeur in stone surrounded by enormous parks and gardens, museums, libraries, palaces, hotels, most of them without visitors, all suggesting vanished prosperity.

I went to see the church of St Rupprecht, the only church known to me dedicated to my patron saint and was told its foundations were laid in the eighth century. But unguided as I was I missed most of the other old buildings of which there are plenty and seemed to move through a nightmare of nineteenth-century architecture imposing rather than beautiful, culminating in the Hofburg, the former imperial palace.

Meanwhile our waggon stood in a smelly backyard in one of the poorer suburbs. We had driven in on a Sunday when the streets were more than usually bleak and sordid and scarcely anyone was to be seen in that neighbourhood. On my first afternoon I found Turkish baths only a few yards from where we had parked and anxious to rid myself of traveller's grime I went in. The rooms were old and frowsty but retained marble evidence of their importance in former times. Round the swimming-pool rather more than a dozen youths, some built like weight-lifters and some delicate and pretty, aged between fourteen and twenty-four, offered their bodies with the artificial wantonness of skilled prostitutes to a few elderly patrons for a shilling or two, their rags left out of sight, a scene from the *Satyricon*. All over the city in cafés and bars there were scenes of similar significance. An empire in decay, one thought inevitably, a great people degraded.

The cafés were for the most part of the old order—red plush and gilt mirrors—as though they had been decorated at great cost and in the most up-to-date style some thirty years ago, and their trade had not justified more than another coat of gold paint since the Empire had fallen. Men would come in to spend an hour or two of the morning, for a great proportion of the bourgeoisie of Vienna had thrown up all attempt at commerce, and if they could scrape together enough to live even in anxious poverty, they preferred it to the imponderable chances against them in any form of enterprise.

Mad dreams were voiced over coffee. There were Royalists who believed Schuschnigg meant to restore the monarchy, there were Nazis who believed that their party would come to power without the intervention of Hitler and rule Austria as an independent country, there were Socialists who hoped to bring back the days of Christian Democrat rule. There were those who thought prosperity would miraculously return and old men who had seen a different city where Vienna now spread and who talked of the Austrian Empire as though somewhere it still existed.

In the little cabarets and night bars there was that kind of cynical and abandoned clowning which I had seen in similar *lokales* in Cologne and Aachen in pre-Hitler days. We went to several of them and watched the lewd idiotic horseplay. Whom the gods wish to destroy they first drive mad.

There was still plenty of eating of excellent food in public restaurants, and of paunchy men to order and demolish large

G

dishes. Women, I thought, were seen in places of entertainment less than in most great cities. But there was begging, too, and though I had known beggars in Spain and Portugal, only here and in London just after the 1914–18 war had I seen able-bodied men reduced to begging in the streets—a sickening phenomenon.

Yet what was both heart-rending and macabre was the ghastly cheerfulness of almost everybody. Vienna positively grinned. The only solemn people I remember were the well-to-do business men in cafés, the anxious Jews and the proprietors of the few flourishing restaurants. The rest of the population showed they had nothing to lose, even if Hitler came.

CHAPTER FIFTEEN

Hungary

[1]

THERE WAS SOMETHING in the very idea of Hungary that was more foreign than anything I had seen, as though it was not part of Europe at all. I had read a little of the history of the Magyar people but as far as I knew had never met any of them and I felt an intense curiosity about them and their city of Budapest.

From our first drive over a frozen and desolate plain to the cathedral town of Gyor, till we crossed the bridge which divided Hungary from Yugoslavia a fortnight later I was in a condition which without much exaggeration might be called one of trance. I thought Budapest the most splendid and attractive city I had seen and even now, after visiting many fine cities of Africa and Asia, I know that if it still existed as it was then I would make my home there. It was not that Hungary was a paradise. In a country of such violent contrast between poverty and riches, between great luxury and conditions of near-starvation, it was impossible merely to enjoy oneself untouched by an uncomfortable shame at eating luxurious food. But it had a quality of surprise, of difference from all I had known or imagined, which gave me back the boyhood thrill of first being abroad.

It was a personal and covetous affection I instantly felt for Budapest. I wanted it to be my home. I wanted to take a flat like those to which I was invited, overlooking the Danube and the city, and live among these strange and beautiful people for the rest of my life, lulled into faith in the future by the unceasing music of Tziganes. I wanted to learn the language which seemed so vigorous and lively, to wear fantastic fur-tipped clothes, to *join* the life I saw about me. No other country had affected me so immediately and so deeply—I was more than captivated, I was bewitched. This was all very young and not a little silly, but it was sincere enough to have given me, from that time till now, such a close interest in the destiny of Hungary and its people that I have studied their history, learned what I can from translations of their literature and been made unhappy by their misfortunes and proud by their heriosm.

Hungary is the only country of eastern Europe that has attempted to defy Russian imperialism, the only country of which one knows for certain that however long she suffers she will never become reconciled to the inhumanity of Marxism, the only country whose example gives hope to the Balkans and Poland. Politically we have misunderstood her motives and actions from 1938 onwards and failed to recognize the daring of Horthy in 1944 when, with Hungary occupied by German troups he ordered that the deportation of Jews by Hitler should cease and—too late to help those of country districts—saved the great Jewish population of Budapest from the gas-chambers. We saw Hungary stripped of equipment, skilled workers, of everything portable and valuable by the slowly retreating Germans and then ravaged—in a very literal sense—by the vast Soviet occupying forces. And when at last she made her despairing attempt to achieve independence all we could send to her aid was a batch of hysterical journalists who wrote stories of their own adventures in Budapest. These things I have felt most keenly, as though of an adopted country, though all I know directly of Hungary was learned in that fortnight's stay, twenty-eight years ago.

[2]

Entering the country at noon we drove in weird and oppressive solitude across a snowy plain, passing no traffic and seeing no human habitation except where a village of one-storey houses seemed itself almost deserted. But at dusk we came to Gyor and it was well-lit and lively after the small towns of Austria.

I had never drunk Tokay and went to a wine-bar to do so. Unprepared for its sweetness, unaware of its qualities as a dessert wine, I was disappointed in the first draught, though I came to enjoy it later. The wine-bar was crowded and we watched a succession of bottles being filled for housewives and workers on their way home. More than anywhere, since we had left England, were the people 'foreign'. Their faces, their clothes, their manner—they brilliantly contrasted with all that I knew—Teuton, Slav, or Latin. I liked their little astrakhan caps, and the scrappy bits of fur that everyone managed to have on his coat collar, and the dark lean intelligent faces, and their vivacity. I remember seeing a student of seventeen or eighteen, his overcoat braided across with lines of cord like a Ruritanian court official's and skirted out from the waist while a bright coloured student's cap was on his head. He was talking excitedly to a group of friends and there was a pleasant swagger in his manner. This was the first time I had seen people dressed in a way that owed more to nineteenth-century Russia than to western Europe.

We dined in a large hotel and I heard my first Tzigane orchestra. Although only about six tables were occupied there were no less than eight violins, an omen of the lack of proportion in all things which amiably characterized Hungary.

As we sat smoking some iniquitous black cigarettes with hollow pasteboard tips to them, one of the Rosaires suggested that we should drive right on to Budapest that night. I wish now I had remained in Gyor for a while and seen its cathedral and driven out to the great Benedictine abbey of Pannonhalma which was founded by the Saint and King Stephen. But although we had left Vienna that morning and had been delayed by documents at the frontier this sudden idea of a long night drive was attractive and I was impatient to reach Budapest. So we set off at about ten o'clock.

It was exciting. We drove along a lonely road with our headlights showing no more than an occasional peasant and a group or two of soldiers. For ten miles the only vehicle we passed was a farm cart on which were hung long lines of dead hares. There must have been a hundred or more of them, and they seemed in our brief glimpse to be abnormal in size.

But suddenly there were lanterns being waved across the road in front of us, and we pulled up. A dozen Hungarian soldiers crowded round our bus, and one of them, a non-commissioned officer I suppose, came to the door and began to talk in Magyar. Hitherto French or German had carried us everywhere, but this was beyond me, and we were reduced to making signs of incomprehension.

"Does anyone speak German?" I asked the group. They shivered slightly but no one answered.

There was a conference among them, and one of them apparently saw the G.B. on the back of our bus, for the non-commissioned officer said something like "Angol" and I nodded. At the same time Ivor, remembering Czechoslovakia, produced our passports, which were handed round the whole group and seemed to have a big success as objects of interest—particularly the photographs.

However, it was cold with the door of the waggon open, and as the conversation did not seem to be leading anywhere we indicated by signs that we wanted to continue on our way. This led to a further, but a briefer, conference, after which the officer saluted and signalled us on.

That was only one of our stops during the long night's drive. By bright moonlight we saw through the trees the gleam of water, and realized that it was the Danube. Within a few hundred yards of it we came to a lighted inn and pulled up again. As soon as our engine was stopped we heard a low rather whining music in the air, and knew that here was yet another Tzigane orchestra.

Inside everything was topsy-turvy and squalid. The inn-keeper was dozing at his bar, and there were two men who (we

gathered later) were the lonely crew of one of the great rafts
going to the Black Sea, and moored here for the night. They
were half tipsy with cheap wine, and lolled over their table.
But in a corner were three gypsies quite self-possessed and happy
in making music. I think they had long since forgotten their
listeners and though they had started playing for pence were
playing now for the sheer pleasure of it. They swept through a
form of the familiar *csardas*, and smiled to us—such unlikely
and welcome intruders.

On again then to a point on a steep hill where the road was
barred by an oncoming cart, far too heavily loaded, which had
a wheel stuck fast. The three men in charge had apparently
given up hope of inducing their team of tired horses to shift it,
and were standing about disconsolately with the fur collars of
their coats up to their ears and their short pipes glowing. This
was the kind of task that appealed most to Ivor and Derrick, as
though it carried them back to their daily round with the
circus for which they were never without some homesickness.
They jumped out and with little or no reference to the carters
set about stirring the horses, shoving, encouraging and leading,
until the men were heartened into joining them, and finally the
wheel was free. It was an odd scene to watch by the light of our
headlamps—the Hungarians bewildered by the arrival of these
competent foreigners, and the brothers shouting instructions to
both men and horses which must have been as incomprehensible
to one as the other.

After that we needed yet another stop for rest and refreshment
and this time were luckier, for we met the first Hungarian on
the road who spoke German. He was a publican in a wayside
tavern, no more than fifteen miles from Budapest. He spoke
most bitterly, not of his government, for he believed that "one
government would be as bad as another", but of living conditions in the rural districts of Hungary.

"A farm labourer", he told us, "is lucky if he earns two
pengos a day. He might have to work ten hours for that. And
even then he is out of work for months in the slack seasons."

I made the inevitable query. "But how does he live?" I asked.

"There is no absolute minimum of wages on which human beings can keep alive. How much does it cost to keep a dog? They live somehow."

We asked for beer, and he laughed.

"Beer? What sale should I have for beer? It costs money. I sell wine here at twopence a litre."

Another half-hour brought us within sight of the city lights, and because it was now past midnight and we had done the longest day's drive of our tour—from Vienna—we stopped there on the verge of the roadside, rather than go down and look for a parking-place for the remaining hours of darkness.

[3]

When we came into the city next morning and asked where we should put the bus, a yard was found for us in an area not five minutes from the busy centre of Pest, yet in one of those unformed, unfinished districts such as I had previously seen only in South American cities. Houses half-built, with no sign of workmen or work on them, a stony piece of field with a new shop facing it, a sudden high tenement block standing starkly and miserably alone. The yard we stood in adjoined a large new garage, equipped with modern contrivances and half a dozen mechanics, while we could scarcely reach our waggon for mud and lean dogs, and the only building on the patch was a lean-to shack of two rooms, in which seemed to live an incalculably large family. Yet as I turned into the main streets I was fascinated at once by the variety and quality of things displayed in shop windows, by the countless inviting restaurants, by the crowded well-dressed and cheerful people, by the air of contented preoccupation.

We went, on our first evening, to a large café called the Ostende, a noisy place which advertised alternating orchestras.

As we came in, the platform was crowded with young gypsies, for a boys' Tzigane orchestra, forty strong, was playing with tremendous zest. Some of the musicians can scarcely have been more than ten years old, and the majority of them, the waiter told us, could not read music, while some could not read at all. There was the usual display of long black hair thrown back impatiently by the violinists, and of brilliant dark eyes and quick grins. But after a time the whole mob scrambled down from the platform and a Spanish orchestra was announced.

Spanish it was—authentic enough. A dozen men took their places, and in a moment were playing flamenco music. They contrasted strongly with their excitable young predecessors—they were grave and confident, their movements seeming automatic. As they began to play a girl joined them on the platform, and for the first time the chattering audience gave its full attention.

She was slim and blonde, and looked barely seventeen. She wore a conventional Spanish dancer's costume, with mantilla and comb. She was exquisite. Her movements had the ripple of rope held high and gently shaken. Ivor and Derrick at once made appropriate exclamations.

When it was over and the gypsy boys were playing again, we went up to a little gallery overlooking the café which was reserved for the musicians. The orchestra, it seemed, was a hastily gathered one of exiled musicians who had escaped from Spain, and when I asked them what it was like in Madrid they all began to talk at once about the horrors, the poverty, the brutality, the madness they had seen. But they spoke with the appalling cynicism which was heard in the stories of exiled Spaniards everywhere and of both sides. They showed the wounds of their country, it seemed, almost as a matter of conversational interest rather than as though they themselves felt the anguish of them. They had stories in all the well-known categories—a mother shot in front of her children, members of the religious communities tortured and killed, arrogance and tyranny of those in power, callous indifference towards all suffering, muddle, selfishness, starvation.

G*

"We are the lucky ones—we who have escaped. That fellow
. . ." the man talking indicated a stout and smiling musician
across the table, "was put in a firing squad to shoot his own
brother. That one was the owner of a big cabaret theatre.
We're all ruined", he ended cheerfully, "and all lucky."

"And your little dancer?"

"Oh you must meet her. She's half English."

He went to fetch the girl who had danced and her mother—
and we found the latter to be a tall Englishwoman who had
lived in Madrid for many years.

"My daughter is less than fifteen years old", she said, "how
did you like her dancing?"

Derrick gave me no chance to reply, and the four of them
were soon happily conversing in English.

These were refugees of a kind new to me, for the great
exodus from Spain across the French frontier had not then
begun. In these weeks while I had been travelling in comfort
and great happiness through Czechoslovakia and Austria there
had been fought what Hugh Thomas calls 'the atrocious battle
of Teruel', one of the grimmest engagements of this bloody
century, unmatched in ghastliness till the battle of Stalingrad.
At Teruel, with the temperature at 18 below zero, the British
volunteers had suffered most cruelly, both in conditions and in
casualties, and there were many who believed that here the
fate of the Spanish Republic was sealed. Rarely seeing an
English newspaper and unable to understand more than the
gist of news in German I knew of this and was surprised to
find that the Spaniards knew nothing at all and seemed to care
less. They had turned their backs on Spain and did not want to
know. They were sardonically cheerful. Nothing, it seemed,
could hurt them any more. There was a callousness in their
stories such as I had not heard in those of any man who had been
through the First World War. They were not interested in
other countries, even as possible refuges. They lived wholly for
the day's bread.

[4]

We lunched next day at the Debreceni Restaurant, a place usually recommended to visitors who asked where they could find 'typical' Hungarian food, a sort of Budapest version of Simpsons. That evening we were taken by a young Hungarian writer to the Café Japon, which might have been called, by those who like to find these parallels, the Café Royal of Budapest. Here we accumulated a considerable party of the writer's friends, journalists, young intellectuals, artists of both sexes, perhaps a dozen in all.

"Come on", suggested one of the young Hungarians at last, "can't you forget about politics for a bit? We'll all go across to a café in Buda and dance. We'll find some gypsies there."

So we climbed on to a creaking tram-car and set out for the other side of the river.

At that time I had nothing but a mild and sentimental interest in gypsies. Later I should come to know them, learn their language (or what remains of it in England) study their history and write three books about them, but in 1938 they were a picturesque and mysterious people to me and no more.

We found them in a café in a narrow street of very old houses. There were only three of them, all elderly men, and they had been playing since six o'clock. Unlike those in the band we had seen on our way to Budapest, and unlike the big orchestra of zigeuner boys at the Café Ostende, these men had lived most of their lives in cities, and though they were of purest gypsy blood, one spoke French and German, another French, and all three fluent Magyar.

The cymbalist had had the most cosmopolitan experience. He was, he told us, in his seventies, and did not look at all out of place in a neat black, rather threadbare suit. The leader, on the other hand, was of the lean-faced, black-eyed type, with lank dark hair, who would have been more at home in the traditional costume.

They had seen a great deal of the world one way and another, always as musicians, with a collecting plate as their sole means of support.

"I have never been paid a salary in my life", said the cymbalist, "and I've had some pretty lean times. But good times too", he added chuckling. "I was in Paris before the War and earned as much as two hundred francs in an evening. You could buy something with a franc in those days."

Ivor and Derrick, who had had more experience of gypsies than I had, were inclined to be sceptical of everything the old man told us. "Didakais are all liars", they said quietly to me, and when I tried to make the three zigeuners talk about their race and its origins, Derrick warned me that they would say nothing even if they knew.

There was a streak of morning light in the sky when we made our way back to Pest.

[5]

Now we had friends who were anxious to show us about and every day seemed to bring some new revelation to life in that dazzling and ragged capital. For instance, there was the *kubikos* whom we met in the Viaduct Bierhaus. A *kubikos*, it was explained to us by the young Hungarian who took us to this place, was the poorest and most wretched of the Budapest workers, a man who in type, occupation, and condition was much like the pre-revolution Russian *moujik*. Strayed somehow from the country, and out of place in the town, he was a creature lost between the two. His entire worldly possessions consisted of a shovel and broom perhaps, which he pushed along in an old barrow, and with which he attempted somehow to earn a living. At the end of a gruelling day in the fierce heat of the summer, or half frozen after ten hours of winter work, he considered himself lucky if he got a couple of pengos.

The Viaduct Bierhaus was a little cave of a pub hollowed out under the road, and filled with thunderous noise whenever a tram ran overhead. It was dark and dirty, and the only customers beside ourselves and the *kubikos* were a drunken group of prostitutes and tram-drivers who were singing as they swayed their heads loosely on their shoulders.

The *kubikos* sat alone. He, too, was half stupid with drink, his large unshaven face lolling over the table.

"What is he drinking?" I asked.

"Probably *palinka*. That's a kind of raw spirit. Villainous stuff—but very cheap. Perhaps he has had a bit of luck today. They don't usually get up this end of the town at all. Wait— I'll call him over."

He made a sign, and the fellow rose slowly to his feet and lurched across the room, then stood over us blinking without a smile. Our friend told him to sit down, and ordered some more *palinka* for him, then began to question him. The other answered in short, grunted sentences, almost like an animal or a half-mute trying to speak.

"He says he slept last night under cover at the Teleketir. His wife has gone today to look for some work."

"What kind of work?"

My friend told me without referring again to the man.

"Oh, she would try to get a few pence by cleaning out someone's yard. They can work like horses, however frail they look."

"And what has he been doing?"

The man grinned when he was asked this, and again grunted a short reply.

"He has been down at the docks since four o'clock this morning." (It was now eight at night.) "And has earned two pengos. He says he is having a drink before he meets his wife."

The waiter brought us some *pogacsa*, little salted cakes made of coarse flour, and the man began to munch earnestly.

"Ask him if he is a Communist."

My friend shook his head. "He won't be", he said. "He

doesn't even know what Communism is, probably. You must remember that he can't read or write."

"But ask him", I insisted.

When he heard the question the *kubikos* looked bewildered and shook his head.

"No, he's just a poor devil who wants food and drink, and will work like two men for them. He knows nothing of politics, or of other nations, except what he learnt in fighting against them during the War. Yes, he was part of the glorious army of the Austrian Empire. Ah, well, he's happy this evening."

[6]

We visited, too, the Telekitér, the market which had provided our *kubikos* with his night's shelter. It covered a large area, and there were avenues of huddled stalls. Articles of every kind from clothes to vegetables, from boots to furniture, new and second-hand, were displayed in astonishing profusion. There was a covered hall in the centre in which the atmosphere defeated our best intentions to explore, but we walked among the open-air stalls inquisitively. Progress was made difficult by continuous and persistent tugging at our arms by the stall-holders, who flatteringly tried every language but our own. Almost all of them were Jews, many of them bearded and dressed in black, proud of their traditional racial appearance, although the first warnings of anti-Semitism were already in the air. From one, a humorous and courtly old man with a handsome son I bought, after an hour's hard bargaining, a rather splendid fur coat which I wore, though never quite without self-consciousness, in every spell of hard weather until I joined the army nearly three years later. Certain changes were made in it by a tailor while I waited listening to the father and son who spoke German. They were deeply religious and at the same time enjoyed a joke, and I have noticed often in my life that

real devoutness and honest piety go with a love of laughter in
people of every creed, the strictest Non-Conformists in England,
Catholics and especially those in monastic orders, Muslims and
Hindus. I have hoped since that the old man and his son and
other gentle people I spoke to in the Telekitér were among
those whom Horthy managed to save from the gas-chambers
but it seems tragically unlikely. That afternoon among the poor
Jews of the Budapest Telekitér returned to me whenever I was
tormented by the nightmare of the Final Solution about which
we all had to read in time.

"What will happen to us?" asked the old man suddenly,
ceasing altogether to smile. "I escaped from Russia to Germany
in 1920, and from Germany here in 1936. Each time I lost a
business which I had built up with years of work. Each time I
lost all my money. *Lieber Herr*, where shall I go next? It is
terrible."

"But why do you suppose you will have to leave here?"

"Already we hear the first warnings. The Government is
beginning to move against us. Before long it will be made
impossible for us here. And I am a good citizen. I pay my taxes.
I don't owe anyone money. I work hard. My boy works here
after school. My daughter, too. I have one daughter married
and in America. I hope we shall all be able to go there to her.
But it is not easy to start yet again."

We watched them and talked to them at a dozen stalls. With
persistence and patience they worked for hours at the difficult
task of selling a few pengos' worth of goods to the impoverished
Hungarians who came to them. Never deriding even the
ridiculous offers, a tenth of the value of some article, with which
the other commenced the work of barter, they would shake
their heads and start the long, unlistened-to explanations
which justified their price before lowering it by a fraction.
They never let a possible customer leave their stall once he
had approached if they could help it. As all over the world they
were industrious, courteous, smiling, and in this work a little
ingratiating.

"I am originally from Syria", another, a young man, told me. "I was in Spain till a year ago, but there is no business there now."

"And here?"

"It is wretched. The people are so poor. But I can make a living. I would like to come to England, though. It is hard to learn English?"

A third was a very old man who was born in Hungary.

"I have five children", he said, "all in different countries. My son is in Germany. He has a business there which he cannot sell or carry on. He must stay and starve, I suppose. My daughter is married and in Palestine. Another son is in France, and another in Spain. And my youngest daughter is in Vienna. They all write to me. I am seventy-four now—I don't want to move, but they say that even here we shall suffer soon."

I looked at the people walking among the stalls—the women with shawls, the men with their bits of fur, poor and a little resentful, I thought, as they examined the merchandise. Underfoot was wet and sticky mud, overhead a dull grey sky. There was none of the resigned cheerfulness of an Oriental bazaar, none of the brisk and pleasant commercialism of a French market. But anxiety everywhere—anxiety on the part of purchasers and vendors alike, and a clouded anxiety which hung over the Jews in Eastern Europe, and particularly in Vienna and Budapest.

[7]

More than any other capital I knew, Budapest seemed in its very architecture to be an assertion of the nation's right to its own way of life, independence, national pride. From the rock of Buda to the plain across the Danube on which Pest is built, the nineteenth-century buildings are ambitious and graceful in contrast to the complacency of the great erections in Vienna.

There was a certain rivalry between the twin capitals of Austria-Hungary, but Budapest with its unique site on both sides of the Danube escaped 'the overshadowing influence of Vienna' to act as the centre and inspiration of its country. Connected by six bridges Buda and Pest had different characteristics. Buda with its citadel and royal palace on a plateau eight hundred feet above the river had an air of antiquity and peace which not all the ostentatious buildings in the last century could destroy.

From here, in a cultured Hungarian home (the flat of my London literary agent's local representative) I looked on that astonishing panorama, the city of Pest across the river. I saw the lights of the city stretching, so far as I could see, to the horizon. It seemed chokingly beautiful to me that evening as I returned to my friends in their warm soft-lighted room lined with books in many languages. My hostess offered me tea, served with a cruet-stand of liquors, rum, whisky, brandy from which one chose one's lacing. Husband and wife were of the liberal and intellectual Left, and we talked without panic of the way the world was going, and about books and people, as though their city was unthreatened and their pleasant way of life could continue for ever.

A very different point of view came from another 'intellectual' I met in Budapest, the German Baron—or was it Count?—Joachim von Kurenberg. Known in his country as a biographer whose books were translated into various languages, he had, he said been 'given permission' to come to Budapest to do some research. He was a fat, smiling man, well-to-do and self-indulgent and it was hard to imagine him as an inhabitant of the disciplined and ascetic country through which I had recently passed. "They have left me in peace so far", he said, with a chuckle. "My books fortunately deal with historical characters and are considered non-controversial. In the future anything may happen."

He sent me an English translation of one of his books later in the year but I heard no more of him.

[8]

At last we drove out of the city one Sunday morning, and made for the shores of Lake Balaton. This, we had been told, provided Hungary with its seaside, and although the little resorts beside it were deserted now, they looked not unlike Norman watering-places, with pinewoods behind them and the lake like an inland sea.

On the way we passed a group of motor cars drawn up to the roadside, with half a dozen chauffeurs among them. Across the field there was a long line of beaters and in the few moments during which we stood there we saw at least a dozen hares.

"It is a hare shoot", explained one of the chauffeurs in German. "The owner of this estate is entertaining his friends from Budapest. He owns thirty or forty square miles of ground including six villages. Oh yes, he is a rich man—but not as rich as some of our landowners. They will take back a hundred or two of these fine hares—as big as foxes most of them. Good sport, eh?"

The irony was clearly audible, and the other chauffeurs smiled delightedly at it as they walked inquisitively round our bus.

"What do they do with them?" I asked.

"Oh, I daresay we shall be given one each to take home to the wife—if we are lucky."

Not far from the town of Keszethely, at which we had planned to stay the night, we ran out of petrol on a lonely stretch of road. It was quite dark, and we had to wait half an hour before anyone approached the place, and then it was only a pair of cyclists who spoke nothing but Hungarian and hurried on nervously when we tried to make them understand. We had begun to discuss the advisability of pushing the bus on to the grass verge and staying the night, when there were footsteps ringing loudly on the frozen road, and a tall young man walked up.

"Petrol. Nafta. Benzine", we explained hopefully.

He smiled and asked us to follow him. A very odd conversation followed. The young man was something of an Anglomaniac, though his knowledge of England and the English language had been gained wholly from listening to our wireless programmes and must seem oddly dated to those who never knew or have forgotten the names and features of broadcasting in the thirties.

"Harry Roy?" he suggested.

"Harry Roy!" we said, not supposing it was a case of mistaken identity, but accepting this limited form of communication for what it was worth.

"In town tonight!" he exclaimed triumphantly.

"In town tonight", we agreed as we walked briskly along beside him.

But his greatest triumph came after longer thought.

"This is the First News, copyright reserved", he stated suddenly.

"The first news", we echoed, without showing surprise.

By this time we could see the lights of a house not far away, and sloshing through the muddy snow we at last reached a small shed beside it. After much searching he got together enough German and English mixed to explain that he was a builder and decorator and owned a motor-cycle.

"Jap. English", he remarked, as he stooped down to draw some petrol from its tank. "Granada, Tooting", he added with apparent irrelevance as he began to accompany us back, bearing a tin of petrol.

The whole incident delighted him. Quite obviously this was his first opportunity of conversing so freely in his favourite language on the topics nearest to his heart. He smiled continuously and poured his last drop of petrol into our tank with gusto.

It was, however, fiercely cold out on that road with a wind coming across the lake and a bare countryside about us. We were grateful, but anxious to move on. We joined as patiently as we could in further repartee of the kind already exchanged, then paid for our petrol and thanked him warmly. He stretched out a large hand to each of us.

"Nat Gonella!" he said rapturously.

"Nat Gonella!" we replied, and with some relief drove on.

[9]

The next morning in Keszethely we were again made to realize sharply that we were in a country with a strange language. Derrick and I went out in the crisp sunshine to do some shopping, and found the streets lined with peasant women who had brought in quantities of produce from their small-holdings. They were fine-looking people, florid and muscular, with big boots and a weight of wide skirts. We stopped before one of them who displayed a stack of eggs.

"How many shall I get?" I asked Derrick, who did the catering.

"A dozen I should think."

"Make it ten, will you?" I suggested, "I can get those on the fingers of two hands." I held them up to the woman.

She let go a flood of Magyar, and called to her neighbours who seemed as bewildered and intrigued as she was. So I tried again—ten fingers, and a nod in the direction of the eggs. More Hungarian, and no move towards counting them. Derrick broke in with similar gestures, but without success.

"Show her some money", he suggested, and I pulled out a handful indicating that she should help herself.

A small crowd had gathered by now, not one of whom spoke anything but Hungarian. But the woman had started to count the eggs.

"What's she doing that for?" asked Derrick, when she had gone through the whole stock twice.

"I've no idea. Let's try the money again. That sets something moving anyway."

This time she carefully took the equivalent of about three shillings from my hand and laid it on the bench beside her.

"Eggs seem to be dear compared with other things in Hungary", I remarked.

A small boy was dispatched to a shop nearby for a large bag, and soon she was counting again. Ten eggs went in, a dozen, two dozen, and nothing seemed likely to stop her.

"How many have you bought?" asked Derrick plaintively.

"I've no idea", I admitted.

But soon we both realized—we had purchased the entire stock. When we had transported it with some difficulty to the waggon it filled most of our drawers and cupboard space, and overflowed into lockers and tumblers. For many days afterwards eggs emerged from the unlikeliest places, including my shoes and Ivor's beret. They lasted us all through Yugoslavia and half-way across Italy on the way home.

But between Keszethely and the frontier we perceived only too plainly what our Budapest acquaintances had meant when they spoke of the poverty of the rural population. The villages of that plain were no more than groups of wretched little one-storey houses round a church. The roads were appalling, and the people tramped solemnly through the mud. When I hear of poverty anywhere, I shall always remember those Hungarian villages and their people.

That they in turn could console themselves with the sight of people more wretched than they were was proved when we met two beggars in a village street a dozen miles from the frontier. No Australian aboriginal could have been nearer to the beast. Man and woman, filthy, diseased, and half-naked, screamed madly at us for nickles. The man's hair, dirty and clogged, hung round his shoulders, and his beard was indistinguishable from it, leaving only a mouth, a nose, and two hungry eyes to peer out from the greasy mass. His clothes were in rags and his feet bare. The woman's hair was in the same condition, one breast showed through her pinned rags, and her feet and legs, too, had nothing to protect them from the snow and slush. We stopped to photograph the woman, but the man refused to be taken, and danced away like a dervish when we asked him. Then the two, like released wild animals, literally screeched and gibbered and clawed at us for money. The sight of them took one beyond pity to revulsion. We were glad, I can frankly admit, to leave them behind and forget them as though they were something obscene.

But after that the clean and smiling Magyar peasants with their baskets and big boots seemed almost comfortable and bourgeois.

CHAPTER SIXTEEN

Yugoslavia

[1]

TWENTY WAGGONS, each drawn by four white oxen with vast buffalo-like horns, met us on the bridge that divided Hungary from Yugoslavia. Each was led by a man on foot, and the whole procession moved forward at an even pace, with woodwork groaning, whips cracking and shouts.

The frontier post itself was more curious. We were invited into a little room, ten foot by ten, in which three Serbian soldiers were asleep on trestle-beds, their jackets and great-coats hung over them and their great flat peasants' feet bare. They woke when we entered, smiled, and accepted cigarettes while the passport official began the long and difficult business of examination.

Outside it was dusk and there was fine snow blown across the plain by a cold wind. In the room the heat was almost unbearable—like the dry room of a Turkish bath. There was a heavy stench of humanity, garlic, and cigarette smoke. But soldiers and officials were friendly, humorous, and hospitable, and did not seem anxious to lose us. We represented not the unexpected, but the impossible—three Englishmen arriving at their post in a motor-waggon in the dead of winter. They lounged back easily, prepared for a long talk.

The passport official unconsciously aided this delay. After examining our papers he pointed out that we had to pay about £2 each for visas. Shocked by this we, too, consulted the list he had examined, and were relieved to find that he was making the mistake of supposing us to be Dutchmen. The Dutch, it appeared, paid most dearly of all for entrance into Yugoslavia.

"But we're not Dutch", I pointed out patiently in German. "What makes you think we're Dutch?"

He took up my passport, and pointed to the words "United Kingdom of Great Britain and Northern Ireland." The "Northern Ireland" had defeated him. He thought it was "Netherlands". It took a long explanation to convince him, and the atmosphere seemed to grow closer until I was in danger of falling asleep. Next we found that we needed only visitors' visas, and that reduced the cost again, and finally there was the question of exchange since we had as yet bought no dinars. We must have been in that room an hour before the customs' men went out to examine the waggon and let us go.

Progress thence was slow. The road—but it was not a road. It was a ribbon of beaten ground between open fields. There were pot-holes and ridges, mud, loose boulders, and puddles a foot deep. The springs of the old Morris-Commercial till now had held their own, but we could not believe that we could cover many miles of this without mishap. In the waggon everything that could rattle did so. The books broke the front of their shelf and tumbled headlong on the bed. The top of the stove beat a tune. But somehow or other, at a risky fifteen miles an hour, we reached the little town of Varazdin, and decided to stay for the night.

The frontier had given the impression that this was some remote country of the pre-war Balkans. The town showed Yugoslavia as far more an integral part of modern Europe than Hungary had seemed to be. The cafés and 'lokals' were of a kind that might have existed in France or Germany, and all the products familiar in different countries were advertised— Café Hag, Byrrh, Johnnie Walker, Bata boots, and Nivea Cream—while hanging above my table at the largest café was a wide selection of foreign papers.

Our waggon, parked in the market square, had not attracted any unusual attention, and we ourselves in the streets got no more than the casual curiosity afforded anywhere to obvious foreigners. Later we went to a couple of 'dancings' rather like the 'saloons' in Wild Western pictures, and heard a Russian orchestra in one and a zigeuner band in another.

Zagreb more than most cities seemed divided into the old and the new, two cities in one with notable contrasts. The streets in the old town were narrow and tortuous round the Gothic cathedral. The new had broad cheerful roadways, lively shops and crowded cafés.

I was interviewed here as I had been in Prague and Budapest and photographs of the bus and the Rosaire boys obligingly doing acrobatics, appeared in the local daily. But this was useful because the journalist who wrote the story, a handsome young giant, spoke English and spent a couple of days showing us the city.

He took us, for instance, to a doss-house where the down-and-outs gathered nightly, washed their clothes, ate if they had food, and slept. As in Hungary we were made to realize that in Eastern Europe it was not possible to say that no one could die of starvation. The young fellows to whom we talked were very far from doing so, but then they were active and cunning and not without hope. They sat about with few or no clothes on while their shirts were drying, and one played a mouth-organ and several sang.

An out-of-work received a little money, fifty dinars[h] a week for three weeks, then all subsidies ceased. I asked what would happen to the young fellows we saw.

"Oh, they won't starve. And sooner or later they'll become absorbed into normal life again. What happens to the men who draw the dole in your country? What happens to the victim of this transitional age anywhere? They starved in Russia in their thousands. But somehow or other here they come through."

The steam-heated atmosphere of the place, the stench of hot flesh, the soup cooking in tin pots, the naked torsos and feet, the mouth-organ music, and dirt—all this made the room oppressive. But after the frozen streets it must have been warm and comfortable for its inmates.

[h] The exchange value of the dinar was then a penny but its purchasing power was more.

"What are their politics?"

"I suppose that in a vague way they are Communists. One or two of them quite knowledgeably and actively perhaps, but most because it promises them something they haven't got. Naturally enough they are anti-society, anti-bourgeois more than anything. But then aren't we all?"

There was a different, a more picturesque kind of poverty to be found in the market place when the peasants from miles around brought in their produce. Many of them wore the complete national costume in all its coloured dignity while others were satisfied with a soiled and compromising version of it. My Croatian friend accompanied me there and interpreted.

First I bought a ham. It was the largest and heaviest I have ever seen and was beautifully cured. It cost seventy dinars— just under six shillings. Small wonder that the people who produce food to sell at this price, complained. The journalist asked one old peasant, a knotted and healthy man in his early eighties, what he foresaw for himself and his fellow small-holders. I saw my friend smiling at the old man's reply.

"They always answer in metaphor", he explained to me. "This one says that very soon, if conditions do not improve, it will not be produce that they bring into the market to be sold, but one another. One man will sell his neighbour, and only the strongest will find a purchaser."

A brisk middle-aged woman selling chickens was less pessimistic.

"We can make a living", she said. "It is hard work, but we manage."

"How much ground have you got?" my friend asked her, and once again smiled when he heard her reply.

"She says", he explained, "that in the centre of her land is a tall tree. When the sun rises in the morning the tip of its shadow touches the boundary on one side of her land, and when the sun sets at night the tree's shadow touches the other boundary. She measures it that way."

The woman spoke again.

"She says that she is lucky. She lives near enough to Zagreb to bring her goods in here and get a fair price for them. It is others, those who live too far from cities for marketing, who are suffering most."

Always the same, I thought. Everywhere, in whatever poverty people found themselves, there were others worse off to be pitied. Even the young men in the doss-house had pitied others who could not stay there for the night. Even the Hungarian peasants had pitied the beggars. If there were people actually dying of starvation they pitied, I suppose, others who had not water to drink.

[2]

Leaving the market we came into a wide square crowded with people, with soldiers drawn up about a central group of priests in the vestments of the Orthodox Church.

"The ceremony of the Three Kings", my friend explained. "You see the soldiers here, being Serbs, belong to the Orthodox religion, though most of the townspeople are Catholics."

There were fusillades and much craning of necks, but the shopkeepers about the square seemed indifferent to the events there, and my guide took me back to a café in the centre of the town where we were to meet some friends of his.

During the long conversation that followed, I was warned not to suppose that I had "visited Yugoslavia".

"These are their main racial divisions", explained a lean-faced lawyer from Sarajevo, "Serbs, Croats, and Slovenes. But there are several minorities, and heaven knows how many languages and dialects. You will have seen something of one of them—the Croats. It would take you a year to study this country even sufficiently to get its people into proportion. So that when you speak of your man in the street remember that it is only one of several races you have met. We think the best", he added smiling, "but you wouldn't hear that in the capital."

In all our tour we never ate better than in Zagreb, or at such phenomenally small expense. A *table d'hôte* dinner at one of the town's best restaurants cost about one and twopence, and I can still picture the big slices of luscious roast goose which was its speciality, the drinkable local wine at a shilling a bottle, the thick Turkish coffee.

Dancing was another matter. After so many evenings spent in listening to political back-chat which was of little interest to them, Ivor and Derrick felt entitled one evening to something more frivolous, and we were taken to a cabaret. This proved to be the usual dull combination of a floor-show by haggard prostitutes, and bad champagne at a price which in that country seemed high. It was difficult, we were told, to find the more modest form of bourgeois dance hall which we had enjoyed in Germany and we left, without feeling much satisfaction, after a conventional conversation with two Viennese women who had told a story equivalent to that of the Wiltshire parson's daughter familiar to their type in London.

Afterwards Derrick nearly got arrested for the serious crime of owning a cigarette lighter. He let it fall from his pocket while we were interrogating a policeman, and it caused such excitement that one would have thought it was a bomb. The policeman made a grab for it, but Derrick was quicker than he, and pushed it back in his pocket. The policeman talked violently for three minutes, indicating that Derrick should produce the lighter.

"Oh no, sonny", Derrick said, "that's mine."

Another volley.

"Does he think I've pinched it?" Derrick asked us. "No—you dam' fool. It's mine. I bought it in Germany. And it's no use your getting excited because you can't have it. See?"

We began to walk away, and the policeman followed, still talking.

"—— off," said Derrick over his shoulder.

This the man seemed to take to heart, for after another ten

yards or so he gave it up, consoling himself probably with the thought that we were foreigners who could not understand him. Afterwards we were told that the making of matches was a Government industry so heavily protected that lighters were severely taxed if not actually forbidden.

With our huge ham swinging from the waggon roof and a piece of smoked goose-breast hanging beside it, we left Zagreb to make for Italy. It was snowing again as we were kept waiting twenty minutes before some much-needed road-mending operations. A few miles farther on we came on a group of school-children which we wanted to photograph, and were amused to see their schoolmaster line them up and tell them to smile for us. Then only fifty miles from Zagreb we stopped for the night at Novo-Mesto, to find that once again, without having crossed a frontier, we had come among a different people, for all with whom we talked in that picturesque village were Slovenes, with little sympathy for the aspirations of their Croatish neighbours.

[3]

To describe Ljubljana I quote from another book of mine written twenty-five years later, after I had returned to Yugoslavia in 1963. In this, I recalled my first visit with the Rosaire brothers: "One grey afternoon when snow threatened but did not fall we came to Ljubljana, the capital of Slovenia, which should have been the very place for material such as I was supposed to be seeking but which had other, very different attractions. We were accustomed to the pitiful cheapness of everything in eastern Europe and particularly in Hungary and Yugoslavia, but nothing prepared us for the Stari Trg.

"This was a street in the poorer part of the town which consisted entirely of little second-hand and antique shops kept by Jews. They were stocked with a confused miscellany of objects, fine old furniture, painted wood-carvings, carpets, silver, pottery, cast-off clothing, chandeliers, paintings, fabrics, glass, old books, skates, toilet ware and books. At the first shop I stopped idly and saw a fine carved statue of St Teresa of Avila, three feet high, probably of the seventeenth century and having its original colour and gilt. I asked the price and was told in dinars a price which hastily translated turned out to be seven and sixpence. Incredulous, I inquired about a pair of altar candle-sticks in beaten silver of about the same height and found they would cost me fifteen shillings. Then I lost my head a little. I went on to other shops and found fine Balkan rugs at half a sovereign each, a painted tray with a brilliant landscape for less than a pound, an eighteenth-century mahogany card-table for thirty shillings, and so on. It was a collector's dream. If I had possessed a hundred pounds and means of transport and had kept what I found I should be a rich man today.

"But I hadn't. I had less than twenty pounds in dinars and I spent it all. The living-waggon had to be arranged to hold my purchases under the bed. Round me still as I write are some of the things I found in that buyer's bedlam. Until war broke out I dreamed of raising the capital to go back to Ljubljana to exhaust the whole market."

I then told how in that same street in a rebuilt Ljubljana in Tito's Yugoslavia I did find on my return one remaining state-owned antique shop and even then made some exciting purchases.

This reminds me that of all the countries of eastern Europe, Yugoslavia is the only one to which I have returned since the war, the only one I have seen as both a kingdom and a Communist state. It tempts me to a doubtless over-simplified and very superficially observed comparison. In 1938 the people were picturesque in their national costumes, frivolous, insouciant and for the most part atrociously poor; prices made a middle-income Englishman feel like a millionaire; public works, education, welfare were at the lowest possible ebb and nobody seemed to care. In 1963 there was no visible poverty or sign of personal wealth and a grey norm had settled on everything. The people's civilian clothes were like a uniform, so small was the choice in the government shops, but they were warm enough. They all seemed earnest and pre-occupied, they were polite but reserved, their places of amusement (where they existed) were dreary and there was an impersonal sameness about hotels and restaurants. Fine new buildings had arisen and the roads were enormously improved. In the old Yugoslavia rebelliousness, individualism and contrariness were openly voiced, in the new if they exist they are out of sight and hearing of the foreigner. One was a Balkan country, chaotic, romantic, needy, the other is efficient by comparison, regimented and drab. But no one starves in it.

CHAPTER SEVENTEEN

Italy

[1]

IT IS WITH SHARP mental discomfort that I read today the chapter I wrote in 1938 about my journey through Italy and the impressions I gained of popular political feeling. It is little comfort that I expressed no admiration of my own for Mussolini—I reported a number of conversations with Italians and British residents from which the reader would gain the impression that the Duce was universally popular in his own country, a big bluff honest fellow with a sense of humour and even a sense of honour, secretly both an Anglophil and a democrat. I do not know how much of this I felt was true, but if I had had the measure of the man, or any idea of it, I simply could not have reported that sickening stuff. I seem to have made no effort at all to hear the other side.

Yet the facts were all known. Mussolini had climbed to prominence on the shoulders of the Socialists, then sold them down the river and been responsible for the murder not of a few but of hundreds of them. He had at first tried to join the movement of workers in their seizure of factories in the north of Italy in 1920, then exploited the general alarm to support the factory-owners and industrialists. He had organized his armed squads of Fascisti and strike-breakers with which he had virtually destroyed the workers' movements; he had renounced his life-long republicanism when he saw that he could get royalist support; he had remained near the frontier to flee if necessary while his followers organized the March on Rome; and as Duce he had never had any policy but the inflation of his own image, ruling by makeshift improvisations and treachery to every ideal he had formerly upheld. He had been acclaimed for his 'efficiency' but the only efficiently organized body in Fascist Italy was the secret police. He had bluffed the French into ceding him territory and the British into giving him Jubaland. He had tried to create not so much an Italian empire as a position for himself as a modern Caesar by his cowardly war on the Abyssinians. He had already agreed (though this was still unknown) to sell Austria to Hitler for German support to his trumpery imperialism in the Mediterranean and Africa. He had made Italy bankrupt and concealed it from the nation. He had used without shame the crudest and most despicable forms of propaganda to promote himself and his own megalomaniac ambitions in the eyes of the people, plastering the whole country with the mad inscription *Mussolini is Always Right*. He had stamped his face, with a jaw out-thrust, on every Italian consciousness; be had smitten a thousand men with the jawbone of an ass.

But anti-Fascist propaganda outside Italy had used little more than ridicule against him, picturing him as a ludicrous poseur, rather than exposing his treacheries with detachment, and this had failed as ridicule always does to move the English to genuine odium and contempt. 'Kaiser Bill' and 'Little Willy' like the early Hitler were cartoonists' jokes and it took Louis Raemaekers and trench warfare in the First World War, and the bombing of our cities in the Second, to give us any sense of reality about our enemies. We laughed a good deal at Mussolini—few people saw him as a murderous blackguard who would let nothing stand in the way of his egomaniac purposes. I certainly did not and when I entered Italy from Yugoslavia I was ready to listen to and report, though not I hope altogether to believe the popular myths of his essential decency. It must be remembered that I had not that fortifying belief in Stalin's Communism which helped so many young men of my generation to perceive the unmitigated beastliness of Fascism. To me there was not then (and is not now) much to choose between those two anti-human heresies.

H

[2]

During the last two centuries a great many Englishmen and particularly writers have loved and lived in one or other of the Mediterranean countries. Greece, Spain, the South of France, Egypt and even Morocco have all had their devoted immigrants escaping from our climate or our puritanism and have inspired English prose and poetry, but none of them more than Italy from Shelley and Browning to Norman Douglas and Ronald Firbank. Indeed, a love for Italy has become almost a convention in English letters.

That I have never subscribed to this has been partly a matter of circumstances—for I was rarely in a position to choose the course of my own early travels—and partly the result of my abiding love for Spain. When I have been in Italy in recent years I have felt that had I come here as a boy instead of going ashore in Spain I should have been captivated as surely an any English lover of Italy in the past. But through a series of mischances I had never had an opportunity of being in the country till my ancient bus jolted across the frontier at Caccia on that unexpectedly sunny day in March 1938.

It was as though the Italians had intended deliberately to show the tourist that he was entering a modern and well-organized state. The road itself changed from the stony cart-track through which we had ploughed for days, to a smooth tarmac kept in excellent condition. The frontier buildings were neat, white-plastered, new, and the guards and officials were spruce and cordial.

Formalities, however, were prolonged owing to one of the economic anomalies of that time when tourists were attracted to Fascist Italy by artificial inducements and a complicated system of petrol and hotel coupons. By buying sufficient of the latter we could get our petrol cheaper, and it was necessary to work out our probable mileage in the country and discover whether it would pay us to get hotel vouchers, since these would in fact be of little use to us, who carried our accommodation with us. The Italians themselves entered into the problem, and after a great deal of arithmetic it was discovered that though we should save little actual money, a hotel for the night for one with dinner and breakfast in each town would cost nothing at all, being paid for by the saving on the price of petrol. Since in Yugoslavia this had cost 3s. 9d. a gallon, we felt that at least we should have an illusion of thrift.

Our first glimpses of Italy after we had left the courteous and benevolent frontier officials were not reassuring, for we were faced with that curious Fascist phenomenon—the writing on the wall. On every available blank space of plastered house-walls were painted extracts from Mussolini's speeches, or tributes to him, in stark block letters, with a profusion of interjection marks. Passers-by were asked to hail the 'founder of our Empire', to be ready to obey and to fight, to believe that the ploughshare was useless without the sword, or merely to see *Duce! Duce! Duce!* in most startling type. One could not help wondering whether this sort of propaganda was not under-rating the intelligence of the people it was designed to attract.

Days later, in fact, when I suggested this to an intelligent Italian, he agreed.

"If Fascism fails, its destroyer will not be Communism but Boredom", he said. "We are suffering from a surfeit of culti-vated nationalism."

Postumia was very evidently a military town. Crowds of soldiers in the streets, groups of officers in the hotels, gave us the impression that more than half the population was in uniform. Yet our bus aroused nothing but passing curiosity when we pulled up in the central square, and not even the civilian police asked us any questions.

As soon as I bought a newspaper, however, I was made aware that the long and bitter onslaught of anti-British propaganda which had continued since the days of the Abyssinian war, had not abated. An incident in Palestine was presented as though this were a Dutch paper describing an episode of the

Boer War. A couple of arrests at a political meeting in the East End of London were described as though Whitechapel had been Dublin in Easter Week, 1916.

On the way to Trieste we stopped in a village square. It was Sunday morning, and people were walking home from Mass in the warm sunshine. Two days ago we had been huddled over our stove in the chill of the Yugoslav winter. That morning we walked about without overcoats, the sun hot on our faces. When we reached Trieste in the afternoon we found that the cafés had their tables out in the square and everybody basked easily in the spring air of the Adriatic. Very attractive it seemed, built in terraces, with its old and new cities joined by handsome Via Corso. But we had not planned to stay here.

We took the new coast road from Trieste, still warmed by sunlight. On these hills, we were reminded by our route sheet, some of the severest of Italy's fighting in the Great War had taken place, and when Ivor and Derrick climbed the steep slope of what appeared to be a quarry near Monfalcone that afternoon they found in the undergrowth an unexploded shell, a twenty-year-old relic of the Austrian retreat.

Then we reached Cervignano-del-Friuli. This appeared to be an ordinary enough little Italian town but like so many of the less spectacular places at which we stopped throughout the tour it proved to be one of the most memorable.

From the first moment we recognized it as the sort of place we liked. With its cinema, its lighted cafés, its animation, it was yet small enough for its activity to be focused in one central square and the streets round it. We went right through this, crossed a bridge, and pulled up on a piece of ground beside a narrow river. There I left the Rosaires to change while I went off to discover what the town had to offer us of entertainment and interest.

In a crowded café near the cinema a wireless was playing too loudly—swing music. Standing over it, manipulating its switches, were three or four young men in grey-green uniform.

"Is that from London?" I asked them.

"No, from Rome. Why, don't you think we have swing music in Italy?"

"Not like that", I admitted.

One of them asked, in perfect English, if I was from London. It appeared that he had spent a couple of years in one of our Northern Universities. He was now doing his eighteen months' military service. Soon we were all talking. They were from the neighbouring barracks—a mechanized unit. These five or six of them were friends who had come from the same city, Milan, and as so often happens in conscript armies everywhere, had kept together throughout the year of their training. They all had nicknames—and there were the usual private jokes. They were gay, bawdy, irresponsible, generous.

Presently, after we had swallowed a few vermouths, I told them about the waggon and Ivor and Derrick, and at once a scheme was evolved for an elaborate practical joke. Rino Mansanti, the boy who spoke English, was to go to the waggon door, and with the other soldiers behind was to challenge the Rosaires in English, examine their passports, and "arrest" them.

So the six or seven of us set out for the waggon. There was a light in it, for night had fallen now. It looked, I thought, rather gypsy-like and travel-worn as it stood by the river, for Ivor and Derrick had insisted that the mud of ten countries should be allowed to accumulate on its flanks. It seemed, suddenly, a comic little ark, in spite of its achivements. Smoke was rising from its chimneys, and the sound of our wireless crossed the water to us.

The soldiers marched straight up to its door while I stood back in the shadow. They knocked sharply.

"What the hell do you want?" It was Ivor's voice, rather sleepy, from the interior. Accustomed to being disturbed by visitors who spoke no English, he was apt to presume that no one abroad could do so.

Rino Mansanti knocked again.

"Go away!" shouted Ivor who had not bothered to look out at the intruders.

"Open the door, please", said Rino curtly.

There was a sudden silence in the waggon. The wireless was switched off. Evidently English speech had its effect. After a moment the door opened and Ivor appeared.

"Good-evening", he said. "I didn't know you spoke English."

Rino, an excellent actor, ignored this.

"Your passports please", he said.

Ivor produced them.

"How many of you are there ?"

"Three. One is in the town."

"What are you doing here?"

"We had just stopped for the night."

"Oh, you had. Did you know that you were in a military area?"

I had suggested this phrase. We had heard so much of military areas in Eastern Europe, that I thought it would sound convincing.

"No, we didn't know that . . . you see . . ."

"I must ask you to come with us please."

This was disturbing. Ivor hesitated.

"Where?" he asked.

"You will see. And your friend also."

Ivor disappeared for a moment to consult with Derrick who had been dozing on the bed when this disturbance began.

"What about our other friend?" Ivor asked.

"Oh, he will be arrested, too, when he returns to the waggon."

"*Arrested*?" gasped Ivor.

"Certainly. Now come along please."

At this point I thought it best to break in. It had not occurred to me till then to wonder what action the brothers might take. I now saw a half a dozen disturbing possibilities. They might start up the waggon and move off at the forty-five miles an hour which the Morris-Commercial could still achieve when she was "all out". They might scrap their way through the soldiers on foot. Or they might flatly refuse to leave the waggon. Any one of these would have embarrassed Rino and his friends. So I gave it away.

We were at once adopted by the soldiers. We were to go with them to "their own little restaurant" for dinner. They were to show us the town. Within half an hour of meeting them we had been absorbed into their fellowship.

Their restaurant proved to be a small clean eating-house on the outskirts of the town. The daughter of the house whose name was Ennia had real beauty. Very Italian, she had dark eyes, thick curling hair which was not quite black, and— surprising to me who had known girls very like her in Spain and Spanish America—a tenderly musical speaking voice. She presided over the restaurant while her mother remained in the kitchen and she was the 'little mother', the sister, *la Madelon* of our group of conscripts. They admired her with extravagant flattery and she flirted publicly with them all, having no favourites. They competed histrionically for her smiles, gave her presents, and expected nothing from her except a show of femininity. She serenely kept them all in their places and probably ended by marrying some steady young townsman. She had great freshness and charm and good-nature.

It was a happy meal. Crowded on one long table, separated from one another so that our hosts could entertain us better, the three of us listened to the noisy clatter of Italian about us, ate *ravioli* and *escalope* of veal, and drank tumblerfuls of sharp red wine. The little room, its only decoration the conventional photos of Mussolini staring glumly out of his frame and the King of Italy looking vaguely outraged, became noisier as our soldier friends assured us that we were welcome to Italy, to Cervignano, and particularly to their circle and their restaurant, and Ennia tried, amid much applause, to make Ivor and Derrick understand what she meant.

We had meant to leave next day, but this was not to be heard of. We were to bring the waggon round to the back of the restaurant and stay there, and our hosts would obtain late leave for tomorrow. Could we get some laundry done? Could they, Ennia? Of course they could. The woman next door would do it. Could they bring the waggon round? *Securamente.*

Subito. So Rino and Ivor went to fetch it while the rest of us drank coffee. We would stay, wouldn't we? Yes, we would. And tomorrow night we should see them rehearse a play. Tomorrow we would dine together again. Ennia would look after us in the day-time—they would all be with us at seven o'clock. Were we going to Milan? We should enjoy that. It was *their* city. They would like to be coming with us. Did we like Italy? Yes? That was good. We should find ourselves welcome anywhere. We were not to believe anything we read in the papers which seemed to show that Italy was unfriendly to England. They, the young men of Italy, wanted friendship with England. Don't let's talk politics. More wine?

Would we like to go to the cinema? It was really the only thing to do in this hole. Come along then. We would see Ennia later. Where were our coats? Ah, here. *Permisso.* That was it. Now this way. If was quite a walk, but we would get in half-price. Of course. If we weren't exactly Italian soldiers we were near enough to it to get the advantage of their reduced entrance charge. We were there. These *signori* were to pay half-price. Of course they were soldiers. Couldn't the manager see? Now upstairs.

Not until the film was half finished did one of them admit by chance that they had been here last night and seen it, only accompanying us this evening because hospitality demanded it.

[3]

So we stayed on in Cervignano-del-Friuli, to see our washing hanging out to dry in the next garden. We were awakened by Ennia and her sister bringing hot coffee to the waggon and, with a good deal of amusement, handing it through the windows while we were still in bed. In the kitchen the mother, a stout and splendid woman, was mixing and cutting paste for the day's *spaghetti* and gossiped with us cheerfully from over her floury board. I was so ignorant of Italian cooking that I had supposed all *pasta* to be factory-made and was unaware that no self-respecting restaurant, or housewife for that matter, would serve any that had not been made in the kitchen that day. I watched fascinated as this big good-humoured woman worked, sieving her flour, dropping in the eggs and stirring them with her fingers, drawing the flour into them, adding a touch of water, till she had a firm, workable dough which she rolled and re-rolled till it was almost paper thin. To my surprise she hung this up for a few minutes, as though it was a cloth, then laid it flat again and rolled it up like a huge pancake to cut it skilfully into the ribbons of *tagliatelle* which was the form it was to take that day. Sometimes, she said, she made *ravioli*, sometimes *cannelloni*, sometimes *spaghetti*—oh and many more. She liked to vary the *pastas* in her menu, but every day of her life she made one or another, she said, as she hung the ribbons of her *tagliatelle* over a clothes-horse to dry. I admired the cool way in which she continued to prepare a three-course meal which would be served by her daughter to some twenty regular customers at midday for five liras each, while she swore good-humouredly at the kitchen girl, joked with Ivor, told her husband what to buy, and sent her son off to school. She was noisy, yet imperturbable, immensely capable and cheerful.

In the afternoon I hired a car and took Ennia and her sister out to Aquilea, to see some fine Roman paving. This was almost the only purely 'sightseeing' expedition of the whole tour. There was much amused comment in the neighbourhood when the girls were dressed for it—and more between the two of them when we passed the army lorries crowded with young soldiers whom they recognized.

"Ah—the *soldatini*!" smiled Ennia, when she had received salutes and shouts and blown kisses from them as we drove by.

At seven o'clock our friends of the previous evening appeared and after dinner we went to see the soldiers' rehearsal at the local Fascist Hall, a new building such as has been put up in most Italian towns for meetings, dances, gymnastics (it contains some fine gymnastic apparatus), and social occasions. But there had been some hitch in the organization and the rehearsal was cancelled. So that it was in the street that we said *Arrivederci* to our friends, who knew that we were setting off early the next morning. It was, after all, the kind of easy acquaintance which might grow suddenly between young men of any nation. It had no political or any other kind of significance. But I used to think of it later during the futile Italian campaigns in Greece and North Africa. Perhaps those decent intelligent young men were disgusted when Mussolini declared war on a fallen France. But what was the use?

Europe is still a mess today but at least we have no imperialist mountebank sending young men to fight for his personal aggrandizement.

[4]

This was certainly not the season for a first visit to Venice nor were the circumstances in any way propitious. The days I spent there, with rain splashing into the canals, the beautiful façades of the palaces dull grey and damp and the piazza deserted, served only to fix my resolve to return in summertime and spend a month between the lido and the beauties of the city. This month I have never achieved and though I have visited that city of unearthly loveliness twice again, the visits were short and one was in winter when Venice was under thick snow.

Of that first brief stay I have only disconnected memories. The bus had to remain on the outskirts and the Rosaires stayed in it while I used some of my hotel vouchers to go to the Danieli which, though even then the best hotel in Venice, was a great deal less grandiose and more Venetian than today. I asked the porter where I might find a modest antique shop and he gave me the address of a palazzo on one of the canals to which I was taken in a gondola to find myself being shown through a series of large apartments by a character in a morning coat. Each stately room was exquisitely furnished in period and everything was for sale. Feeling that in common politeness I should ask the price of something I looked at a carved walnut coffer in a magnificent *salon*, and whispered an enquiry.

"That, I fear, cannot be sold, Signor", said my guide. "The whole contents of this room, including the carved fireplace by Rovezzano, the frescoes by Perugino, the ceiling by Diziano, were purchased by Mr. Randolph Hearst some years ago and we have not yet received his instructions."

"A pity", I said, and went on to a room with settees and chairs covered with Beauvais tapestry. I was not a valuable customer.

I can see the Rosaire brothers in an ornate gondola propelled as most of them were still, by a man wearing the traditional black clothes. I remember the Renaissance staircase in the Ducal Palace—though why that should stand out in memory amongst so much splendour I do not know, unless I was impressed with the vastness of it and the colossal statues at its head. I remember being rather lost and unguided in that incredible city, feeling that I should have come to it with money and leisure as Englishmen making the Grand Tour had done, or as a humble writer or artist who could give himself the sense of living here for a time, or, as Frederick Rolfe did, to starve and freeze to death rather than leave it. I was conscious of the inadequacy of my knowledge and taste, my powers of proportion. I felt like a child in a great museum staring in uninformed wonder at this or that. It was, in fact, too much for me.

But at least I knew it and should not return to England to talk in that fake-sophisticated manner I have heard adopted by even less initiated visitors than I. ("What I liked in Venice was the forecourt and screen in the Scuola of S. Giovanni Evangelista at Frari. Pietro Lombardo, you know.") I found the city beautiful, exciting, an entirely new experience—but who does not? It made me feel ignorant and provincial. That, too, must be a common sensation among all but the most brash or self-deceiving. I sensed a little, but only a little, of what it might

mean to me, what it had meant to generations of Englishmen
better prepared for it than I. No more than that.

[5]

I had to adopt an even more philistine attitude as we hurried
across northern Italy, stopping in Padua only to see the basilica
of St Anthony. He was a saint for whom I had felt a particular
devotion, complete with Burns and Oates statuette, since boyhood. I thought now that the Basilica was much grander than
that modest Portuguese Franciscan would have wished. At the
Palladian grandeurs of Vicenza I could give no more than a
glance, though here again I, or any sight-seer for that matter,
could have spent weeks, and the most I gained from it and from
the drive across the breadth of northern Italy was a belief that
the riches of that country are inexhaustible and that it would
scarcely matter where one landed there in order to see beauty,
antiquity, petrified history and great pictures.

But Verona was another matter for its little central square
made an instant appeal not only to me but to the Rosaires
who decided that among all things bright and beautiful they
had seen in Venice and three East European capitals this was
'the winner'. Yet no one I have met has seemed to find it
remarkable. The frescoes at St Zeno's, the Romanesque sculp-
ture of the cathedral, Pisanello's painting of St George in the
church of S. Anastasia, the Castel Vecchio, the many great
paintings and the sculptured tombs fill them with enthusiasm
but they seem to take for granted the two adjoining piazzas,
the Piazza delle Erbe on the site of the Forum and the Piazza
dei Signori. If these are anything like as lovely and as redolent
of the past as they seem in my recollection there are no more
beautiful city squares in the world, and they are worthy of
the legend and the play of Romeo and Juliet. But I may have
idealized them.

Of my first visit to Milan I remember very little except its brilliance of illumination, its vast central square, a *galeria* or arcade somewhere, impressions of space, commerce, civic importance, loquacious and busy crowds and the incredible cathedral, the third largest church in Europe, which has been called a forest of stone. I went to see a young English couple I had met on the ship going to South America eighteen months before and found them occupying a flat in a huge new block overlooking the highly illuminated Piazza del Duomo.

Mussolini and his antics seemed somehow improbable and remote in that city, as though its huge population of business-like and intelligent people would not be bothered with such nonsense. Yet it was a stronghold of Fascism.

Leaving Milan we had only one more night in Italy which we spent in the pleasant Piedmontese town of Cuneo. Its name, 'The Wedge', denotes its position on a hill between the Sturo and the Gesso rivers. It seemed very lively and cheerful that evening.

Next morning, on our way to the French frontier, we climbed the Col di Tenda, which our route-sheet told us was 4331 feet. We had grown almost blasé about the achievements of the old bus and were scarcely surprised when she came up without a stutter. Now that her head was turned towards home and the countries of bad roads were behind her, she seemed in fact to tackle the difficulties of the Maritime Alps with a new zest. She rounded the hair-pin bends one after the other, and the water in her radiator did not even boil—this at the end of three or four thousand miles without repairs. The occupants of other GB cars we met near the Col di Tenda tunnel—smart saloon cars, of course, driven by people who had chosen this region for ski-ing—may have smiled rather dubiously at our battered paintwork and chimney, but we were proud of them. Our last words in Italian were of warm thanks to an Italian official who had troubled to cycle half a mile down the road after us to return some papers which I had carelessly left in his office.

CHAPTER EIGHTEEN

France and Home

[1]

WE TOOK A WRONG road somewhere just over the frontier and found ourselves climbing the Col de Bruis by a rough track, but with the motorists' obstinate dislike of turning back we continued. On that windy evening of March, with snow still on the ground, failing lights, no skid chains, and an eight-year-old vehicle, it gave us what even the Rosaires, too case-hardened to be much impressed by the difficulties of the road, described as a 'thrill'. I should use a less cheerful word, for there were moments of sickening anxiety.

The ascent was about one in eleven, and the track was narrow and poor. All the morning we had been winding our way up the Alps in sunlight on the smooth, broad surfaces of the new roads of Italy. This was very different. The hair-pin bends were as sharp, the ascent as endless, but the surface was rough and half-frozen, with loose stones and ruts, while nothing fenced the road from the fall of several thousand feet below us. We had panted about half-way up when the accumulator ceased to charge, and after a few moments we had to dispense with headlights.

Derrick was driving and Ivor, who had a rather good crooner's voice, began to sing. But the fact that he kept the door beside him open rather belied his apparent indifference. Then, on the last and stiffest piece of hill, the Morris-Commercial made her one protest at the task which had been set her in her old age. Derrick had changed down and was moving in bottom gear at 7–8 miles an hour.

"She's slipping," he said quietly, and a moment later she

stopped. Ivor and I got out and tried to push her forward, but her protest was a determined one, and she stayed where she was.

It was as though that old engine after six years of propelling a daily busload of heavy people over the Welsh hill-sides, after these weeks of rough travel and after climbing the Col di Tenda that day, was making a protest. Understanding this, the Rosaires left her to cool down with stones behind her wheels.

Derrick turned her lights off, though he remained at the wheel to switch them on if other traffic should approach—a remote possibility at that hour and place. I walked on alone to examine the road ahead, and to see how much more of this steep incline there might be.

I had gone perhaps a hundred yards when I came on something rather frightening. Road-workers had laid a rough, wooden bridge over what might have been a gap caused by a landside, but was probably only a break in the surface of the road where it was under repair. But there was no sign of the red lamps hung on such temporary structures in England, and the little pontoon was only just wide enough for our bus to negotiate.

I began to hurry back to where I had left the others, but as I did so the engine started again, and the waggon approached. I knew it was no good shouting to warn the Rosaires as even if they heard me above the wind and the noise of the engine, they would probably think I was calling for them to wait for me. So I stood at the roadside hoping that the door would still be open so that I could jump aboard as she passed. It was, and I did, so that Derrick had warning of the bridge ahead, and with the help of our headlights, switched on for a moment in approaching, we came over it safely. Nor did the bus hesitate again till she crested the hill.

Down in Sospel, with its cheerful lights on a quickly flowing river, its stone bridge and its pleasant hotel, we felt immensely pleased with ourselves, the old bus, and this French village. Food and wine would have been reason enough, for there was the usual excellent *table d'hôte* and a good *vin du pays*, but there was also the practised courtesy of the skilled *hotelier*, the brilliance of the young waiter, the charm and welcome of the hotel which we happened to choose, and for me a happiness, associated perhaps with other days, which is peculiar to being in France.

"M. Neville Chamberlain lunched here when he was in the South of France a few weeks back", the *hotelier* informed us. We felt he had chosen well.

Conversation here, even about politics, seemed more like inquiring after an old friend than discovering new theories. The *hotelier*, like most of his class, spoke as he supposed would be most reassuring to us.

"The Communist movement in France is virtually no more", he said, "if there was a general election tomorrow I doubt if they would get more than a couple of seats. The country has realized that it must hold together in the face of all menaces from the outside. You will see no evidence of the strikes and disorders of 1936. All is industrious and serene now . . ."

This was obviously a complacent summary calculated to please English visitors, as one saw from a glance at almost any newspaper. But it made it hard to guess the man's real sympathies, particularly as a few minutes later he brought us an evening paper and indicated an account, under minor headlines, of a curious incident in Genoa. It appeared that several arrests had been made following the discovery one daybreak of two huge skeletons painted on a housewall, with the inscription: "To this Mussolini has reduced us."

"You see?" said the *hotelier*, "things are not so wonderfully smooth on the other side of the frontier."

[2]

Arriving in Mentone was a new kind of experience and one which I enjoyed, as I had enjoyed entering an English pub with the Rosaires to be looked at dubiously as 'one of the circus

people', as I always in young manhood enjoyed, I think harm-
lessly, not so much *epater les bourgeois* as to tease the over-
correct and conventionally-minded of whatever caste. It may be
thought ostentatious and childish in me to take pleasure in
driving that battered bus with its now blackened chimney
smoking along the promenade road of Mentone during its
smart winter season, but vanity of that kind went with youth
and I find nothing to be seriously deplored in my inverted
snobbery. I would have enjoyed driving a Rolls or a noticeable
sports car no less, probably, had the chance been given me. Who
doesn't want to show off in some way or other? Car, wife,
garden, clothes, horses, dogs, balance sheet, skill at sport, in art,
in oratory? And how far from the caves would mankind have
come if it were not for this exhibitionism? The most dangerous
men have surely been those who have gone beyond it, who no
longer want to impress their fellows except as a means to an end
who, like Hitler, have darker manias and hatreds than mere
swank.

All this because as we drove into Mentone, a town of brightly-
painted buildings and people, a resort then considered the most
discreetly chic on the coast, we attracted some notice from the
generally rich and rather elegant English people wintering
there, and enjoyed attracting it. As usual we had some trouble
in finding a place to park, but after a search in modest streets
we took the coastal road in the direction of Monte Carlo and a
quarter of a mile from Mentone casino, we came on a piece of
ground between the road and the promenade. It adjoined a
hotel and it was open and gravelled, with a few trees along its
side.

"What about this?" Derrick suggested.

I pointed out that it was a sort of public garden, that there
was no sign of it ever having been used as a car park, that it was
probably municipal property, and that we certainly should not
be allowed to stay there long.

"No harm in trying", Derrick replied, as he gently mounted
the kerb, ran over the pavement and came to rest on a level

space in the open square. There was only a stretch of promenade between us and the beach, and in the strong sunlight of the early afternoon the sea was smooth and sparkling. Certainly the spot was ideal, and from our windows we had the sort of view for which people who went to the Côte D'Azur in winter paid exaggerated sums. I like to think we were responsible for turning that square into a parking site for trailers. Within an hour of our settlement there two French cars with large modern trailer-caravans came along the road, and seeing us encamped, drove on some yards away.

We stayed there, unmolested, for a week. We bathed every day, and played roulette every evening. We lounged about in the sunshine, the frozen chill of Prague and the Austrian snow-storms seeming very far behind. We had a good many English visitors who were attracted by curiosity and our GB plate and came to ask questions and we made friends with a likeable Englishwoman called Grace Jeans, the wife of a mathematician and astonomer famous at the time for his popular books and articles.

"Where do you come from?" asked an inquisitive old English gentleman, with a touch of patronage as he examined our travel-stained bus.

"From England", Derrick told him.

The old gentleman seemed surprised that such a vehicle could have made so long a journey.

"Really? which way?"

"Via Budapest and Zagreb," replied Derrick innocently.

This was taken for a piece of senseless impertinence by his questioner, who moved stiffly away.

To realize the extraneousness of it all, our travel-worn bus with its battered paintwork, ourselves in foreign clothes bought on the way, the Rosaires particularly alien in appearance and unconventional in manner, our smoking chimney under the windows of a smart hotel, one should have an idea of what 'the South of France in winter' meant before the war. The very words had their snob value and in those days of photographers busy for the 'society' weeklies, taking pictures of 'Lady-So-and-So with Friends at Cannes' 'Miss the Other fresh from her triumph at Daly's Theatre relaxing on the beach at Nice', the Blue Train, the Côte d'Azur, the Casino at Monte Carlo were passwords among social climbers and publicity seekers. In nothing were British class distinctions more emphasized than in the matter of holiday resorts, the charabanc-borne prole-tariat being expected to spend no more than a day on the beach at Margate or Blackpool, the middle classes appearing at the 'nice end of the town' in Eastbourne, Bournemouth or Lytham St Annes, while those who could afford it, or had to find the means to afford it as part of their campaign for recognition, stretched themselves in the sunlight for a week or two on the French Riviera, or played golf at Le Touquet or disported them-selves in Biarritz or Deauville. Cornwall, St Jean de Luz, St Tropez were 'artistic', Ostend and the Belgian coast, Llandudno the Channel Isles and Boulogne were 'common', Spain, the Norwegian fjords, Southern Italy and Portugal were 'remote' if not 'adventurous', Ireland, the Highlands of Scotland, Majorca and Madeira were 'eccentric'. Of all places and sea-sons the surest bet for an appearance in the *Tatler* (the very goal of much holidaymaking), was St Moritz and the South of France in winter. It was generally agreed that only smart, famous, wealthy or at any rate *nice* people were to be found in these. So we had driven into the midst of a self-conscious Vanity Fair and found it amusing, cheerful and surprisingly kind and friendly.

[3]

When at last we left Mentone it was to dawdle along the coast, stopping for drinks or meals, enjoying the sunshine of that splendid March. There was bathing everywhere and brilliant colour in the outside cafés. Monte Carlo, Villefranche,

Nice, Antibes, Cannes, they are all in memory full of an unnatural, summery brightness, full of impossibly gay people and holiday abandon.

We stopped a night at the old town of Frejus where the bus stood in front of a convent. The coast was only two miles away and in a foolish moment Derrick and I decided to return to St Raphael for a last fling in the casino. I should have known better than to turn back to something already left behind and I should certainly have had more sense than to play the idiotic game of *boule*. But when we reached the Casino it appeared that there was not sufficient season here to open the main rooms, and a *boule* table was all that functioned. I had not played it since 1922 at Le Touquet, for even so poor a mathematician as I could see that the punter has no real chance at those odds. However, having walked two miles for a gamble, we gambled. When we left the casino we had lost everything but a few francs —enough, used with care, to buy petrol to get us to Troyes where a small sum awaited us. Ivor, who had refused to come, nobly refrained from saying 'I told you so' and we set out at once, in the small hours, on that dash across France. "We shall have to do a John Audley", the Rosaires said in circus lingo. (John Audley was a long-ago American showman who had spent his life in a hurry.)

We passed though Avignon next afternoon and did not pause. When on a later visit I suffered the weary boredom of being led by a lecturing guide through the palace of the popes with its interminable empty halls I thought we had missed very little, at least in that monstrous building. Early in the small hours we entered Orange. The streets were deserted as we drove through, and the sound of our engine seemed magnified out of all proportion as it was thrown back at us from the walls of the houses.

We went through villages in darkness guessing their names, when they were not displayed on blue boards, from our route-sheet. Then through the little town of Montelimar seemingly bare and cold, with nobody awake in the streets. Then more

names, Derbierre, Loriol, Fiance. Ivor slept till we reached
Valence-sur-Rhône when he took the wheel while Derrick lay
down.

A conscript soldier had begged a lift to Lyons and was
snoring on the seat beside me. I slept a little too; nodding with
the jerking of the waggon as it went on steadily through the
darkness. Suddenly I sat up, wide awake. I did not know
for a moment what had happened, my mind still swaying with
the bus. Then I realized that it was the silence; for we had
stopped. We appeared to be in the middle of a small village, or
at least among low buildings. The only sound was the heavy
breathing of the soldier lolling beside me as he continued to sleep.

"What's the matter?" I asked Ivor, who was just beginning
to climb out of the cab.

"Petrol", he answered briefly.

It could not have been later than three or four in the morning, and I looked around at the still village hopelessly.

"We passed a garage a few yards back", said Ivor. "Let's
knock them up. If we stay here until the morning the soldier
won't get to Lyons until dinner-time."

We woke the soldier and took him back with us to the little
one-pump garage Ivor had seen at the entrance to the village,
and all three of us began to bang on the wooden doors. Above
the garage there were curtained windows so we guessed that
the proprietor lived here. The door shivered as the soldier
thumped it with the butt of his rifle, and the sound echoed in
the narrow streets. For a long time nothing happened. We
banged again, and heard the sound of a window sash being
raised somewhere down the road.

"*Qu'est c'qui s'passe?*" demanded a querulous voice.

The soldier left us to go and explain and as his voice rose
other windows began to fly up and more and more people
joined in the discussion. But there was no stir or sound from the
garage. The soldier returned, still discussing the problem, with
the man who had awakened first. The latter had thrown a coat
over a flowing night-gown, and shuffled along in a pair of

plimsols. He regarded the wooden doors in silence for a while, then bending he peered through the keyhole. Others had by now arrived and stood in a crescent behind the old chaps' bent back.

"That's the mayor", one of them whispered to me. "He'll do it. You see."

M. le Maire shook the door ceremoniously. Nothing happened. He took a clod of earth and threw it against the closed window. He rained blows on the door.

"Open up", he shouted.

"Open for M. le Maire", chorused the crowd.

At last the window opened and a tousled head appeared. The Mayor turned to me with a bow. He shook hands all round and then gathering his night-gown out of the mud, he stalked off down the street. The crowd dispersed quietly to their homes, and in a little while we were carrying two cans of petrol up the road to the waggon.

Vienne was just waking up when we stopped to get some breakfast at a little café which had scarcely opened. A large, six-wheeled Dubonnet lorry stood in the street outside and its driver was alone in the bare room when we entered. A short stocky man, his grimy face told of an all-night drive. He swallowed his coffee in silence throwing a casual glance at Derrick who was yawning cavernously.

"Driving all night?" he said at last.

"Yes, and you?"

"From nine o'clock. Look, here it is." He fumbled in his breast pocket and drew out a bunch of thin wax-paper discs. They were perforated with tiny pin-pricks running in zig-zag lines from the centre to the edge and back again. They appeared to vary both in the distance between the holes and the angle of the zig-zag. He explained it to us.

"See, these go in a little machine on the dashboard of the lorry. Each little hole means one kilometre and the number of holes between these lines is the number I have travelled in an hour. If I stop—no holes, see," and he pointed to a space in the line.

"They are clever ones," he went on. "How many miles, how many hours, how much rest, they know everything from this. Too clever for business men; they ought to be in the Chamber with the other crooks."

"You wouldn't trust your own mother", shouted the café proprietor from behind the counter.

Our 'John Audley' continued. Derrick, who had had some sort of sleep, took over the wheel and I went to the back to lie down. I was too tired for the rumbling and bumping of the waggon to disturb me much, and although I woke for a few minutes in Lyons, where we dropped the soldier, I saw nothing of the town except the straight grey sides of the buildings, though I heard the heavy traffic already moving through its streets.

When I awoke again it was about eleven in the morning and the Morris-Commercial was going steadily along the quiet road between Macon and Tournus. Derrick was whistling cheerfully to himself and I joined him in front while Ivor in turn went back for a 'kip'.

Our midday meal that day consisted of a clearance of the larder. But there was a bottle of Tokay which had somehow stood forgotten in the corner since we had left Hungary, and a glass or two of *slivovice* which Vincy Schwarz had given us in Prague. As we started the engine and drove on I no longer resented quite so strongly that we were passing through the famous vineyards of Burgundy without a single pause to drink. On either side of the road the rows and rows of little bushes which were grape vines stretched away in the misty rain.

It was dark by the time we passed through Dijon, and I took over the wheel while Ivor and Derrick slumbered in the back. It was lonely, driving between the sombre woods on either side of a road. The moon appeared washily for a moment or two and showed the Côte d'Or hills as black humps lying just off our track. As fast as I left one group of them behind me there were more sitting stolidly in front, till I began to feel that they were interminable, and the old car would have to jolt on through the darkness for ever. But there was a certain exhilaration in that long night drive, however tiring. I suppose the strain of the last few days had begun to tell, for when Ivor woke up to relieve me I was driving almost automatically. We were just approaching Bar-sur-Seine, a little more than twenty miles from Troyes. It was two hours from the dawn and a slight mist had risen which hung along the sides of the road.

I was too tired to sleep now. Ivor and Derrick had awakened cheerful and talkative. They saw Troyes as a last stop on the way home, and they talked about the animals that had to be trained before the circus went on the road again, and the three lion cubs which had been bought for this year's tour while they had been away.

Almost unexpectedly we entered Troyes. The town was grey and silent with the street lamps extinguished, and it was with some difficulty that we found the post office. With a flourish Ivor drew the waggon up against the kerb in front of it and turned off the engine. The only sound as we waited for the morning was the creaking of the hot engine as it cooled and the slow ticking of the post office clock. But we were not on the doorstep when it opened, for at ten o'clock, in broad daylight, we were all three awakened from a heavy sleep to be asked by an amused policeman if we intended to keep our 'van' standing in front of Troyes post office all day.

The money for which I had wired was comfortingly there however, and the meal we enjoyed on the strength of it was one of the most welcome of the whole trip.

We reached the coast in the small hours of a stormy night which promised an uncomfortable crossing next day. But the thing was done, the five thousand odd miles covered without mishap. Our rush through France had brought us home slightly ahead of schedule—but that had been my fault for playing the asinine game of *boule*.

That we were not behind it was to the credit of my sterling companions and the indefatigable old bus. Less anxiously but more affectionately than on the outward journey we watched her lifted across to the channel boat, and went below to sleep.

[4]

The book I wrote, full of political conversations, was not a good one, and the publishers had folded up before I received anything from it but the initial advance which did not quite pay for the trip. But I sent out a good many copies of it to prominent politicians of the time which brought me some gratifying letters,[1] including characteristic ones from Winston Churchill, Ernest Brown, Anthony Eden, and Josef Goebbels, while from Lord Nuffield it brought not only two interesting letters but—through the Morris company's advertising agent—a pleasant sum of money in recognition of the sincere admiration I had expressed for the performance of the old Morris-Commercial bus. What seems much more to me now, the book has served as an *aide-mémoire* as I have written the story of the whole exploit.

Obviously I could not see it then as a last look at Europe before the lights went out. Nor was it that in fact because I made two more long journeys in Western Europe before the outbreak of war seventeen months after our return. But in the eastern countries, Czechoslovakia, Hungary and Yugoslavia I saw the last of freedom for at least the next thirty years—and for how much longer?—while in Germany and Italy I saw Fascism in what I suppose must be called its heyday.

This I did with enormous enjoyment, in the best of company, unafflicted by any morbid fears. I had less comfortable emotions, of indignation, of pity, of fellow-feeling with the unfortunate, but in sanguine young manhood, in health and high spirits, it was difficult to be saddened by the poverty of whole nations or fully to appreciate its effects, and impossible actually to suffer on account of the hidden misfortunes of the masses. Of the deliberate cruelty which I know now was at work in Germany I saw nothing, and I had no clairvoyant forebodings in Czechoslovakia. So I have no shame in saying that those months of travel, observation, and adventure were among the happiest I have known.

[1] All these are now in the library of Texas University.

L'Envoi

AS I CAME NEARER HOME, however, I decided that I could
not return to the rural peace of Smarden or to the life, however
active, which I had followed there. A glimpse at so many
capitals and talk with so many city-dwellers had given me an
urge to be 'nearer the centre of things', to see 'what was going
on', to meet 'those in the know'—all the traditional illusions
which cause people to live gregariously. I felt that I had been
away long enough and for the sake of my career should be 'more
in the swim'. I recognized that most other writers were pro-
fessionally cliquish and I began to think my attempted isolation
was too costly. This came partly from my realization in Prague,
Vienna and Budapest that I was unable to answer the questions
of artists and writers there about the intellectual life of my own
country and was, in many respects, a very provincial young man
in spite of the travels of which I was so proud. I had never been
to a Promenade Concert or to more than three or four exhibi-
tions of paintings. I had seen no ballet since 1925, and no plays
—except my own at the St Martins on a Sunday evening—since
1932. I belonged to no club, society or movement. I knew
almost no one of distinction in the arts or in the pettier worlds
of politics, society, commerce or law. My ambitions and abilities
were wholly literary and what other expertise I claimed was
fortuitous rather than impressive—some knowledge of food, drink
and first editions and a facility, inherited from my father, for
surmounting the obstacles and competently solving the problems
of everyday existence. I had read voraciously but I had little
understanding of the tendencies of the day in poetry and fiction.

So I was out of touch naïvely and believed that the remedy
for this was to live in London, which had been twice my home

since I had come of age, but to which I had been no more than an occasional visitor during the past six years. I felt for the first time in doing so I should be following my star.

It never occurred to me to think of London as the storm centre of the coming war. It was to me, for all its philistinism, its ugliness, its obsession with commerce, a place of great beauty, of immense possibilities, a home of all the arts I understood or cared about. I saw it at last after so much wandering as a promised land.

Always, in all those moves and ventures, I believed I was working towards an objective which would justify every disorientation, disaster and experience, that there was some final goal which I as a writer would reach, not by study or practice, but by fruitful activity, by seizing opportunities to travel and observe, by empiric and intense living. It is not without irony, yet in a sense comforting, these thirty years later to recognize that although its nature was then unforeseen a fulfilment of a sort has taken shape, a notably direct and simple one—the writing of these books. All that experience which, in my young intention, was to ferment and fall bright then emerge in some sparkling irresistible form to dazzle and intoxicate posterity has in fact come out of storage with its pristine simplicity uncomplicated by time as a plain chronicle of other days. This, if it does nothing else, satisfies the craving which I share with philosophers both Greek and Oriental, to uncover some pattern in the past and achieve some vindication for its absurdities.

The story I am writing lacks shadow and I have been unable to find self-pity with which to darken its colours. "Prick him where you will", invites a knowing critic in discussing one of this series of books,[j] "he still bleeds rose-petal jam", an understandable (if somewhat luridly worded) complaint, since there is nothing harder for the cynic to forgive than the happiness and exuberance of others. But if gusto is a fault I owe it to circumstances as well as to my own nature. We can only 'speak as we find' of life, and I have no complaints.

[j] *The Observer*, February 13th 1966.